ESSAYS ON THE PRESIDENTS

PRINCIPLES AND POLITICS

BOOKS BY PAUL F. BOLLER JR.

George Washington and Religion (1963)

This Is Our Nation (1963), with Jean Tilford

Quotemanship (1967)

American Thought in Transition (1969)

American Transcendentalism (1974)

Freedom and Fate in American Thought (1978)

Presidential Anecdotes (1981; rev. ed., 1996)

Presidential Campaigns (1984; rev. ed., 1996)

A More Perfect Union (1984), with Ron Story

Hollywood Anecdotes (1987), with Ron Davis

Presidential Wives (1988)

They Never Said It (1989), with John George

Congressional Anecdotes (1991)

Memoirs of an Obscure Professor (1992)

Not So! Popular Myths About America (1995)

Presidential Inaugurations (2001)

Presidential Diversions (2007)

ESSAYS
ON THE
PRESIDENTS

PRINCIPLES
AND
POLITICS

PAUL F. BOLLER JR.

TCU Press
Fort Worth, Texas

Library of Congress Cataloging-in-Publication Data

Boller, Paul F.
  Essays on the presidents : principles and politics / Paul F. Boller Jr.
    p. cm.
  ISBN-13: 978-0-87565-443-0 (hardcover : alk. paper)
  ISBN-10: 0-87565-443-6 (hardcover : alk. paper)
  1. Presidents--United States. 2. United States--Politics and government.
I. Title.
  JK516.B66 2012
  973.09'9--dc23

                                     2011051245

TCU Press
P. O. Box 298300
Fort Worth, Texas 76129
817.257.7822
http://www.prs.tcu.edu

To order books: 1.800.826.8911

Designed by fusion29.com

With gratitude for the help and encouragement in the preparation of this book from Dan Williams, Director of the TCU Press, Kathy Walton, Editor, and Melinda Esco, Production Manager.

CONTENTS

During my academic career as a specialist in American Studies, I have given lectures and written essays and reviews, as well as books, and I'm presenting twenty-six of them together here, with forewords to each putting them in context. Many of them no doubt reflect the times in which they were written as well as my thinking about various features of American life and thought. I trust, though, that they also reveal some growth on my part through the years, both in knowledge and in my way of looking at various developments in American culture and civilization. To save space, I'm omitting the footnotes that accompanied many of the essays presented here, but the original editions, located in the Boller Papers in the Archives of the Mary Couts Burnett Library at Texas Christian University in Fort Worth, Texas, are readily available.

Ah, history! Several years ago a woman I met in Boston wanted to know what I did for a living, and when I told her I taught American history, her eyes lit up and she exclaimed: "Gadsden's Purchase! 1853!" Of course I congratulated her on her good memory, but I was amused by her notion of history as being simply a collection of facts and dates and names that one memorized. I call it the college-bowl conception of history.

For myself, I prefer to think of history as a quest. The word history comes from an ancient Greek word, *historia*, which means inquiry, and there are good grounds for thinking of history as essentially a set of questions that we ask about the past. Some of the questions historians ask are obvious and easy; others are tremendously difficult; and still others, in the nature of things, can never be satisfactorily answered.

The first question historians ask is the most basic, but also the simplest: what exactly happened and precisely when did it happen? This is the area of historical specificity, the area my Boston friend concentrated on. What, for example, was the Yalta agreement and when was it made? What was the Emancipation Proclamation? Exactly when was it issued and by whom? History, after all, is to some extent a collection of facts and dates. Historians keep records of treaties, elections, legislative enactments, conferences, battles, US Supreme Court decisions, and a host of other significant happenings for lawyers, judges, public officials, journalists, biographers, historians, and other interested parties. Some history books are little more than reference books, filled with facts, names, and dates for consultation. Factual information is the foundation for all the other questions we ask of the past.

But history is more than a collection of facts; it's more than something you look up in a reference book or encyclopedia. A second question that historians ask of the past is this: how did things happen? What actually went on in the past? And in answering this kind of question, we get into historical narrative. From this point of view, history may be regarded as a story. It's a factual narrative of what people said, did, and thought about in the past. For some people, history is mainly story. When they think of history, they don't think of Gadsden's Purchase, 1853; they think of George Washington chopping down a cherry tree (which, by the way, isn't a true story). Or they think of Christopher Columbus's daring voyage across the Atlantic.

History is filled with dramatic, even breathtaking stories: the Trojan War, the Norman conquest of Britain, Martin Luther's defiance of the Catholic authorities, the collapse of the stock market on Wall Street in 1929, the attack on Pearl Harbor by the Japanese in 1941. Some of our greatest historians have written narrative histories of the United States, filled with fascinating information about colonial settlements, the fight for American independence, the drafting of the US Constitution in 1787, the settling of the West, and so on. These narrative historians recreated the events of the American past with elegance and excitement. Historian Henry Steele Commager once wrote that "History is a story," and if a historian "forgets or neglects to tell a story, it will inevitably forfeit much of its appeal and much of its authority as well."

But history is more than story. Narrative history hits only the high spots of the recorded past; it tends to single out dramatic events for emphasis. It's a fact, of course, that American life contains dramatic moments; but mostly, our lives consist of habit, ritual, convention, schedule, and routine. That was true of people in the past, too. And one of the historian's tasks is to inquire into life as it was lived in the past.

A third question historians ask when dealing with the past is, what was it like then? How did people really live back in those days? In answering questions like these, the historian attempts to reconstruct life as it was lived in times and places quite different from our own times: ancient Greece, for example, or Renaissance Italy, Elizabethan England, or colonial Virginia. History, according to Herbert Butterfield, is "attempting to see life with the eyes of another century than our own." It's extremely difficult to enter into the mind and spirit of another age. We're all culture-bound; we all tend to judge other people, places, and periods in history by our own standards and principles. It's difficult for us to understand other cultures in their deepest reaches. "Understanding the past," Paul Fussell reminds us, "requires pretending that you don't know the present." It's hard to see people in other ages with their eyes rather than with our own. But if, after mastering our materials, we succeed, by an act of imagination, in overcoming the parochialism of the present and penetrating to the central vision of some bygone age, we achieve the exhilarating freedom that comes from transcending our own cultural bonds.

If we become thoroughly familiar with another period of history, we can put our own age in better perspective. Putting our own age into a larger context enables us to understand it better, its limitations as well as its opportunities. Knowing the past enlarges our understanding of human experiences; we become wiser and more knowledgeable about what human beings have accomplished in other times and places, and we become more realistic about our own opportunities and achievements. When historians concentrate on describing past societies and civilizations, they're engaging in what used to be called cultural anthropology.

But historians have special questions of their own that cultural anthropologists don't normally ask. There's the indispensable historical question: how did things get to be the way they are today? How did they get started, and for what reason? How did they change with the passage of time? What were they like before they became as we see them today? We can ask this question of material objects—how did this particular object come into being and when? We can ask it of the telephone, for example, or men's ties, or kitchen utensils. We can ask this question about social customs, too: why do people in the United States greet each other by shaking hands? When did handshaking get started, and why?

We can ask questions about origins when it comes to political and social institutions as well. How did the US Supreme Court get to be the way it is today? Where did the organization called the Red Cross come from? What's the origin of presidential primaries? We can also ask questions about the emergence of ideas, concepts, attitudes, and opinions. When did the idea of progress become influential and why? How did the notion of enlightened self-interest enter the picture? When did the idea of evolution begin to emerge and alter our thinking about the universe? Why did the idea that there's a special category of human beings known as "teenagers" come into existence, and when? Every event—every custom, habit, political institution, social organization, and every concept and opinion—has a history, sometimes a long history. By asking how things got to be the way they are today, we end up understanding them better.

A final question the historian asks is perhaps the most difficult of all. The question asks, "Why do things change?" From the dawn of history until the present moment, there have been continual changes, some trivial, and some momentous in the history of humankind. But why do things continually change? How do you account for the vast changes that have occurred in the past? How do you explain the rise and the fall of the Roman Empire? How do you explain the outbreak of the French Revolution, with its enormous influence on history? How do you explain the outburst of European exploration of the world, with its tremendous effects on subsequent history? How do you explain the eruption of the Protestant Reformation? How do you explain the great population explosion that began in the sixteenth century and continues unabated today? Why did modern science emerge in seventeenth-century Europe? Why did modern music take form in the West instead of in the East?

Historians disagree violently on reasons for social change. Some of them think that technological innovations are at the root of historical change: the invention of gunpowder, of printing, of the compass, or the development of the steam engine, of the dynamo, the electric generator, the automobile, airplane, television, computer. Other historians insist that changes in the way people produce and distribute material goods are the basic motors in social development. Still other historians think that novelty of outlook—the appearance of new ideas—has transforming effects. New ideas, they say, bring about changes in the way people think, and therefore in the way they behave. Ideas like the Christian religion, or the idea of progress, or the concept of evolution all have profound effects on the way people behave. And the ideas themselves are creative responses to the world in which we find ourselves.

Personally, I'm what philosopher William James called a "pluralist." I think that both ideas and economic behavior are at work in the process of historical change. I'm also aware of the fact that chance and accident also play an important part in historical development. William James placed emphasis on what he called "the contingent and unforeseen" in human life and history, and I think he was right to do so. Chance and random change do play an important part in life, and the student of the past will always have to take them into account in explaining what's going on in history.

William James also emphasized the part that individuals, particularly creative individuals, play in bringing about social change. Napoleon certainly had a major influence on modern history, but so did the inventor Thomas A. Edison, and so, for that matter, did Albert Einstein. But historians have a final question. Why did this event take place exactly when it did? Why did colonial Americans decide to seek independence from Britain in 1776, rather than in 1775 or 1778? Why did Lincoln issue the Emancipation Proclamation in 1863, rather than in 1862 or 1865? Why did the second World War break out in 1939 rather than in 1938 or 1940? We can ask this kind of question when dealing with general developments as well as precise events. Why did the Industrial

Revolution take place when it did—the eighteenth century—and why did it take place in Western Europe rather than elsewhere? Why did democracy emerge in Western Europe and America in the late eighteenth century? Why did the antislavery movement begin to develop power and influence, for the first time in history, in the late eighteenth century in Western Europe?

History, in short, is full of questions. And if the historian comes up with thoughtful answers to these questions, we will know something we didn't know before. That new knowledge about the past may help us to understand the present situation more deeply and enable us to consider present-day problems more thoughtfully. Knowing something about the past is absolutely essential for making sensible choices in the present. Without putting our questions into the great world of the past, our choices and actions are likely to be simplistic, hit-or-miss, or even reckless.

When the Founding Fathers met in Philadelphia in the summer of 1787 to write the US Constitution, one of the delegates announced: "Experience must be our only guide. Reason may mislead us." His point was that the constitution-makers would do a better job of organizing a government for the new nation if they kept in mind the experiences people had in the past with different kinds of governments, especially republics. The Founding Fathers were indeed historically minded.

There was something else that the Founding Fathers were aware of: history is always in action; it moves, changes, and develops, no matter what the situation is. Human beings cannot freeze history; they cannot impose ideologies, deemed to be near-perfect, successfully onto human endeavors, though dictators do the best they can. Trying to enforce rigid ideologies will, of course, produce changes, but history will continue to move on. There are no fixities and finalities, as John Dewey put it, among human beings; the future is always open to change. History never ends. And, as one Brit put it, coping with problems is more fruitful than trying to solve problems for all time.

Paul F. Boller Jr.
Professor Emeritus
Texas Christian University
Fort Worth, Texas

CHAPTER 1

The First American Presidency, 1789-1829

What kind of president did the founding fathers want when they produced the US Constitution in 1787 and submitted it to the states for ratification? They certainly hoped for a highly moral chief executive who set a good model for the American people he governed, though they didn't mention it in the document they prepared. The first president, remarked Benjamin Franklin, will be a good one—he was thinking of George Washington as the choice—but after that, he wasn't sure what kind of president would succeed him. In his book on *Presidents Above Party*, Ralph Ketcham singled out the first six presidents—George Washington, John Adams, Thomas Jefferson, James Madison, James Monroe, John Quincy Adams—as taking the moral view of the presidency that the constitution-makers had in mind. He called them "the First American Presidency, 1789–1829." With the election of Andrew Jackson as chief executive in 1828 came a new period in the history of the presidency that was quite different from what most of the constitution-makers had in mind. Apparently US Supreme Court Justice Antonin Scalia, an "originalist," stands with the "First American Presidency" rather than the presidents who came later.

★ ★ ★

"The whole community," ran an old Latin proverb that Benjamin Franklin liked to quote, "is regulated by the example of the King." What about the example of the president? Ralph Ketcham's *Presidents Above Party*, a painstaking study of the concept of the presidency held by America's first six chief executives, stresses the fact that until the Age of Jackson the notion that the president should provide moral leadership for the nation—transcending party politics—held powerful sway in the young republic. His point is not new. But he is the first to develop it in all its richness and complexity, and he succeeds in making the "first American presidency," as he calls it, more accessible to us than ever before.

Our earliest presidents, Ketcham points out, were all familiar with Henry St. John, Lord Bolingbroke's *Idea of a Patriot King*, published in 1749, and liked what it said. They were, to be sure, devoted to individual freedom and government by consent; in varying degrees, too, they came to terms with the commercial ethic which was rapidly replacing older values while they held office. But at the same time they heartily endorsed Bolingbroke's call for a high-minded, disinterested leadership which put the public welfare above private interest and sought to encourage virtue in the people at large. All of them scorned party politics; they wanted to be patriot presidents. "We are all Federalists, we are all Republicans," asserted Jefferson in his inaugural address in 1801. "If I could not go to heaven but with a party," he once confessed, "I would not go there at all." His position was unexceptionable. From George Washington to John Quincy Adams the nonpartisan presidency, not party leadership, was the great ideal.

The heart of Ketcham's book is his analysis of the views of the first six presidents. But he provides the necessary background for their opinions, both in seventeenth- and eighteenth-century British and American thought and in the swirling world of competitive capitalism that was transforming the Western world. He discusses, too, the increasingly popular view that self-interest is the basic motor of human behavior, that "private vice is public benefit," and that the main task of executive leadership is to preserve law and order and let the push and pull of competing factions produce a compromise of some kind. He also examines the new party-oriented presidency developed by Martin Van Buren and other politicians in the 1820s and 1830s and tries to see what remained of the older ideal in administrations following that of Andrew Jackson. "The longing, indeed the imperative, that the president be more than a party leader, that he retain something of the aura, posture, and power of the patriot king," he concludes, has persisted to the present.

Ketcham probably could have organized his book more adroitly; there are too many flashbacks, montages, and periodic replications of themes already well developed. It would have helped, too, if he had introduced in his text the names of the twentieth-century writers he quotes instead of relegating them to the footnotes. But these are minor flaws. His book, like all thoughtful historical studies, throws a great deal of light on current events as well as ancient happenings. It makes clear, for one thing, that the appeal of Ronald Reagan rests more on his intuitive allegiance to Bolingbrokean principles than on his predilection for supply-side economics. And it forces us, for another, to recognize that with declining party attachments, nominating primaries that stress *personalismo* rather than principle, and the gradual transformation of American voters into a "telectorate," we may well be entering a new political age as different from the one the Jacksonians ushered in as the Jacksonian age was from the era of the "first presidency."

REVIEW OF RALPH KETCHAM, *Presidents Above Party: The First American Presidents* (1984), *Journal of American History*, 1984.

CHAPTER 2

The Log Cabin Myth about American Presidents

There haven't been log cabin presidents for decades. Presidential campaigns cost millions of dollars these days, and candidates must collect a lot of it themselves if they're going to win nominations in the primaries and elections in the presidential contest.

Campaigns are more costly in 2011 than they were in 1984, when Edward Pessen published his book pointing out that few American presidents started out life in log cabins. Even a nice little home and yard are not enough. You must become a millionaire at some point, after begging for dough, if you are going to pay for campaign expenses these days. The US Supreme Court hails the million-dollar presidential contests as wondrous examples of freedom of speech.

★ ★ ★

Years ago Charles Beard made a career-line study of the men who drafted the US Constitution and discovered that they were mostly men of wealth. In *The Log Cabin Myth* Edward Pessen does a somewhat similar study of the thirty-nine presidents, from Washington to Reagan, who have been elected under that constitution, and discovers that, like the constitution-makers, they too for the most part have come from the ranks of the privileged. Pessen's analysis, the first ever made of our presidents' social backgrounds, is based largely on published sources, particularly presidential biographies; though it suffers at times from repetition, it is a convincing corrective to the popular notion that anyone can rise from rags to riches in this country if he tries hard enough.

Once when Lyndon Johnson was showing friends around his Texas ranch he pointed out a ramshackle cabin as his birthplace. "Why, Lyndon," cried his mother afterward, "you know you were born in a much better house closer to town which has been torn down." "I know, Mama," said Johnson, "but everybody has to have a birthplace." To be sure. But the birthplaces of all our presidents—Johnson's included—have almost invariably been good ones. To demolish the log cabin myth, Pessen first examines the social and economic circumstances of the presidents' families and then takes a look at the careers of each of the presidents before he entered the White House. His conclusion: "Very few began at or near the bottom. The lives of the presidents only illustrate this principle: Americans who attain great worldly success, whether in wealth and property accumulation, occupational prestige, or politics, have typically been born to youthful advantages that were instrumental in accounting for their adult success." One does not become a president (or, I would presume, a professor) without special advantages at the outset that are denied the vast majority of Americans.

Pessen describes all thirty-nine presidents, including FDR, as basically conservative, that is, as upholders of the capitalist system, and he thinks the major parties pick candidates mainly for their ideological "soundness." Hence conventionality and mediocrity have been the rule, and our presidents have mainly served "not the general interests of the people as a whole, but the narrow interests of the small privileged and wealthy minority." If intelligence and character were the criteria for high office, says Pessen, there is no reason why our leaders would not be drawn as often from the ranks of skilled mechanics, farmers, teachers, and architects as from the upper classes.

I don't find classifying both FDR and Reagan as conservatives especially illuminating; I am bothered by the fact that Pessen says nothing about the essential conservatism of the masses of Americans who were not born to privilege. Still, it is hard not to sympathize with his plea, at the end of his stimulating (and occasionally sardonic) survey, that "we seek in the future, as we have not sought in the past, to select candidates of commanding intelligence, learning, and above all patience, wisdom, and humanity—traits all that are not necessarily revealed by high social standing and the ideological preferences that typically accompany such standing."

REVIEW OF EDWARD PESSEN, *The Log Cabin Myth: The Social Backgrounds of the Presidents* (1985), *Journal of Southern History,* May 1985.

CHAPTER 3

Pennsylvania: The Avenue of the Presidents

W hen Sheldon Meyer, the wonderful senior editor at the Oxford University Press, decided to retire, William E. Leuchtenburg, one of the American historians with whom he had worked, arranged for the publication of a book in his honor containing essays by various historians whom Meyer had guided through editing and publication at Oxford. The book was entitled *American Places: Encounters with History*, with each essay centered on some place in the United States that the writers were able to link to the development of American history. As the book jacket put it: "America's Leading Historians Talk About the Sites Where the Past Comes Alive for Them."

When Professor Leuchtenburg invited me to write one of the essays, I had begun research on presidential inaugurations, and I decided to pick Pennsylvania Avenue in Washington as my site and the use of the avenue during inaugurations as my historical interest. I was a runner in those days, and whenever I visited Washington I always did my sightseeing while jogging. I'd done some running on the avenue, but not nearly enough, I thought, to nail down my topic. Shortly before commencing my work on the essay, I took a trip to Washington, ran down Pennsylvania Avenue between the White House and the Capitol, and then walked back, taking notes on some of the buildings along the route. What I did reminded me of Abraham Lincoln. During the 1860 presidential campaign, a biography of Lincoln appeared and it mentioned some books he had read. It turned out that he had never gone through one of the books, so "Honest Abe" promptly acquired the book and zipped through it.

I felt deeply honored when Sheldon wrote me a letter after the book appeared telling me how much he enjoyed my trip down Pennsylvania Avenue.

★ ★ ★

As a sport, running (like swimming laps) can be boring at times, at least for an amateur, and a few years after taking it up I began combining it, whenever possible, with sightseeing. It seemed like a bright idea: keeping fit while learning something about cities I visited. I did runs around the Emperor's Palace in Tokyo, down Riverside Drive in Manhattan, along the waterfront in Seattle, on the river walk in San Antonio, near Golden Gate Bridge in San Francisco, and in Rock Creek Park and down Pennsylvania Avenue in Washington, DC.

Pennsylvania Avenue was a favorite. The sights along the way were impressive: museums, monuments, memorials, statues, imposing government buildings, parks, plazas. The association with presidents, a major interest of mine, was also powerful. Most presidents, I knew, traveled along the "Grand Avenue" from the White House to the Capitol to be sworn into office on Inauguration Day, and then returned to review the big parade in their honor that afternoon from a stand erected for that purpose in front of the executive mansion. A few went to the Capitol by foot or on horseback; more made the trip in fancy phaetons and barouches and, later on, in automobiles and limousines. At my leisurely pace I made the trip (1.7 miles) in about fifteen minutes. It took the presidents longer because they were usually part of a stately procession witnessed by hundreds, and then thousands, lining the avenue. Three presidents—Jimmy Carter, George H. W. Bush, Bill Clinton—were runners, but none ventured to jog down Pennsylvania Avenue on Inauguration Day, though Carter and Clinton walked part of the way on their return to the White House.

Time gallops on, of course, and in retirement I substituted swimming for running, but I still take walks along America's "Appian Way" (as it used to be called) whenever I am in Washington, admiring the Romanesque Post Office, with its 315-foot clock tower, the East Building of the National Gallery of Art (designed by I. M. Pei), and the Willard Hotel (self-styled "the crown jewel of Pennsylvania Avenue"), the host for American presidents since Franklin Pierce in 1853. As I stroll down the avenue (at a slower pace than Harry Truman used in his daily walks), I take time out to visit the exhibits in the National Gallery of Art and the National Archives, chat with attendants at the Willard who have witnessed inaugural parades, and examine the sketches, maps, and quotations inscribed on the flagstone surface of the Freedom Plaza between 13th and 14th streets. Two quotes I find especially pertinent. One is an utterance of Samuel C. Busby, president of the Medical Society of

Washington, in 1898: "There is not a street in any city in this country entitled to the eminent distinction which crowns the history of Pennsylvania Avenue." The other is from Thomas Jefferson, writing in 1791: "The Grand Avenue connecting both the palace and the federal House will be most significant and most convenient."

Jefferson preferred the dreams of the future to the history of the past, as John Adams put it, but it took a lot of history to transform the Grand Avenue from what it was when he became the first president to be inaugurated in Washington to what it is today. In 1801, Jefferson used New Jersey rather than Pennsylvania Avenue in walking from his boardinghouse to Capitol Hill, because Pennsylvania was still too much of a "Serbonian bog." But after becoming president he saw to it that the avenue was graded and paved, and he used it when riding in a carriage to the Capitol for his second swearing-in. On both occasions, he received praise for his "Republican simplicity." He avoided fancy garb and insisted on simpler oath-taking ceremonies than those accompanying George Washington's and John Adams's inductions into office. And he soon rechristened the "President's Palace" the "President's House."

Jeffersonian simplicity, I found, was short-lived. Soldiers accompanied James Madison to the Capitol in 1809, perhaps because of strained relations with Britain, and became indispensable features of inaugural processions thereafter. Andrew Jackson returned to Jeffersonian austerity in 1829, walking informally with a few Revolutionary veterans along the avenue, nodding and waving to his fans along the way, as he headed for Capitol Hill. "It is true greatness," exclaimed one observer, "which needs not the aid of ornament and pomp." I expected ornament and pomp in William Henry Harrison's inauguration in 1841, and I got plenty of it. The Whigs, I learned, sponsored the first big, colorful parade (reminiscent of their "log cabin and hard cider" campaign), made up of members of Tippecanoe Clubs and log cabin floats, as well as military units and bands. The most striking float (since it showed that the Whigs tried to keep up with the times) was a large platform on wheels, drawn by six white horses, displaying a power loom, with several operators busily weaving pieces of cloth and tossing them out to people lining the avenue. It was a frigid day, but Harrison joined the procession to and from the Capitol on "Old Whitey," his white charger, and the paraders trooped back and forth for a couple of hours after the inaugural ceremony to entertain the crowds. John Quincy Adams called the procession "showy-shabby," but he meant it as a compliment: elegant but not undemocratic.

Floats became a big thing after 1841. In 1857 two floats demonstrating that Liberty and Union were in good shape (though they weren't) dominated the parade for James Buchanan, and in 1865 three ambitious floats proceeded down the avenue to celebrate Abraham Lincoln's second oath-taking: a replica of the *Monitor*, from which sailors fired salutes; a structure representing the Temple of Liberty, filled with women wearing costumes signifying the different states; and a platform containing a hand-run press, with members of the Typographical Union turning out inaugural programs for the parade-watchers.

Lincoln's first inauguration in 1861 was inevitably unique. With the nation on the brink of civil war on March 4, the inaugural planners realized that the safety of Lincoln and the security of Washington itself were their most urgent tasks. To meet the crisis, General Winfield Scott, the army's general in chief, moved several hundred regular troops into the city and arranged for the presidential carriage to move along Pennsylvania Avenue on inauguration morning between double files of District cavalry, with a company of sappers and miners marching in front of the carriage and the infantry and riflemen of the District following behind. He also stationed soldiers on streets paralleling the parade route and cavalrymen on the side streets crossing Pennsylvania Avenue, and put riflemen on the roofs and at the windows of buildings along the parade route as well.

Fortunately there was no trouble that momentous day, and the inaugural procession, with soldiers, bands, marching clubs, governors, war veterans, congressmen, and Washington officials, went off nicely. The crowds lining the avenue especially liked the float decorated in red, white, and blue, drawn by four white horses, and carrying thirty-four pretty little girls, one for each state (including the seceded ones), wearing white frocks and waving little flags. The story that Lincoln took time out to kiss each little girl is charming but spurious. So, probably, is the tale told by one of Buchanan's biographers about the exchange Lincoln had with his predecessor en route to the Capitol. "My dear sir," Buchanan supposedly said, "if you are as happy in entering the White House as I shall feel on returning to Wheatland, you are a happy man indeed." "Mr. President," Lincoln is said to have replied, with uncharacteristic stiltedness, "I cannot say that I shall enter it with much pleasure, but I assure you that I shall do what I can to maintain the high standards set by my illustrious predecessors who have occupied it." Later, when General Scott, stationed on a hill nearby, learned that the inauguration had gone off peacefully, he raised his hands and exclaimed: "God be praised! God in His goodness be praised!" I couldn't help liking old "Fuss and Feathers" as I read about his last hurrah.

Four years later, at Lincoln's second swearing-in, American blacks marched in the inaugural parade for the first time, both as soldiers wearing the Union Army blue and as members of an Odd Fellows lodge in full regalia. Though some people objected, participation of blacks in their country's quadrennial celebrations continued and increased in importance until the day came when Margaret Truman could boast that at her father's inauguration in 1949, all the activities, including the inaugural ball, were at last fully integrated.

After the Civil War, the military component of inaugural parades increased in importance, and the parades themselves, originally a minor supplement to the task of getting presidents to and from the Capitol, gradually became featured events, were moved to the afternoon, and were scheduled to take place after the inaugural ceremonies at the Capitol. Meanwhile, the morning processions to the Capitol became less significant and, with the arrival of automobiles in the early part of the twentieth century, turned into little motorcades, with the president and the president-elect in the first car, the vice president and his successor in the second car, the presidential wives in the third, and members of Congress, cabinet members, government officials, and Secret Service men in succeeding cars. Crowds continued to gather along the historic thoroughfare on inauguration morning, hoping to get a glimpse of the presidents and their wives as well as to get good seats in the bleachers erected along the way for the afternoon parade. Helen Taft was the first presidential wife to get into the act when she insisted on riding with her husband back to the White House after the inaugural ceremony in 1909.

Automobiles replaced horse-drawn carriages in 1921, when Warren G. Harding succeeded Woodrow Wilson as president. The motorcade from the White House to the Capitol on the morning of Harding's inauguration contained a dozen cars, and the mounted cavalry accompanying the cars came close to galloping in order to stay ahead of them. Cheers greeted the little procession moving down the avenue, but Wilson purposely ignored them; he assumed they were all for Harding, and he tried to convince himself that he didn't mind a bit. But he was amused by the turn the conversation took soon after they left the White House. Harding began telling Wilson about an elephant he'd heard of whose devotion to his keeper was almost unbelievable. "You know," he said, "I've always wanted to own an elephant some day." Murmured Wilson, "I hope it won't turn out to be a white elephant." History, the New York Times observed in 1953, "is an outgoing President riding up Pennsylvania Avenue with his successor, each trying to make pleasant conversation while each hears the loud ticking of the clock that brings noon nearer."

The clock-ticking chats weren't always as amiable as the Harding-Wilson exchange. One of the unpleasantest (and among my favorites) occurred in 1933, when Herbert Hoover and Franklin Roosevelt rode to the Capitol together for the latter's swearing-in. Thousands of people lined the avenue that morning, waving, shouting, cheering, and singing "Happy Days Are Here Again," and FDR smiled, waved, and raised his silk hat in obvious pleasure as the presidential limousine lumbered along. But Hoover, aghast at his successor's determination to go ahead with his New Deal, stared bleakly straight ahead, utterly unresponsive to FDR's efforts to get a conversation going. FDR prided himself on his skill in engaging people in small talk, but with the ponderously glum Hoover his efforts came to naught. Spying a building under construction on one side of the avenue, he suddenly exclaimed, almost in desperation, "My dear Mr. President, aren't those the nicest steel girders you ever saw?" There was no response from Hoover, and FDR gave up at this point. As he told Grace Tully, his secretary, later on: "I said to myself, 'Spinach! Protocol or no protocol, somebody had to do something. The two of us simply couldn't sit there on our hands, ignoring each other and everybody else.' So I began to wave my own response with my top hat and kept waving it until I got to the inauguration stand and was sworn in."

Harry Truman's ride to the Capitol with Dwight D. Eisenhower in 1953 was more strained, if anything, than the Hoover-Roosevelt trip. Once on good terms, the two men had come to dislike each other thoroughly during the 1952 campaign, when Truman went out on the stump for Adlai Stevenson, and just before Ike touched base with Truman on inauguration morning, he told aides he wondered "if I can stand sitting next to the guy." He refused to meet Truman in the White House, as protocol dictated, forcing the president to go out front to join him in the presidential car. In his diary for January 20, Truman wrote that the conversation en route to the Capitol was at first about "the crowd, the pleasant day, the orderly turnover," and then Eisenhower suddenly remarked that Kenneth Royall (Truman's secretary of war) "tried to order him home" for Truman's inauguration in 1949, "but he wouldn't come because half the people cheering me at that time had told him they were for him." "Ike," Truman retorted, "I didn't ask you to come—or you'd have been here." At that, New Hampshire Senator Styles Bridges, one of the congressional escorts, "gasped," according to Truman, and Massachusetts's Joe Martin, Speaker of the House, "changed the subject."

Eisenhower's remark continued to rankle Truman long after Ike became president, and when he came to publish *Mr. Citizen* in 1960, he gave a fuller and more confrontational account of the episode. But both Truman and Eisenhower seem to have had faulty memories. Newspapers covering the 1949 inauguration reported that Ike was actually on hand for the celebration; he appeared in the afternoon parade. The crowds along Pennsylvania Avenue, according to the New York Times, applauded enthusiastically "when they spotted Gen. Dwight D. Eisenhower in a car whose placard bore only the name of his host, Secretary of the Army Kenneth Royall." Eisenhower said nothing in his memoirs about the curt exchange with Truman in 1953, but he did recall asking Truman who ordered his son John, a colonel stationed in Korea, to

Washington for the inauguration, and when Truman said, "I did," he "thanked him sincerely for his thoughtfulness." Truman remembered it differently; he interpreted Ike's query (which came after they reached the Capitol) hostilely, and in *Mr. Citizen* reported another angry retort on his part. But he said nothing about the friendly letter he received from Ike's son three days after the inauguration, thanking him for enabling him to attend his father's swearing-in. He never forgave Eisenhower for his discourteous behavior in 1953.

The ceremonies of 1933 and 1953 were exceptions to the clock-ticking encounters on inauguration morning. Most journeys of presidents and presidents-elect to Capitol Hill seem to have been polite, if not cordial. The transitional trip of Gerald Ford and Jimmy Carter in 1977 was certainly friendly; Ford reminisced about his days in Congress and explained to Carter that Republicans and Democrats could have their scraps in the House and still remain friends. George Bush and Bill Clinton got along fine, too, in 1993; Clinton was never at a loss for friendly words.

In the twentieth century, the newly installed president usually had lunch with members of Congress in the Capitol after the inaugural address and then returned to the White House to review the parade down Pennsylvania Avenue. Some presidents enjoyed the parades enormously; others simply took them in their stride. But for at least one president, Calvin Coolidge, the parade after the inauguration in 1925 seems to have been an ordeal, though it lasted only an hour and consisted mainly of army, navy, and marine forces. "Silent Cal" was so quiet throughout that some people called it "a review in silence." In an attempt to explain Coolidge's apparent indifference, "Ike" Hoover, the White House's chief usher, mentioned the president's "lack of appreciation for such demonstrations. The people certainly like to be noticed and the President could not or would not warm up to them." *The Emporia Gazette's* William Allen White put it more colorfully: "It takes two to wake up the hurrahs of a crowd, the harrahers and the harrahee. That fine, fair Coolidge day the hurrahee's emotions—never tenacious—were spent by four o'clock." Thoroughly exhausted by the experience, Coolidge returned to the White House afterward for a bite to eat and a good nap.

Theodore Roosevelt was more typical. Like Franklin Roosevelt, John F. Kennedy, and Ronald Reagan after him, he thoroughly enjoyed the afternoon performance, and it was probably the high point of the day for him in 1905. As the inaugural parade passed his reviewing stand in front of the White House, he grinned, smiled, laughed, nodded, waved his hat, clapped his hands, stamped his feet, swayed to the rhythm of the band music, and at times almost danced, as more than thirty thousand men, representing hundreds of military and civilian organizations, passed in review. He liked the band music: the Sousa marches, the ragtime, and tunes like "Maryland, My Maryland," "Marching through Georgia," "America," "Dixie," and especially "There'll Be a Hot Time in the Old Town Tonight." He liked the signs and banners too: "The President's Neighbors" (people from Oyster Bay), "All I Ask is a Square Deal for Every Man" (a Roosevelt political club), and, in particular, the banner carried by some coal miners in overalls, with lamps on their caps, celebrating his intervention in the anthracite coal walkout in 1902: "We Honor the Man Who Settled Our Strike."

With his affection for things military, Roosevelt was particularly proud of the army and navy units, which saluted as they passed in the parade. "Those are the boys," he exclaimed, as the West Point cadets and the midshipmen from the Naval Academy appeared: "They're superb." When the Seventh Cavalry passed by, its band playing "Garry Owen," TR remarked, "That is a bully fighting tune, and this is Custer's old regiment, one of the finest in the service." As a squadron of the Ninth Regular Cavalry, a black regiment, went by, he cried, "Ah, they were with me at Santiago!" He got a big kick out of the Rough Riders, of course, and joined in the laughter when one of them lassoed a spectator and carried him along with the march. Seeing soldiers from the "Territories" (Puerto Rico and the Philippines) gave him special pleasure, and when a battalion of Puerto Rican militiamen came by, he turned to antiexpansionist senator Augustus O. Bacon of Georgia and chortled, "They look pretty well for an oppressed people, eh, Senator?" The arrival of some Filipino scouts (with their band playing, for some reason, "The Irish Washerwoman") led him to lean far over the railing and clap his hands vigorously. "The wretched serfs disguise their feelings admirably," he teased Senator Bacon. A little later he remarked to Senator Henry Cabot Lodge in a voice loud enough for the Georgia senator to hear: "You should have seen Bacon hide his face when the Filipinos went by. The 'slaves' were rejoicing in their shackles!" Bacon was too polite to remind the president of how many lives were lost putting down the Filipino insurrection that broke out after the United States took over the Philippines from Spain.

There were civilian groups in the parade that gave Roosevelt a great deal of pleasure too. When fifty or so cowboys, headed by his friend Seth Bullock, came dashing along Pennsylvania Avenue, waving their sombreros and cheering like mad, TR yelled back his greetings and waved his hat frantically. One cowboy, putting spurs on his steed, raced up under TR's very nose at such speed that he almost fell over the railing but, to TR's delight, skillfully spun his bronco around on its haunches and rejoined his companions. Then, as TR watched with a big smile, the entire bunch rolled merrily away, yelling and hollering, and snaring unwary bystanders with their lariats. When it was all over, TR exclaimed: "It was a great success. Bully. And did you note that bunch of cowboys?

Oh, they are the boys who can ride! It was all superb. It really touched me to the heart."

Like TR, most other presidents had their favorites in the parades down the grand boulevard. In 1933, FDR's seems to have been the three hundred members of the Electoral College marching in the inaugural parade (at his request) to remind people of the role that electoral as well as popular votes play in American presidential contests. But he admired, too, the model of the War of 1812's famous frigate, the *Constitution*, and exchanged friendly greetings with former New York governor Alfred E. Smith as the latter passed with a contingent from Tammany Hall. (Smith received a thunderous ovation from the people thronging the avenue, but the cowboy star Tom Mix, in town to promote a new movie, received even more applause.) For John F. Kennedy, the pièce de résistance in 1961 was the reproduction of PT boat 109, carrying members of his wartime crew; as it passed the reviewing stand, he waved vigorously and cried, "Great work!"

Kennedy enjoyed the parade, but he was distressed by the shabby condition Pennsylvania Avenue had fallen into after World War II, and soon after becoming president, he sponsored a program of renovation that by the early 1980s had produced the majestic boulevard that I was privileged to traverse when I first began jogging in Washington. Unfortunately, JFK didn't live to see any of the redevelopment, and it was the old avenue that was used for his funeral on November 25, 1963, three days after his assassination in Dallas. Thousands of people crowded the sidewalks that day to watch his casket, placed on a black caisson (the same one that carried FDR's coffin eighteen years before), proceed slowly down Pennsylvania Avenue, followed by a riderless horse carrying empty boots reversed in the stirrups, signifying that the warrior would never mount again.

The transformation of Pennsylvania Avenue was almost complete when Ronald Reagan became president in 1981 and reviewed the customary parade on the afternoon of his inauguration. Reagan's enthusiasm was mainly for the military formations in the parade. He was thrilled as he watched the soldiers and sailors march by the White House reviewing stand and execute an eyes right and a brisk salute as they passed. "Is it appropriate for me to return their salute?" he asked an army general sitting near him in the reviewing stand. "It is appropriate, sir," returned the officer a bit officiously, "if your head is covered." Since he wasn't wearing a hat, Reagan simply nodded, his hand over his heart, when receiving salutes after that, but, as he told his friend Michael Deaver later on: "I really felt uncomfortable not returning those salutes the men gave me, just standing there, motionless." Deaver reassured him. "Mr. President," he said, "you are commander in chief now, you can do whatever you want." Reagan's eyes lit up, Deaver wrote later, and "to this day, he salutes everything that moves." George Bush followed Reagan's practice, and the two of them exchanged spirited salutes as they parted after Bush's oath-taking in 1989, even though Reagan was no longer commander in chief.

What about the twentieth century's last president? In 1993, Bill Clinton omitted the military gesture when the troops marched by on the afternoon of his first inauguration. Reporters covering the parade were condescendingly amused when they saw a high-ranking army officer walk over to Clinton at one point and salute him, while the latter "froze for a few seconds before he realized that his new status as commander in chief required him to salute back." In fact, I learned, after a little research, that there is no such requirement. Most presidents, including Eisenhower and Kennedy, refrained from returning military salutes in kind because, as civilian commanders of America's armed forces, they were not in uniform and they symbolized the principle of civil supremacy over the military in the American system. A smile, a wave, nod, or friendly "Hello" sufficed for them and would have been just right for Clinton. But in the end Clinton yielded to reportorial importunities, took up saluting, and then received taunts for not matching President Reagan's panache. It was hard for me to understand why Clinton bothered to go in for saluting, since he didn't have to. I had never felt comfortable saluting the quarterdeck when I boarded ships as an ensign during World War II. Snappy salutes by nonprofessionals set my teeth on edge. Even in uniform I was a civilian at heart.

For people lining Pennsylvania Avenue to see the big show every four years, such matters were of little or no account. They were there to see the president in the morning, if they could, and to watch the parade in his honor in the afternoon. The crowds attending inaugurations increased steadily in numbers as Washington's population grew and as the ways of getting to the city—train, bus, automobile, airplane—multiplied. On stormy days, only the hardiest and most determined ventured to take up positions on the avenue for the morning procession and the afternoon parade, but on pleasant days the avenue was a hub of activity from dawn until dark. There were decorations everywhere: flags, bunting, banners, flowers. Hundreds of vendors—called "fakirs" in the nineteenth century—swarmed the avenue throughout the day, hawking soda pop, snacks, and souvenirs. The inaugural trinkets were frequently tailored to the president-elect. For TR there were Rough Rider hats, little brown teddy bears wound up to dance, pieces of wood bound together called "Teddy's Big Stick"; for Wilson there were professorial blackboard pointers, yardsticks labeled "Wilson's Rule" bearing the words "A full measure of prosperity for all," songs and ballads announcing "Woody's a jolly good fellow," and even a restaurant on the avenue with a big sign: "White House Lunches Like Mrs. Wilson Will Cook

Them, for 50 Cents." With Lyndon B. Johnson came inaugural medals, bracelets, plaques, and ashtrays bearing his likeness; with Jimmy Carter, a former peanut farmer, came scads of inaugural buttons, key chains, scarves, lapels, and tie pins inscribed with the peanut logo; and with Bill Clinton came medallions featuring his face, pens featuring his name, envelopes featuring his hometown postmark (Hope, Arkansas), books featuring his ideas, and license plates emblazoned with a promise "to build a bridge to the future" (one of his favorite fin-de-siècle catchphrases). For rainy days, there were umbrellas for sale, with prices rising as supplies declined. And for any day, rain or shine, window seats inside some of the buildings along the parade route were available for rent. On icy days, some groups paid as much as five hundred dollars for comfortable window views of the Pennsylvania Avenue parade.

In the twentieth century America's inaugural celebrations became so elaborate—lasting several days and featuring hundreds of events on and off Pennsylvania Avenue—that a few people began lamenting the egregious departure from the Jeffersonian simplicities of the early nineteenth century. A few presidents even requested simpler celebrations—Wilson in 1917, Harding in 1921, Coolidge in 1925, and FDR in 1941 and 1945—and from time to time the inaugural planners shortened the afternoon parades or omitted them entirely.

But the opulence persisted. Richard Nixon's first inauguration, in 1969, was the costliest up to that time, and his second, in 1973, was even more expensive. Carter economized in 1977, and then Ronald Reagan threw an "Inauguration Special" that Time called "the biggest, most lavish, expensive presidential welcome ever." In 1993, Clinton took a page from Carter's book—he walked some of the way with his family down the avenue after the inaugural ceremony—but the four-day inaugural festivities on his behalf were Reaganesque in their extravagance. The 1997 inauguration was costly, too, and contained, wrote one reporter, the usual "mishmash of patriotism, pride, and silliness." Clinton apparently reveled in the whole mishmash; reading about his boyish glee at the passing parade reminded me of TR's exuberance in 1905. But Library of Congress historian Marvin W. Krinz defended 1997's lavishness. A presidential inauguration, he insisted, was really "a celebration of the American civil religion. It shows the diversity and the oneness of the nation. There's a certain amount of hokiness in it, after all, but so what?"

One participant denied the hokiness: John Pinter, vice president of the Wisconsin Hall of Fame in Milwaukee. When the White House asked him to arrange a polka float for the inaugural parade, he regarded the opportunity for the president to exchange greetings with Frank Yankovic, the King of American Polkadom, during 1997's parade as momentous, not hokey. Crowned the Polka King in 1948, the eighty-one-year-old Yankovic and his wife Ida, an accordion player, arrived in Washington just before Inauguration Day with a contingent of polka dancers from Milwaukee, ready, willing, and able to take part in the inaugural parade past the White House reviewing stand. "He is an icon; he is a legend," a Hall of Fame spokesman told reporters. "He is to polka what Elvis Presley was to rock-and-roll." In the parade the following day, Yankovic sat on a throne attached to the Hall of Fame float, while all around him musicians played and dancers performed the polka and Barbara Lane, the Polka Queen of Milwaukee, sang "The White House Polka," which she had written for the president:

> We're on our way to the White House
> Pennsylvania Avenue
> We're on our way to the White House
> And we're proud of our red, white, and blue.
> The polka is our state dance,
> A dance that sets the pace.
> It's great to play for the President,
> But Wisconsin's our home state.

Well, there it was, in a scraggly nutshell: diversity and oneness. Hokey or not, the polka performance seems to have charmed the president. So did the parade as a whole, with its University of Arkansas marching band, the Democratic donkey (Irene from Alabama), schoolchildren singing "It Takes a Village" based on Mrs. Clinton's best-selling book, and the Chicago Rope Warrior who jumped rope while in a sitting position (he called it a "tush-up"). From polka to tush-up, Clinton thoroughly enjoyed the lively procession in his honor down Pennsylvania Avenue. It was just as well, I can't help thinking. It was the last bit of serious fun he was to have as he began his second term as president.

....

WILLIAM E. LEUCHTENBURG, ED., *American Places: Encounters with History* (Oxford: New York, 2000).

CHAPTER 4

The Story of Presidential Campaigns: From Electioneering to Taking to the Stump

Times change. Everything human has a history. The idea that for many years it was considered indecent for a candidate for the presidency to go out making speeches about his policies seems incredible today. But the rule at the birth of the American republic was that the man doesn't seek the office, but the office seeks the man. In 1789, George Washington didn't seek the presidency, but the Electoral College, established by the US Constitution, gave all its votes to Washington, and he quietly accepted the office—though he felt a little like a prisoner at first. The early presidents, beginning with Washington, did no campaigning. They let the political parties campaign on their behalf. Gradually, though, candidates began to deviate from the rule of silence during the nineteenth century, and by the twentieth century the practice of going out on the stump to present their opinions to the voters became acceptable. By 1908, when William Howard Taft sought the presidency, it was acceptable for him to travel around and make campaign speeches. Electioneering was replaced with stump speaking that year.

★ ★ ★

Until the twentieth century, it was considered improper, even demeaning, for America's presidential candidates to take to the stump. George Washington did no campaigning before being chosen president in 1789 and 1792, and his discreet behavior set a precedent for future presidential candidates. There was a nasty word for the behavior of people who actively sought votes when running for high office: "electioneering."

If "a man sollicites [sic] you earnestly for your vote," warned a pamphlet appearing in 1771, "avoid him; self-interest and sordid avarice lurk under his forced smiles, hearty shakes by the hand, and deceitful . . . enquir[i]es after your wife and family." Even if Washington had been eager to become the nation's first president—which he emphatically was not—he would have carefully avoided any semblance of "electioneering." Only at the local level, it seems, was it permissible to go out on the campaign trail.

Washington was fully aware of the constraints on seeking office. He knew that candidates were expected to "stand," not "run," for office. He also knew that for America's experiment in self-government to succeed, people had to avoid picking leaders who might abuse their powers once in office, and he carefully refrained from saying or doing anything, after the US Constitution was adopted, that might give the impression he sought to become president. To the discomfit of his admirers, in fact, he barely let them know ahead of time that he would accept the presidency if he was the choice of the Electoral College.

By placing electioneering out of bounds when it came to picking the president, the Founding Fathers hoped to avoid both corruption and the abuse of power in the presidential office. Only with men of character and virtue at the head of state, they thought, men who were devoted to the public good and not to the advancement of their own interests, were the liberties of the people safe and secure. Public-spirited men did not seek office; the office sought them. Washington was the ideal leader; his character, exclaimed the *Massachusetts Centinel*, was a "TISSUE OF VIRTUES."

But the rise of political parties, not contemplated by the constitution-makers, posed a threat to the self-recusing rules for men eligible for the presidency. Political parties, which emerged during Washington's second administration, chose candidates for president, launched vigorous efforts on their behalf, utilized stump speakers on the state and local levels, and did not hesitate to denigrate their opponents. The first real presidential campaign came in 1796, with John Adams the candidate of the Federalist Party and Thomas Jefferson the choice of the Republicans, and it contained a great deal of mudslinging the Founding Fathers had hoped to avoid in contests for the presidency. Neither Adams nor Jefferson did any electioneering, but unlike Washington, they followed with interest the work of the parties on their behalf (especially Adams), and made no effort to restrain the party excesses. Adams won, but four years later, when he faced Jefferson again, both candidates—Jefferson in particular this time—were active behind the scenes.

After 1800, it became acceptable for presidential candidates to keep in touch with party workers during their campaigns, and to make known their political views through letters accepting their nominations and through communications to party leaders, which were released to the press. In 1828, Andrew Jackson was tirelessly busy behind the scenes organizing his forces and directing the campaign to put him in the White House, but he refrained (or was restrained by party leaders) from making any public remarks that could be construed as attempts to push his own cause. When the Davidson County Bible Society invited him to speak on the occasion of one of its anniversaries, he politely declined. "I might be charged by my public enemies," he explained, "with having come forth hypocritically under the sacred garb of religion thus to electioneer." He did, though, accept Louisiana's invitation to attend a ceremony in New Orleans commemorating his victory over the British in 1815, insisting that it was "non-political."

William Henry Harrison, put forward as a military hero ("The Hero of Tippecanoe") by the Whigs in 1840, was the first presidential candidate to go out on the stump on his own behalf. Frustrated by Democratic charges that he was concealing his opinions on controversial issues from the public, he finally decided to accept an invitation to appear at a celebration in Perrysburg, Ohio, of the Battle of Fort Meigs (fought during the War of 1812), and to utilize the occasion to say something about his views in public. His appearance at Fort Meigs shocked some people. "When was there ever before such a spectacle . . . as a candidate for the presidency, traversing the country," exclaimed the *Cleveland Advertiser*, "advocating his own claims for that high and responsible station? Never!" The "precedent" thus set by Harrison "appears to be a bad one."

Despite the criticism, Harrison went on to make twenty or so more speeches in Indiana and Ohio, improvising remarks lasting from one to three hours to audiences ranging from fifteen thousand to one hundred thousand people, thrilling them by his performances, if not especially clarifying the basic issues in the campaign. His opponent, Martin Van Buren, a Democrat running for reelection, was convinced that "the people will never make a man president who is so importunate as to show by his life and conversation that he not only has an eye on, but is in active pursuit of the office." But he was wrong. If Harrison's stumping was not really the main event of the 1840 campaign—the Whigs' lively "log cabin and hard cider campaign" contained many other innovative features that ensured victory—it seems not to have done him any harm. In 1852, the Whigs picked another military hero as their candidate—General Winfield Scott—and when their campaign seemed to be getting nowhere, they sent him out on the hustings to whip up some "fife-and-drum enthusiasm" for their cause. Unfortunately, Scott was something of a prima donna as well as a fussbudget ("Old Fuss and Feathers"), and a babe in the woods when it came to politics, and he quickly became an object of ridicule for the Democrats, who were running Franklin Pierce for president and keeping him quietly at home. Mindful of the continued taboo on electioneering (despite Harrison's tour in 1840), the Whigs found a nonpolitical excuse for sending Scott out to appear before the public. Congress, they learned, had recently authorized the establishment of "soldiers' asylums" in Kentucky to take care of elderly and disabled veterans in their final years, and they decided that General Scott was just the man to send to Kentucky to inspect possible sites for the asylums. They arranged for him to leave Washington in mid-September, saw to it that his itinerary was well-publicized, and hoped that the speeches he made in towns and cities along the way would liven up their campaign.

Scott livened things up all right, but not exactly the way he intended. There were mishaps along the way. At one rally a gunner misloaded the cannon for a salute to Scott and it exploded, taking the gunner's arm off and then his life. Scott visited his widow that night, offered condolences, and left her with some money to tide her over. At another gathering, delegates of Irish and Germans cornered him to charge that he had treated their countrymen cruelly when they were serving as soldiers under his command. Scott insisted that he punished all soldiers, regardless of ethnic background and nationality, for serious misbehavior and that he had nothing against the Irish and Germans per se, but he didn't succeed in placating his critics. On another occasion, when his train passed through a rainy region and arrived at a town which was bone-dry, Scott apologized to the townspeople for having sat comfortably in a seat on the train during the storm while his auditors had trudged through mud and water to hear him speak. The crowd was bewildered.

Most of the time, though, the crowds were friendly and the encounter was pleasant. Carefully avoiding political issues, Scott talked about the weather, singled out for praise the veterans who happened to live in the town he visited, and, to revise his reputation as an anti-immigration nativist, said nice things about the Irish and the Germans whenever he got the opportunity. "Fellow citizens of Cleveland!" he liked to begin, in a typical speech, "—and when I say *fellow citizens*, I mean all American citizens, both native and adopted citizens." When someone in the crowd interrupted to shout, "Hurrah for Lundy's Lane!" (a War of 1812 battle), Scott, who had been there, exclaimed: "I love the Irish brogue. I have heard it before on many battlefields, and I wish to hear it many times more!" In Columbus, when someone interrupted his remarks about a site for "worn-out and infirm soldiers" in Kentucky to demand that he say something about naturalization and Irish-American citizenship, he shook his head and said with a big smile: "I think I hear again that rich brogue that betokens a son of Old Ireland. I love to hear it! I heard it on the Niagara in '14 and again in the Valley of Mexico. It will always remind me of the gallant men of Erin who in such great numbers have followed me to victory." Elsewhere, he was able to work in a comment on the "mellifluous accents" of the Germans living in the locality.

Scott's corny speeches irked some Whigs. After hearing one of Scott's talks, a Michigan Whig called Scott "a d——d old fool!—a brainless bundle of wind." An Ohio Whig felt the same way. "For God's sake. . . . Keep Scott at home," he told party workers. "Just write him some speeches and forward [them] as soon as possible. Dont [*sic*] trust him a single minute *alone*." The Democrats didn't even bother to blast him for electioneering; they simply made fun of his oratorical forays. "In every speech," huffed the *New York World's* James Gordon Bennett, "he has talked of nothing but campaigns and battles and old soldiers," with occasional references to the weather or some blarney on the "rich Irish brogue." His speeches, according to Bennett, were "as alike as eggs, and have as little variety." The *Democratic Review* scoffed that on only one day of his tour did Scott avoid hurting his chances of election—the day he arrived in a New York town, immediately ate supper, and went straight to bed. The *Review* wondered why the Whigs didn't always get him to bed when he hit town, "instead of letting him roam rampant through the country, making bad worse and demolishing the slender chances of his party."

Scott gave more than fifty speeches in all, and though some Democrats claimed he had only one speech and kept repeating it over and over again, he may well have helped his cause a bit. A study of election returns from cities and counties where he spoke suggested that he picked up Whig votes there. Hopeful to the end, Scott took his enormous defeat—he carried only four states—with, as it was nicely put, "soldierly fortitude," convinced he had run a good campaign. Afterward, a friendly Whig editor in Ohio resorted to a pun to explain the General's defeat. Scott's career as a soldier, the editor noted, disqualified him from "running." Scott "never had RUN," he said, and "he couldn't learn how."

There was no electioneering in 1856, and then, in 1860, Illinois senator Stephen A. Douglas, a nominee of the Northern Democrats, became the third presidential candidate to go out on the campaign trail. But it took a major crisis—the impending breakup of the Union—to convince him that he should go before the public to plead for a peaceful settlement of the sectional dispute dividing the nation. "I did not come here to purchase your votes," he told one crowd. "I came here to compare notes, and to see if there is not some common principle, some line of policy around which all Union-loving men, North and South, may rally to preserve the glorious Union against Northern and Southern agitators." The other candidates—Abraham Lincoln (Republican), John C. Breckinridge (Southern Democrats), and John Bell (Constitutional Union)—remained quietly at home during the contest.

Senator Douglas's open campaign pleased some people, but it also drew much criticism. "Douglas is going about peddling his opinions as a tin man peddles his wares," sneered the *Jonesboro* (Illinois) *Gazette*. "The only excuse for him is that since he is a small man, he has a right to be engaged in small business, and small business it is for a candidate for the presidency to be strolling around the country begging for votes like a town constable." The *North Iowan* declared that Douglas "demeans himself as no other candidate ever yet has, who goes about begging, imploring, and beseeching the people to grant him his wish. . . . He should be attended by some Italian, with his hand organ to grind out an accompaniment."

To mute the criticism when he headed for the Northeast, Douglas tried to give the impression that he was on his way to visit his mother in Clifton Springs, New York. But the trip took a month, with numerous stopovers and speeches, and the Republicans showered him with scornful taunts. "A Boy Lost!" exclaimed one Republican handout. "Left Washington, DC, some time in July. He has not yet reached his mother, who is very anxious about him. He has been seen in Philadelphia, New York City, Hartford, Connecticut, at a clambake in Rhode Island. He has been heard from at Boston, Portland, Augusta, and Bangor, Maine. . . . Answers to the name of Little Giant, talks a great deal, very loud, always about himself. He has an idea that he is a candidate for president."

Douglas also took his campaign to the South, where he urged people to accept the outcome of the election peacefully, even if Lincoln was the victor. "The election of a man to the presidency of the American people in conformity with the Constitution of the United States," he declared, "would not justify any attempt at dissolving this glorious confederacy." For the most part, though, he was preaching to the deaf. "The South," announced the *Southern Confederacy* in Atlanta, Georgia, "will never permit Abraham Lincoln to be inaugurated president of the United States; this is a settled and sealed fact. It is the determination of all parties in the South. Let the consequences be what they may."

Douglas was in Iowa when he heard that Lincoln had carried Pennsylvania and would probably win the election. "Mr. Lincoln is the president," he exclaimed. "We must try to save the Union. I will go south." So he returned to the South and gave scores of speeches to hostile crowds from balconies and car platforms, begging them to uphold the Union. "I am not here on an electioneering tour," he insisted. "I am here to make a plea, an appeal for the invincibility of the Constitution and the perpetuation of the union." His efforts, he soon realized, were fruitless, and when he ended his tour he was, said an associate, "more hopeless than I had ever before seen him." He was despairingly downcast when he left the South. "I think the Union is gone," he sighed.

After the Civil War, when the Republicans picked Ulysses S. Grant as their candidate in 1868, the "Hero of Appomattox" played such a passive role in the campaign—he refused even to release statements on the issues—that he was called the "Dummy Candidate" and described as being "as dumb as a mute." His Democratic opponent, Horatio Seymour, former governor of New York, was an excellent speaker, and party leaders were eager to have him use his oratorical skills against the popular but taciturn Civil War general. The *New York World* insisted that the ban on stump speaking by presidential candidates had "no foundation in reason," and journalist William Cassidy pointed out that in Britain, members of the House of Commons all went out on the stump during elections, and there was no reason why America's presidential candidates couldn't do the same.

Until late in the 1868 campaign, however, Seymour refused to make any speeches except nonpolitical ones, and when he finally gave in to his party's demands, he did so with some doubts about the proprieties. "I go to speak to this people," he told party leaders, "not because I wish to do so, but because you have called upon me to go into this along side of you." In one speech, he told the audience: "It is said that I am an interested man, and so I am, and so is every man who pays taxes and helps to support this government. How would it be if none of those who had an interest in this contest were to take part in it?"

There were objections to Seymour's electioneering, to be sure, especially among Republicans—the *Cincinnati Gazette* deplored this "most strange . . . departure from former precedents"—but the *Utica* (New York) *Observer*, Seymour's hometown newspaper, heaped praise on him. "He is moved by no ambition," wrote the editors; "he is deterred by no obloquy. Now, as ever, he meets the emergency of the hour and treads the road that duty points." When the Republicans sneered that "Grant takes his cigar—Seymour takes the stump," the Democrats shot back: "Seymour for president—No Dummy for us." Seymour's tour lasted two weeks and took him into cities and towns in Ohio, Indiana, Illinois, and Pennsylvania, ending in New York City the day before the election. Grant won the election handily in electoral votes, but in a total of six million votes cast, his popular majority was only 310,000.

In 1872, when Grant ran for a second term, the Democrats tried stump speaking again. This time their candidate was the celebrated New York editor Horace Greeley ("Go west, young man"), and though he never had much of a chance of beating Grant, he put on a campaign of impassioned speech-making that dwarfed Seymour's efforts four years before. Like Seymour, Greeley, the choice of the liberal Republicans as well as of the Democrats, had initial qualms about going on the campaign trail. At first he simply received visitors at his farm in Chappaqua, New York, after resigning from his paper, the *New York*

Tribune, though, as always, he answered all the letters he received about the campaign. In September, however, he hit the road, and in a series of earnest speeches he denounced the Republicans for "waving the bloody shirt" and called for a "New Departure" centering on the end of military reconstruction of the South after the Civil War and reconciliation between the North and the South.

Some observers, previously hostile, were surprised and impressed by Greeley's eloquence. "THE VOICE OF A STATESMAN," conceded the *New York Sun.* "Magnificent Speeches of Dr. Horace Greeley." But others were offended by his frank departure from the metes and bounds of presidential campaigning, which they thought should continue to govern the behavior of presidential hopefuls. "For the first time in the history of the country, a prominent candidate for the presidency has found it necessary to to take the stump in his own behalf," wheezed the *Hartford* (Connecticut) *Courant*, forgetting the electioneering of Harrison, Scott, Seymour, and Douglas. It went on to call Greeley the "great American office beggar" who believed that "man should seek the office rather than the office the man."

But Greeley was well aware of what he was doing. In a speech in Portland, Maine, he mentioned "the unwritten law of our country that a candidate for president may not make speeches," and then defended his own speech-making by insisting that there was "a truth to be uttered in behalf of those who have placed me before the American people." President Grant, of course, remained aloof from the campaign, as he had done in 1868, confident that he could win reelection that way. "My judgment," he told New York senator Roscoe Conkling, "is that it will be better that I should not attend any convention or political meeting during the campaign. It has been done, as far as I remember, by but two presidential candidates heretofore, and both of them were public speakers and both were beaten. I am not a speaker, and don't want to be beaten."

Grant had it right. His own silence and Greeley's garrulousness produced victory for Grant. Greeley got off to a good start, to be sure, but, thoroughly inexperienced in the art of politics, he soon ran into trouble. He succeeded in alienating both Union veterans and black voters by tactless remarks he made about them in some of his speeches. And his general demeanor—erratic, crochety, unpredictable—as well as his personal appearance—cherubic face, big blue eyes, bald pate, steel-rimmed glasses, and shuffling gait—seemed hilariously unpresidential to many people, and he was an easy target for his Republican opponents.

Republican ridicule was cruel and relentless. In *Harper's Weekly*, cartoonist Thomas Nast looked upon Greeley as a hopelessly nearsighted and pumpkin-headed clown, and in a particularly savage takeoff on his plea for North and South to "clasp their hands across the bloody chasm," he pictured the Democratic candidate shaking hands with a rebel who had just shot a Union soldier, stretching out his hand to John Wilkes Booth across Lincoln's grave, and turning a defenseless black over to a member of the Ku Klux Klan who had just lynched a black man and knifed a black mother and her child. "I have been assailed so bitterly," Greeley wailed at the end of the campaign, "that I hardly knew whether I was running for the presidency or the penitentiary."

The denouement was dolorous. Shortly before election day, Greeley's ailing wife Mary died, and he told a friend, "I am not dead, but I wish I were." After the election he exclaimed, "I was the worst beaten man who ever ran for high office." Three weeks later he was dead. Actually Greeley did better than Seymour had in 1868 and about as well as Van Buren in 1840. And four years later, the Republicans ended Reconstruction, as he had recommended, as well as their efforts to help blacks in the South. But it is doubtful that Greeley had much, if anything, to do with Republican policies.

In 1880, Republican candidate James A. Garfield gave a few nonpolitical speeches (three of them to veterans' groups) during his campaign for president, and he got neatly around the nonelectioneering tradition by arranging to receive thousands of his well-wishers at his home in Mentor, Ohio, and making little speeches of welcome in response to their pledges of support for his candidacy. It was the first of what came to be called "front-porch campaigns," which several of his successors—Benjamin Harrison (1884), William McKinley (1896), and Harding (1920)—were to utilize, as Garfield did, with great success.

Garfield's visitations went nicely. Politicians, veterans, businessmen, members of political clubs, and plain citizens, singly and in groups, took the train to Mentor bearing campaign banners, petitions, and gifts for the Republican nominee, and some of them sang for him, gave complimentary little speeches, and quoted poetry (Garfield was known as a literary man) for his edification. They arrived in such large numbers, at times, that the local railroad manager offered to run the trains out to Garfield's farm, but the townspeople turned down the proposal, preferring the profits made from conveying visitors by horse and buggy from the railroad station to the Garfield residence. Sometimes, if the crowds weren't too large, Garfield's wife Crete served refreshments after her husband had thanked his guests for their support and encouragement. On the occasions when Garfield left home to appear elsewhere and make a few remarks from the railroad platform along the way, he never forgot the rule he adopted from the outset: "Say but little, beyond thanks and an occasional remark on the localities through which we pass." Maine's Republican senator James G. Blaine was impressed with the deftness with which Garfield avoided charges of electioneering while appearing in public so often during the campaign. "With innumerable critics," he wrote later, "watchful and eager to catch a phrase that might be turned into ridicule or odium, or a sentence that might be distorted to his own or the party's injury, Garfield did not halt nor trip in any one of his seventy speeches. This seems all the more remarkable when it is remembered that he did not write what he said, and yet spoke with such logical consecutiveness of thought and such admirable precision of phrase as to defy the accident of misreport and the malignity of misrepresentation."

Over seventy-eight percent of the eligible voters participated in the 1880 election, and they gave Garfield a stunning victory in electoral votes over General W. S. Hancock, the Democratic candidate; in popular votes, however, he won a majority of less than ten thousand votes out of nine million. General James B. Weaver, candidate of the tiny Greenback-Labor Party, actually went boldly out on the stump during the campaign and made serious proposals for bettering America's industrial order, but he won only about three hundred thousand votes. Most people hardly noticed him.

In 1884, James G. Blaine became the first Republican to take to the hustings when he faced Democratic candidate Grover Cleveland in the heated presidential campaign that year. Blaine admired the way Garfield got around lingering reservations about open campaigning by his "front porch" strategy, but early in his own campaign he toyed with the idea of making a speaking tour to whip up interest in his candidacy. At first, party leaders discouraged the idea. Asking for people's votes would put Blaine "in the attitude of a supplicant," warned one Republican. "To suppose that any intelligent men who have made up their minds are going to change them after gazing at Mr. Blaine a few minutes seems to me absurd." But some Republicans thought stumping was crucial for the "aggressive campaign" Blaine promised to wage. "I see no reason against it," exclaimed one Republican senator; "it would inspire the party with zeal."

Soon after the campaign began, party workers in New England and the Middle West started clamoring for Blaine to visit their states in order to add his "personal power"—he was a magnetic speaker—to the contest. Blaine was eager to go; he enjoyed public speaking and he hoped that a lively tour around the country might divert attention from revelations of his shady dealings with a railroad company when he was in the Senate. In the end, he spent six weeks on the road, made four hundred short speeches praising the protective tariff as the key to prosperity, and excoriated the Democrats as "free traders" and "agents of foreign interests" for sponsoring tariff reduction. "We are full of hope," John Hay wrote him from Warsaw, Illinois, "and your visit is worth 10,000 votes."

The Democrats scoffed at Blaine's stump-speaking. They called him a "hippodrome," said he was "exhibiting himself like a dime-museum," and recalled that Greeley's tour in 1872 had ended in defeat and death. Blaine's incessant speech-making, according to the *Cleveland Plain Dealer*, was having pernicious effects on him; his eyes had "a peculiarly singular appearance," like those of a madman. Blaine's schedule was certainly wearing him down, but he was reluctant to turn down requests for personal appearances, "peculiarly singular" or not. Meanwhile, his Democratic opponent, New York governor Grover Cleveland, declined to respond to Blaine's sallies. Except for some nonpolitical appearances at county fairs and two speeches about civil service reform, Cleveland stayed quietly in Albany, New York, during the campaign, conscientiously attending to his duties as governor. When the story broke that he had fathered an illegitimate child when he was a young man in Buffalo years before, he let Democratic party workers handle the crisis. At that point, the campaign turned into a choice between a Republican who was "delinquent in office, but blameless in private life," and a Democrat who was "a model of official integrity, but culpable in his personal relations."

Despite the attacks on Blaine's character, the Republicans were hopeful. His campaign in the Middle West went swimmingly, and it looked as though the states there were safely in the Republican fold. But New York was crucial for success, too, and since the Democrats were running scared there, the Republicans persuaded Blaine to extend his campaign by giving some talks in cities and towns in the Empire State, making a final grand appearance in New York City before returning to his home in Maine just before election day. Blaine's tour across the state went nicely, but his appearance in New York City was a disaster. At a meeting of pro-Blaine Protestant clergymen which he attended in Manhattan, a Presbyterian minister named Samuel H. Burchard delivered a welcoming address in which he blasted the Democratic Party as the party of "Rum, Romanism, and Rebellion," thus infuriating the city's Irish-American voters, previously friendly to Blaine, who had some Irish in his background, and costing him thousands of votes. Turning up at a fancy dinner at Delmonico's restaurant that evening, to give a talk and mingle with some of New York's wealthiest citizens, didn't help either. On election day, he lost New York by 1,149 votes out of more than a million cast—and with it, the election.

Four years later, the Republican candidate, Benjamin Harrison, copied neither Blaine nor his own grandfather—William Henry Harrison—in the campaign he undertook in the fall of 1888. Instead of going out on the hustings as they had done, he chose to stage a front-porcher like Garfield's in 1880. Both Harrison and Matthew Quay, the National Republican Party chairman, were convinced that Blaine's tour, by exposing him to tactless windbags like Burchard, was largely responsible for his defeat. Quay didn't even want a front-porcher at first, though he was soon won over to it by the enthusiasm Harrison generated in the crowds visiting him at his home in Indianapolis. Grover Cleveland, running for reelection, did even less than he had done in 1884 to advance his cause, insisting that it was undignified for a president to go out hustling for votes. He let his running mate, the aged and ailing Allen Thurman, do all the campaigning. Thurman did the best he could, but sometimes he got to talking to his audiences about his ailments—neuralgia, cholera, head colds—instead of the issues, and several times he came close to collapsing on the podium.

There was nothing casual about Harrison's front-porcher. The Republicans set up a committee of arrangements to plan the visits to Indianapolis by delegations from all over the country: businessmen, politicians, veterans, farmers, workingmen, and even youngsters. ("Children have always been attractive to me," Harrison told a junior Harrison club made up of girls between the ages of seven and fifteen. "Some of the best friends I have are under ten years of age.") Harrison's little speeches, centered on the tariff and on Americanism, seem to have enchanted his callers. When he told one group he was sorry his house was not large enough for him to invite all in, someone yelled: "There will be more room in the White House. . . . We will take your order and deliver the goods in November." From an old college classmate, now in Congress, came high praise. "I want to tell you how much you have gained by your meaty speeches—without making a mistake," he wrote. "Both sides here recognize the severity of the task and the very great ability you have displayed. . . . You don't know how rapidly you are growing in public esteem for common sense and great intellectual ability."

Harrison did leave his porch for a couple of speeches on the tariff to large crowds outside Indianapolis, but for the most part he stayed home, though pressed to do more elsewhere. "I have a great risk of meeting a fool at home," he told Whitelaw Reid (with Blaine's Samuel Burchard in mind), "but the candidate who travels cannot escape him." The day before the election a delegation from Terre Haute, Indiana, presented him with a miniature silver-mounted plush chair labeled the "Presidential Chair," and later in the day a great big "Harrison Ball" (similar to the campaign balls utilized in his grandfather's campaign in 1840) came rolling into Indianapolis, after starting off in Cumberland, Maryland, in mid-August, and traveling five thousand miles through a half dozen states to greet the Republican candidate in his home city at the end of the campaign. The following day Harrison won the presidency in the Electoral College, though his popular votes were one hundred thousand fewer than Cleveland's.

In 1896 came the most famous stumping campaign in American

presidential history up to that day: Democratic candidate William Jennings Bryan's populistic campaign against the Republican's pro-business William McKinley. Right after his nomination, Bryan went out on the campaign trail with no qualms about electioneering, and by election day in November he had traveled over eighteen thousand miles by train in the East, the Middle West, and the Upper South and had given over six hundred speeches (sometimes as many as twenty-seven in one day) discussing the leading social and economic problems (especially the currency) which he thought confronted the country. "I make no apology for presenting myself before those who are called upon to vote," he declared, "because they have a right to know where I stand on public questions." McKinley, by contrast, conducted a front-porch campaign, like Garfield's and Harrison's, in his hometown, Canton, Ohio, but it was even better organized than theirs, brought far more people to his home, and featured carefully written and edited speeches both by the delegations traveling to Canton and by McKinley in his response to them. McKinley in effect "stumped in place." He knew he couldn't match Bryan when it came to public speaking, but he didn't really need to go on the stump. His party had far more funds at its disposal than the Democrats did to spend on leaflets, pamphlets, and stump speakers, and from the outset he had the support of most of the leading newspapers in the country.

Unfortunately for Bryan, the first major speech he gave—his acceptance address in Madison Square Garden in New York City—was a disappointment. Eager to impress Easterners with his seriousness, "the Great Commoner," as he was called, deliberately avoided the improvisational excitement with which he customarily thrilled audiences, and on this occasion read calmly from a carefully prepared manuscript, with no oratorical flourishes, for an hour and forty minutes. People were walking out on him long before he finished. His supporters were crestfallen, and the Republicans breathed sighs of relief. But it was Bryan's last dull speech in 1896. As he made his way around the country in the weeks that followed, he pulled out all the stops in his rhetorical repertoire, attracting enormous and tremendous ovations wherever he went. He was also the recipient of tons of telegrams and letters from his spellbound admirers, as well as hundreds of gifts (including four live eagles, a mule, an ostrich egg, and a huge stuffed alligator).

The attacks on Bryan's character and intellect during the 1896 campaign were almost unbelievably savage and unremitting. Not only was his call for replacing the gold standard with a bimetallic policy involving the coinage of silver as well as gold regarded as reckless and irresponsible, his assaults on banks and corporations and his championing of the average American—farmers, workers, small businessmen—were excoriated as demagogic, rabble-rising, and dangerous to the social order. Bryan's opponents found it hard to come up with epithets powerful enough to convey their contempt and hatred for him: anarchist, socialist, communist, revolutionary, lunatic, madman, rabble-rouser, thief, traitor, murderer. The *New York Times* called him "an irresponsible, unregulated, ignorant, prejudiced, pathetically honest and enthusiastic crank"; the Philadelphia Press said his supporters were "hideous and repulsive vipers," and the *New York Tribune* dismissed him as a "wretched, rattle-pated boy, posing in vanity and mouthing resounding rottenness." One New York "alienist" (psychologist) threw the book at him: Bryan, he huffed and puffed, was suffering from megalomania, fixed ideas, delusions, and from "paranoia querulenta," "gueralent logorrhea," and oratorical monomania.

For a man regarded as mentally unbalanced by his political enemies, Bryan remained amazingly restrained amid the attacks on his decency and respectability. Charged with lacking dignity for going around making campaign speeches, he told audiences, "I would rather have it said that I lacked dignity than . . . that I lack backbones to meet the enemies of the government who work against its welfare in Wall Street." In Philadelphia, he asked, "What other presidential candidates did they ever charge with lack of dignity?" When someone in the crowd said Lincoln, he replied, "Yes, my friends, they said Lincoln." When someone else suggested Andrew Jackson, Bryan nodded: "Yes, they said it of Jackson." "And Jefferson," volunteered another Bryan supporter. "Yes," cried Bryan, "and of Jefferson; he was lacking in dignity, too."

From train platforms as well as in large auditoriums, after bands played Sousa's "El Capitan" (a favorite of his) as he came out to speak, Bryan talked feelingly about the average American in small towns as well as big cities. Bryan's major theme was currency reform, centered on the free coinage of silver. "Where there is more money in circulation," he told his followers, "there is a better chance for each man to get money than there is when money is scarce." With free silver and more money in circulation, the hard-pressed farmer would get more for his produce, said Bryan, pay off his debts, and live a better life. Gold, Bryan insisted, helped only the classes; silver helped both the masses and the classes. He scornfully rejected what was later called the "trickle-down" theory of economics. "There are those," he said, "who believe that, if you will only legislate to make the well-to-do prosperous, their prosperity will leak through on those below. The Democratic idea, however, has been that if you legislate to make the masses prosperous, their property will find its way up through every class that rests upon them." Bryan talked of many things in his speeches—farm prices, mortgage rates, the need for credit, railroad regulation, the inordinate power of the big banks and corporations—but he looked upon "free silver" as the central issue. Free silver for Bryan meant democracy and the people; gold meant Wall Street, special interests, privilege, and plutocracy. No doubt he was simplistic in his view of free silver as a cure-all for the nation's economic ills, but the "goldbugs," as he called them, weren't all that sophisticated either in regarding the gold standard as the heart of the American system.

Just before the campaign of 1896 ended, Mark Hanna, McKinley's major campaign adviser, announced a Flag Day on which all good Republicans would display the American flag as a gesture of support for McKinley. Bryan then asked his supporters to fly the flag, too, but as a symbol of patriotism. By this time, a revival of business, accompanied by rising prices, seemed to be taking the heart out of Bryan's campaign, and on election day, November 5, McKinley swept the country with six hundred thousand more popular votes than Bryan and ninety-five more electoral votes. In Chicago, elderly businessmen and bankers, as they sat nursing drinks in the Chicago Club, were so overjoyed when they heard the news that they started playing "Follow the Leader," running up and down stairs, jumping over tables, chairs, and sofas, and dancing gleefully in each other's arms. As for Bryan, he cabled his congratulations to McKinley (something new in campaign history) and then made it clear he would try again in 1900.

A few Republicans couldn't help being impressed by the gallant fight that the "Great Commoner" waged in 1896 against such great odds. In a letter to the British ambassador after the election, the wife of Republican senator Henry Cabot Lodge wrote a surprisingly sympathetic retrospective view of the Bryan campaign. "The great fight is over," she wrote, "and a fight conducted by trained and experienced and organized forces, with both hands full of money, with the full power of the press—and of prestige—on the one side; on the other a distinguished mob at first, out of which there burst into sight, hearing, and force— one man, but such a man!" Lodge went on in her praise of Bryan:

> Alone, penniless, without backing, without money, with scarce
> a paper, without speakers, that man fought such a fight that
> even those in the East can call him a crusader, an inspired fanatic
> —a prophet! It has been marvellous. Hampered by such a following,
> such a platform . . . he almost won. We acknowledge to 7 millions
> campaign fund, as against his 300,000. We had during the last
> week of the campaign 18,000 speakers on the stump. He alone
> spoke for his party, but speeches which spoke to the intelligence
> and hearts of the people, and with a capital P. It is over now, but
> the vote is 7 millions to 16 millions and a half!

Bryan's second campaign against McKinley in 1900 wasn't exactly a duplicate of the first one, but it did contain more discussion of the free-silver issue, to the dismay of his followers, as well as renewed emphasis on the threat Bryan thought the big corporations posed to the American democratic system. But there was a new issue for Bryan this time around: anti-imperialism. Though Bryan had supported the war with Spain in 1898, he was troubled by the expansionist bent of Republican policymakers and repelled by the thought of the American republic becoming an American empire, possessing colonies around the world. But anti-imperialism, then as now, wasn't much of a vote-getter at election time.

In 1900, McKinley was so sure of himself that he didn't even bother to sponsor another front-porch campaign. He was no longer a private citizen, he told his associates, and "the proprieties demand that the president should refrain from making a political canvass in his own behalf." Some people criticized a speech-making tour he made in the Middle West in 1899 as an "electioneering enterprise," but he didn't look at it that way. In any case, he stayed in the background in 1900 and let his running mate, Theodore Roosevelt, do all the campaigning, and the latter quickly became "the central figure" (as Henry Cabot Lodge put it) of the campaign. "I am as strong as a bull moose," TR told the chairman of the Republican National Committee, "and you can use me to the limit, taking heed of but one thing, and that is my throat."

Roosevelt turned out to be as energetic (if not as riveting) a stump speaker as Bryan; he traveled twenty-one thousand miles during the campaign, spoke in hundreds of towns and cities around the land, and attracted huge crowds wherever he appeared. In his speeches, TR warned that Bryan's economic policies would wreck the American economy and that his anti-imperialistic views, if adopted, would transform the United States from a "nation of men" ready to face their responsibilities in Eastern Asia into a "nation of weaklings." TR was the first vice-presidential candidate to play a major role in a presidential campaign. Thurman's efforts in 1888 were hard to take seriously.

Bryan campaigned as vigorously as he had four years before, and he rang the changes on the three issues he singled out for special attention: the money question, the trusts, and imperialism. "I would not exchange the glory of this republic," he exclaimed, "for the glory of all the empires that have risen and fallen since time began." He also linked the trusts, gold, and empire together into a kind of unholy trinity by which the plutocracy tightened its grip on the country. But his campaign tour didn't match Roosevelt's. TR covered twenty-one thousand miles to Bryan's nineteen thousand, and he delivered 673 speeches to Bryan's 546. He also outdid Bryan in denigrating his political opponents.

Still, there were fewer hyperbolic slurs on Bryan's character in 1900; his enemies had come close to exhausting their store of invectives in 1896. There was also less talk about undignified electioneering, this time, for with Roosevelt in the fray, the Republicans could hardly condemn stump-speaking with a straight face. The *New York Times*, to be sure, criticized TR for neglecting his duties as governor of New York in order to engage in "unseemly" campaign activity; stumping, the *Times* lectured him, was "undignified and obsolete." But New York's Republican boss, Thomas Platt, was delighted by TR's efforts on behalf of McKinley. "No candidate for vice president in the whole history of the republic," he exclaimed, "made such a canvass in a national campaign." TR unquestionably gave a big boost to McKinley's campaign for reelection, and on election day McKinley's victory over Bryan was even greater in both popular and electoral votes than it had been in 1896.

With McKinley's assassination in 1901, TR became president, and in 1904, when he ran for president on his own, he decided to follow McKinley's view that although it was acceptable for vice-presidential candidates to make campaign speeches, as he had done in 1900, it was improper for presidents themselves to go out on the hustings. Like McKinley in 1900, though, he kept in close touch with campaign workers and issued scores of directives to party leaders on strategy and tactics.

Roosevelt didn't find it easy to abstain from speech-making, particularly when the Democrats attacked his policies. "I think it depresses you a little," Senator Lodge teased him, "to be the only man in the country who cannot take part in the campaign for the presidency." Roosevelt admitted as much. He felt, he said, "as if I were lying still under shell fire just as on the afternoon of the first of July at Santiago," during the Spanish-American War. "I have continually wished that I could be on the stump myself." But he confined himself to releasing a lengthy acceptance letter to the press after receiving his party's nomination, and to issuing another letter toward the end of the campaign defending himself against various Democratic attacks on his presidency.

Roosevelt's Democratic opponent, Judge Alton B. Parker, was more openly active than TR. He began his campaign with front-porch appearances at his Hudson River estate in Esopus, New York, but was goaded into making some stump speeches at the end of the campaign by Republican taunts that he avoided stumping because he had nothing worth saying. But his electioneering didn't help him a bit. On election day, TR thoroughly trounced him; Parker did worse than Bryan did in 1900, and four years later the Democrats turned to the "Great Commoner" for the third time.

In 1908, when Bryan ran and lost his bid for the presidency again, he wasn't alone in ignoring the traditional restraints on campaigning. This time around, his Republican opponent, William Howard Taft, went out on the stump, too, despite initial reservations about doing so. During the 1908 campaign, moreover, the two candidates turned up at the same banquet in Chicago at one point, shook hands, exchanged small talk, and gave speeches, though not on campaign issues. Some people even proposed a debate between the two men on the issues—perhaps in Galesburg, Illinois, where Abraham Lincoln and Stephen A. Douglas had faced each other in a senatorial race fifty years before—but nothing came of the idea. It took television years later to bring presidential candidates together in public debates.

In a new twist in 1908, some Republicans wanted the retiring president Roosevelt himself to stump the country on Taft's behalf. Roosevelt had picked Taft, his Secretary of War, as his successor, and he acted as his major adviser behind the scenes during the campaign. When things didn't seem to be going well for Taft at first, some Republicans urged TR to get into the fray himself to rescue Taft. In an editorial, "Roosevelt on the Stump," on September 27, the *Washington Post* insisted that if Taft didn't do better on the hustings, "it will become imperative for President Roosevelt to take the stump and defend his policies from the assaults of the Democratic party. . . . As for the dignity of the thing—who was the prime minister that failed to go on the stump for his country? . . . Let us have done with the foolishness of politics. . . . Let Roosevelt take the stump." In later editorials, the *Post* proposed that TR accompany Taft on a campaign tour to the West Coast, with both of them addressing crowds along the way. "Tradition and precedent do not bother the president," the Post reminded its readers. "If he should be convinced that a personal appeal to the people" was required for a Taft victory, "he will not hesitate to brush tradition aside and make a transcontinental stumping tour." But Taft gradually improved his public speaking, and TR ended by going public only with letters and interviews in order to criticize Bryan, defend his own records, and express confidence that Taft would carry on his own principles if he became president.

For Bryan, the basic issue of the campaign was "Shall the People Rule?", and he centered his speeches on contrasting government devoted to the people's rights to government by privilege. But Taft, with TR's coaching, took a critical view of the big trusts (just as TR had done as president), and some people professed to see no great differences between McKinley and Bryan on the great issues of the day. "What is the *real difference*," cried the *New York World's* Joseph Pulitzer, "between the Democrat and Republican parties?" The voters, declared the *Washington Post*, "refuse to go into hysteria in 1908 over the puny little questions that divide the two parties." Bryan expressed pleasure over the fact that the Republicans had come around to his way of thinking after all these years, and he even claimed that TR had borrowed some of his principles from him. But he went farther than TR and Taft did in his proposals for reform, and continued to be regarded as outlandish by many Republicans.

Bryan attributed the decision of the Republicans to send Taft on a campaign tour to a "GOP Panic," and he took satisfaction in knowing that his opponents were running scared. But he couldn't help gloating over the fact that the Republicans felt obliged to sponsor stump speaking in 1908 after having denounced him for breaking precedent and violating the proprieties when he took his case to the public in 1896 and 1900. "They said it was demagogic to run around the country hunting for votes," he pointed out. "Now it is eminently proper since Mr. Taft is going to do it. My greatest sin is to be made a virtue by imitation." It was hard, he added, "to keep your patents from being infringed upon this year." He also criticized TR's open support of Taft as his successor. Roosevelt was president of all the people, he pointed out, and he degraded the high office of president by using his position to push a particular candidate. Apparently for Bryan, there were still proprieties to be observed in presidential contests.

Bryan was right to be disturbed by the part TR played in the 1908 campaign. There is no doubt that the president's open backing of Taft was crucial to the Republican victory that year. After helping Taft get the Republican nomination in July, TR advised him to launch a hard-hitting campaign against Bryan. "My own voice is always for aggressive warfare," he told Taft, "and in your position I should go hard at Bryan and the Bryanites." When Taft expressed reservations about campaigning—at first he wanted to do only front porches—TR tried to bolster his spirits. "Poor boy!" he cried. "Of course, you are not enjoying the campaign. I wish you had some of my bad temper. It is at times a real aid to enjoyment."

Roosevelt's pressure, along with urgent requests from Republicans in the West to go on the road, finally convinced Taft that "the necessity for stirring up interest in the campaign is so imperative that I am willing to run the risk of breaking a precedent or following the course that Blaine took." Taft's first speeches were disappointing; he wrote them out, filled them with statistics and references to judicial decisions he had made as a judge, and produced bewilderment, not acclaim. Still, he came across as open, friendly, and likable (his hearty chuckle endeared him to audiences), and his confessions from time to time that he didn't really want to run for president convinced people of his sincerity and straightforwardness. With TR's help, moreover, he steadily improved his style and began, on occasion, to speak extemporaneously, the way Bryan did.

But TR's coaching was unremittant. "You are now the leader," he told Taft, "and there must be nothing that looks like self-deprecation or undue subordination of yourself." He also admonished him to be "very careful to say nothing, not one sentence that can be misconstrued. . . .

I have always had to exercise a lynx-eyed care over my own utterances." Above all, he continually urged him to be always on the offensive. "Do not *answer* Bryan; attack him!" he emphasized. "Don't let *him* make the issues. . . . Hit them hard, old man!" Avoid religion, he advised him (Taft was a Unitarian), and "Smile, always!" He also urged him to avoid playing golf in public because many people regarded it as a "dude's" game. "I have received literally hundreds of letters from the West protesting about it," he wrote Taft. "It is just like my tennis. I never let a photograph of me in tennis costume appear." At times, TR practically merged himself with Taft when talking about the campaign. "I believe you will be elected," he wrote in one letter, "*If we can keep things as they are.*" Elsewhere he wrote, "I want us to choose our ground and make the fight aggressively." And when Taft rode to a comfortable victory in November, he exulted, "We have beaten them to a frazzle!"

Taft and Roosevelt also beat the old anti-electioneering tradition (already much frayed) to a frazzle in 1908. It was practically a dead issue by the end of the campaign. Neither Bryan's third active campaign nor Taft's busy stump speaking came under fire on the ground of impropriety during the contest. Initially, the *Washington Post* dismissed stumping as useless (only William Henry Harrison won by it), not improper, and then decided it was worthwhile after all and began beating the drum for tours around the country by both Taft and TR "It is not undignified, it is not improper," claimed the *Washington Times*. "The people want to see and listen to the men asking their votes." The Nation chimed in. As Taft traveled around the country, the editors declared he "will get a clearer idea than a thousand delegations could give him of the temper of the people and of their desires in the way of political changes." What had once been regarded as self-seeking and demeaning finally turned out to be—as Bryan had long maintained—the truly democratic way of running presidential elections.

Four years later, in 1912, Taft took to the campaign trail again, with no ifs, ands, or buts about it, in his quest for reelection. So did Theodore Roosevelt, after receiving the nomination of the newly organized Progressive Party. Woodrow Wilson, the Democratic candidate, had reservations about stumping at first, chiefly because he doubted its effectiveness. "I have tried discussing the big questions of this campaign from the rear end of a train," he said. "It can't be done. They are too big. . . . By the time you get started and begin to explain yourself the train moves on." But he delivered a series of thoughtful speeches around the country, as Taft and TR were doing, making clear his political views to the voters. The 1912 campaign, with three presidential candidates electioneering, so to speak, was one of the most enlightening in campaign history.

After 1912, there was a steady expansion of the role candidates for the presidency played when running their campaigns: they gave acceptance speeches at the party nominating conventions, they submitted to newspaper and magazine interviews, they made speeches on the radio as well as on tours around the country, and they participated in televised debates. In addition to discussing the issues, they entered primaries and raised money for their campaigns. During the twentieth century, moreover, the candidates' wives began joining their husbands in the quest for the presidency. They advised them on the issues, helped out on the speeches, appeared in public by their sides (to great approval), coached them for televised debates, gave interviews on their behalf, made little talks of their own, and then went on to take independent speech-making tours to promote their husbands' candidacies.

By the end of the twentieth century the old idea that the office sought the man, not the man the office, had disappeared into the dustbin of history. The man—and in 2009, the woman—was now free to seek the office with all means at his or her disposal. No doubt Bryan would have been pleased by the turnabout. He would have been dismayed, however, by the money-begging that has come to dominate contests for the presidency.

CHAPTER 5

No Need to Salute the Troops, Sir

There are more reasons than my *Star-Telegram* column (1982) cited for presidents to refrain from behaving like military men. They didn't rise from the ranks to their status as commanders in chief; they are not in uniform; and by putting themselves on the same level with military professionals, they lose the status the founding fathers assigned them as civilians, elected by the people, with superior power over the military. Presidents like John F. Kennedy and Gerald R. Ford served in the military during World War II, but neither of them did any saluting when they became presidents. They smiled, nodded, or said, "Hello"; there were no bowings or civilian salutes.

★ ★ ★

Soon after entering the White House, Ronald Reagan learned that it was customary for men and women in the armed forces to greet the president with a salute, but that because the president was a civilian, he did not salute in return. The tradition bothered Reagan.

"I think there ought to be a regulation that the president could return a salute," he told a Marine commandant, "inasmuch as he is commander in chief and civilian clothes are his uniform."

"Well," said the commandant amiably, "if you did return a salute, I don't think anyone would say anything about it."

The little chat emboldened the former Hollywoodian. From that moment he began returning salutes with the precision and dash of a professional, and, upon leaving the White House, he encouraged his successor to do the same. President George Bush happily obliged. In

January 1989, when the two men parted after Bush's inaugural ceremony, they exchanged brisk military salutes that looked awesome on television. (Apparently an ex-president may salute too, in his capacity as ex-commander in chief.)

Well, George Washington and Thomas Jefferson seem to have gotten along nicely without saluting when they were in the president's house. So did John Adams, for all his love of ceremony. James Madison ventured into the field when he was president during the War of 1812 (and was almost captured by the British), but he did no saluting while inspecting the troops. Neither did Abraham Lincoln when he visited one of the forts defending Washington during the Civil War (and almost got himself killed). Woodrow Wilson did no saluting, so far as I know, during World War I, nor did Franklin Roosevelt during World War II. Harry Truman did plenty of saluting when he was in the army during World War I, but when he visited West Point (celebrating its bicentennial) in 1952, it never occurred to him as president to return the salutes of the high-ranking military officials he encountered there. Dwight Eisenhower, like George Washington years before, apparently quit saluting when he quit the army and became president.

When William Clinton became president a few weeks ago, he continued to behave like a civilian at first, the way our earliest presidents had done. Then, possibly because one prominent journalist chided him for failing to return the salutes of military personnel, he decided to adopt President Reagan's innovation after all. But his performance had none of the impressive showbiz panache that Reagan brought to the act. "Oxford University isn't the best place to learn American military habits," teased *Time* magazine. "Word is that President Clinton's sloppy salute is drawing winces from the Pentagon. Aides are subtly suggesting that he work on it."

Clinton's aides might better advise the new president that he doesn't need to return salutes, that in fact it would be wiser for him to abandon them once for all. He is, to be sure, commander in chief of US armed forces, as the Constitution provides, but he remains a civilian all the same and an important symbol of a basic principle established by the Founding Fathers: the supremacy of the civilian branch of government over the military. In an age in which the Pentagon plays so influential a role in American life, it is more important than ever before, it seems to me, for the president by his behavior to remind Americans of what President Eisenhower called "the necessary and wise subordination of the military to civil power."

Fort Worth Star-Telegram, March 27, 1982 (1993).

CHAPTER 6

To Bigotry No Sanction

In a collection of essays entitled *Character Counts*, Os Guiness put together a book about four men of character whom he admired: George Washington, William Wilberforce, Abraham Lincoln, and Aleksandr I. Solzhenitsyn. There were two essays for each of the men, written by various specialists. Since I had published a book on *George Washington and Religion* (1962), he asked me to do one of the two essays for the first president. I centered my essay on Washington's firm belief in religious freedom and his friendly relations with Jewish as well as Christian believers. The title of my essay, "To Bigotry No Sanction," is a phrase taken from Washington's response to the greetings that the Jewish synagogue in Newport, Rhode Island, gave him when he visited the town in August 1790.

★ ★ ★

During the course of a speech delivered in October 1958, on the occasion of the laying of the cornerstone of the Inter-Church Center in New York City, President Eisenhower declared:

> We are politically free people because each of us is free to express his individual faith. As Washington said in 1793, so we can say today: "We have abundant reason to rejoice that in this land the light of truth and reason has triumphed over the power of bigotry and superstition, and that every person may here worship God according to the dictates of his own heart."

Then, expressing his "horror" at the recent bombing of a Jewish synagogue in Atlanta, Georgia, he added, "You can imagine the outrage that would have been expressed by our first president today had he read in the news dispatches of the bombing of a synagogue."

Washington would indeed have been outraged. More than once, in private letters and in public statements, the first president voiced his utter detestation of intolerance, prejudice, and "every species of religious persecution." His often-expressed wish was, as he told the New Church Society (Swedenborgian) in Baltimore in an address from which President Eisenhower quoted, that "bigotry and superstition" would be overcome by "truth and reason" in the United States.

And in the fight against bigotry Washington himself played a role second to none. Both as commander in chief of the Continental army and as president of the United States, he always used his immense prestige and influence to encourage mutual tolerance and good will among American Protestants, Catholics, and Jews, and to create a climate of opinion in which every citizen (as he told the Jewish community in Newport, Rhode Island) "shall sit in safety under his own vine and fig tree and there shall be none to make him afraid."

The fact is that Washington was no less firmly committed to religious liberty and freedom of conscience than were Thomas Jefferson and James Madison. Like Jefferson and Madison, he looked upon the new nation over whose fortunes he presided as a pluralistic society in which people with varied religious persuasions and national backgrounds learned to live peacefully and rationally together instead of resorting to force and violence. In his opinion, what was unique about the United States, in fact, in addition to "cheapness of land," was the existence of "civil and religious liberty," which "stand perhaps unrivaled by any civilized nation of earth."

In his General Orders for April 18, 1783, announcing the cessation of hostilities with Great Britain, he congratulated his soldiers, "of whatever condition they may be," for, among other things, having "assisted in protecting the rights of human nature and establishing an Asylum for the poor and oppressed of all nations and religions." The "bosom of America," he declared a few months later, was "open to receive . . . the oppressed and persecuted of all Nations and Religions; whom we shall welcome to a participation of all our rights and privileges."

The following year, when asking Tench Tilghman to secure a carpenter and a bricklayer for his Mount Vernon estate, he remarked: "If they are good workmen, they may be of Asia, Africa, or Europe. They may be Mohometans, Jews or Christians of any Sect, or they may be Atheists."

As he told a Mennonite minister who sought refuge in the United States after the Revolution: "I had always hoped that this land might become a safe and agreeable Asylum to the virtuous and persecuted part of mankind, to whatever nation they might belong." He was, as John

Bell pointed out in 1779, "a total stranger to religious prejudices, which have so often excited Christians of one denomination to cut the throats of those of another."

FROM DIFFERENCES TO INQUIRY, FROM INQUIRY TO TRUTH

It is clear that Washington's devotion to religious liberty was not based, like Roger Williams's, upon a profound and passionate conviction that freedom was crucial for the Christian earthly pilgrimage. Washington seems to have had the characteristic unconcern of the eighteenth-century Deist for the forms and creeds of institutional religion. He had, moreover, the strong aversion of the upper-class Deist for sectarian quarrels that threatened to upset the "peace of Society." It is a truism that indifference leads to toleration, and no doubt Washington's Deist indifference to sectarian concerns was an important factor in producing the broad-minded tolerance in matters of religion that he displayed throughout his life.

Still, like most American Deists (and unlike many European Deists), Washington had little or none of the anticlerical spirit. In addition to attending his own church with a fair degree of regularity, he also visited other churches, including the Roman Catholic, on occasion. Moreover, from time to time, like Franklin and Jefferson, he contributed money to the building funds of denominations other than his own. But it would be wrong to assume that Washington's views were shaped solely by social expediency and theological indifference. Though Washington was not given much to philosophical reflection, he did, on one occasion at least, try to work out a more fundamental basis for his views on liberty. In a fragmentary passage in his handwriting that he apparently intended to use in his inaugural address or in his first annual message to Congress, Washington asked:

> [Should I] set up my judgment as the standard of perfection?
> And shall I arrogantly pronounce that whosoever differs
> from me, must discern the subject through a distorting
> medium, or be influenced by some nefarious scheme?
> The mind is so formed in different persons as to contemplate
> the same objects in different points of view. Hence originates
> the difference on questions of the greatest import, human
> and divine.

Without reading too much into this isolated passage, it may be noted that Washington's apparent attempt here to find a basis for liberty in a pluralistic view of human perceptions sounds very much like Jefferson. Differences of opinion, Jefferson always insisted, "like differences of face, are a law of our own nature, and should be viewed with the same tolerance." Furthermore, such differences lead to inquiry and "inquiry to truth." Freedom, therefore, for Jefferson, was a necessary condition for the moral and intellectual progress of mankind. Washington's musings on the eve of his inauguration are so Jeffersonian in spirit that one cannot help wondering whether his association with Jefferson had something to do with the clear-cut enunciation of his views on religious liberty that he made while he was president.

At any rate, it was unquestionably a matter of principle with Washington to treat the "different points of view" of the religious organizations of his day on "questions of the greatest import" with sincere respect, even if he could not share these points of view. As he told Joseph Hopkinson toward the end of his life: "To expect that all men should think alike upon political, more than on Religious, or other subjects, would be to look for a change in the order of nature." And since, as he said elsewhere, important questions are invariably "viewed through different mediums by different men, all that can be expected in such cases is charity [and] mutual forbearance." Charity and mutual forbearance in matters of religion were for Washington prime desiderata in the life of the new nation.

A REVOLUTIONARY AIM
During the Revolution Washington had little occasion to make formal pronouncements on the subject of religious freedom. Nevertheless, he made it clear, as commander in chief of the Continental army, that he was firmly opposed to all expressions of religious bigotry among his soldiers. Roman Catholic historians frequently single out the fourteenth item of his instructions to Colonel Benedict Arnold on the eve of the Canadian expedition in the fall of 1775 to show that the American commander was "one of the very few men of the Revolution who had, in 1770, outgrown or overcome all religious prejudices in religious matters." Washington's instructions on September 14 were these:

> As the Contempt of the Religion of a Country by ridiculing any of its Ceremonies or affronting its Ministers or Votaries has ever been deeply resented, you are to be particularly careful to restrain every Officer and Soldier from such Imprudence and Folly and to punish every Instance of it. On the other hand, as far as lays in your power, you are to protect and support the free Exercise of the Religion of the Country and the undisturbed Enjoyment of the rights of Conscience in religious Matters, with your utmost Influence and Authority.

In an accompanying letter to Arnold, Washington added:

> I also give it in Charge to you to avoid all Disrespect to or Contempt of the Religion of the Country and its Ceremonies. Prudence, Policy, and a true Christian spirit, will lead us to look with Compassion upon their Errors without insulting them. While we are contending for our own Liberty, we should be very cautious of violating the Rights of Conscience in others, ever considering that God alone is the Judge of the Hearts of Men, and to him only in this Case, they are answerable.

Although Washington's associations during the Revolution with the Quakers, Catholics, and Universalists showed that he was sensitive to the rights of conscience and "a total stranger to religious prejudices," only once, as Continental commander, did he single out religious liberty, in a formal public statement, as one of the objectives for which the war was being fought. This was on November 16, 1782, when he was responding to a welcoming address made by the ministers, elders, and deacons of the Reformed Protestant Dutch Church of Kingston, New York, on the occasion of his visit to the town. During the course of their address, the officers of the Kingston church declared that "our Religious Rights" were "partly involved in our Civil," and Washington, in his reply, declared:

> Convinced that our Religious Liberties were as essential as our Civil, my endeavours have never been wanting to encourage and promote the one, while I have been contending for the other; and I am highly flattered by finding that my efforts have met the approbation of so respectable a body.

No doubt Washington had assumed all along that "Religious Rights" were involved in civil rights. In an address to the United Dutch Reformed churches of Hackensack and Schalenburg, New Jersey, shortly after the close of the war, he mentioned the "protection of our Civil and Religious Liberties" as one of the achievements of the Revolution. He also told the German Reformed congregation of New York City about the same time that the "establishment of Civil and Religious Liberty was the Motive which induced me to the field."

If, on the whole, he had said little about this during the war, he had much to say publicly and of an explicit nature on the subject after he became president. In each case what he said grew out of some point raised in a formal address of congratulations similar to that delivered to him by the Kingston church.

SHOUTS OF CONGRATULATIONS

Among these many exchanges of compliments twenty-two were with the major religious bodies of his day. There is, as one would expect, much in the addresses of these groups and in Washington's responses of a ceremonial, platitudinous, and even pompous nature. The addresses were, as the Virginia Baptists put it, largely "shouts of congratulations" upon Washington's elevation to the highest office in the land. They consisted of praise for Washington's services in both war and peace, pledges of loyal support for the new national government, expressions of hope for the flourishing of religion and morality in the new nation, and invocations of divine blessings upon the president.

Washington's replies, for their part, were properly modest regarding himself, expressed gratification at the professions of loyalty to the federal government, and, regarding religion, frequently consisted of little more than paraphrases of what had been said by his congratulators. Nevertheless, there is also much that is valuable in these exchanges for the insight that they give us into Washington's views both on the subject of religious freedom and on the question of the relation between church and state in the young republic.

In thirteen of the twenty-two exchanges there are direct references to religious liberty. Three of the references are largely conventional in nature. When the Synod of the Dutch Reformed Church, for example, pointed out that "just government protects all in their religious rights," Washington said simply that he "readily" agreed with this sentiment. Similarly, when the Methodists praised Washington's concern for the "preservation of those civil and religious liberties which have been transmitted to us by . . . the glorious revolution," Washington assured them of his "desires to contribute whatever may be in my power towards the preservation of the civil and religious liberties of the American People." In the same manner, when responding to a statement by John Murray on behalf of the Universalists that "the peculiar doctrine which we hold is . . . friendly to the order and happiness of Society," Washington merely voiced his hope that citizens of every faith would enjoy "the auspicious years of Peace, liberty and free enquiry, with which they are now favored."

More interesting, perhaps, is Washington's response to felicitations from the General Convention of the Protestant Episcopal Church meeting in Philadelphia, when the Episcopalians, during the course of their long letter, expressed pleasure at " the election of a civil Ruler . . . who has happily united a tender regard for other churches with which we, as a society, had unusual strugglings of mind; fearing that the *liberty of conscience*, dearer to us than property or life, was not sufficiently secured." The letter continued:

Perhaps our jealousies were heightened on account of the
usage that we received under the royal government, when
Mobs, Bonds, Fines, and Prisons were our frequent attendants.—Convinced on one hand that without an effective
national government we should fall into disunion and all the
consequent evils; and on the other fearing that we should be
accessory to some religious oppression, should any one Society in the Union preponderate over all the rest. But amidst
all the inquietudes of mind, our consolation arose from
this consideration: "The plan must be good for it bears the
signature of a tried, trusty friend"—and if religious liberty is
rather insecure, "The administration will certainly prevent all
oppression for a Washington will preside. . . ."
Should the horrid evils of faction, ambition, war, perfidy,
fraud and persecution, for conscience sake, which have been
so pestiferous in Asia and Europe, ever approach the borders
of our happy nation, may the name and administration of
our beloved *President*, like the radiant source of day, drive
all those dark clouds from the American hemisphere.

In his reply, Washington praised the Baptists as "firm friends to civil
liberty" and as "persevering Promoters of our glorious revolution" and
tried to quiet their fears about the Constitution:

If I could have entertained the slightest apprehension that
the Constitution framed in the Convention, where I had
the honor to preside, might possibly endanger the religious
rights of any ecclesiastical Society, certainly I would never
have placed my signature to it; and if I could now conceive
that the general government might ever be so administered
as to render the liberty of conscience insecure, I beg you will
be persuaded that no one would be more zealous than myself
to establish effectual barriers against the horrors of spiritual
tyranny, and every species of religious persecution—For you,
doubtless, remember that I have often expressed my sentiments, that every man, conducting himself as a good citizen,
and being accountable to God alone for his religious opinions, ought to be protected in worshipping the Deity according to the dictates of his own conscience.

A NEUTRAL DOCUMENT

If the Baptists and the Quakers were particularly interested in liberty
of conscience under the new Constitution, there were other religionists

who deplored the omission of any reference to deity in the document. The Constitution is, in fact, completely secular in nature.

The Constitution-makers were by no means hostile to organized religion, but they were undoubtedly eager to avoid embroiling the new government in religious controversies. The clause prohibiting religious tests for officeholding was adopted, as Luther Martin acknowledged, "by a great majority of the convention and without much debate," and it was certainly welcomed by fervent church-state separationists like the Baptists.

Presbyterians in northern New England, however, were somewhat less enthusiastic about this constitutional aloofness from religion. In October 1789, when Washington was traveling in New England, the ministers and elders of the first Presbytery of the Eastward (composed of Presbyterian churches in northeastern Massachusetts and in New Hampshire) sent him a long welcoming address from Newburyport in which they commented in some detail on the Constitution. They had no objection, they declared, to "the want of a *religious test*, that grand engine of persecution in every tyrant's hand." Moreover, they praised Washington for his toleration in religious matters:

> The catholic spirit breathed in all your public acts supports us in the pleasing assurance that no religious establish-ments—no exclusive privileges tending to elevate one denom-ination of Christians to the depression of the rest, shall ever be ratified by the signature of the *President* during your ad-ministration. On the contrary we bless God that your whole deportment bids all denominations confidently to expect to find in you the watchful guardian of their equal liberties.

Nevertheless, they continued, "we should not have been alone in rejoic-ing to have seen some explicit acknowledgment of the *only true God and Jesus Christ, he hath sent* inserted some where in the *Magna Charta* of our country."

Washington's reply was a clear statement of his views on the rela-tion between church and state under the new Constitution. After thank-ing the Presbytery for its "affectionate welcome," he declared:

> And here, I am persuaded, you will permit me to observe, that the path of true piety is so plain as to require but little political attention. To this consideration we ought to as-cribe the absence of any regulation respecting religion from the Magna Charta of our country. To the guidance of the ministers of the gospel this important object is, perhaps, more properly committed. It will be your care to instruct the

ignorant, to reclaim the devious; and in the progress of morality and science, to which our government will give every furtherance, we may expect confidently, the advancement of true religion and the completion of happiness.

Washington's response was tactfully phrased, as were all his responses to addresses of religious organizations, but there is every reason to believe that the policy of "friendly separation" that he enunciated here represented his own considered opinions and those of most of his associates in the Constitutional Convention.

AN INSTRUMENT OF CHANGE
Nevertheless, a few days after Washington's inauguration, an article appeared on page one of the *Gazette of the United States* (New York), insisting that the foundations of the American republic had been laid by the Protestant religion and that Protestants therefore deserved special consideration under the federal government. In a long letter to the Gazette the following month, Father John Carroll vigorously challenged this point of view. "Every friend to the rights of conscience," he declared, "must have felt pain" at this evidence of "religious intolerance." "Perhaps," he continued, the writer

> is one of those who think it consistent with justice to exclude certain citizens from the honors and emoluments of society merely on account of their religious opinions, provided they be not restrained by racks and forfeitures from the exercise of that worship which their consciences approve. If such be his views, in vain then have Americans associated into one great national Union, under the firm persuasion that they were to retain, when associated, every natural right not expressly surrendered.

Pointing out that the "blood of Catholics flowed as freely" as that of "any of their fellow citizens" during the Revolution, and that American Catholics had "concurred with perhaps greater unanimity than any other body of men" in the work of the Constitutional Convention, Father Carroll concluded, "The establishment of the American empire was not the work of this or that religion, but arose from the exertion of all her citizens to redress their wrongs, to assert their rights, and lay its foundation on the soundest principles of justice and equal liberty." It is not surprising that American Catholics, like the Virginia Baptists, looked upon the friendly sentiments that Washington expressed to them a few months later as of major importance in the development of religious toleration in the new nation.

In a congratulatory address, signed by John Carroll and presented to Washington on March 15, 1790, by Charles Carroll of Carrollton, Daniel Carroll, Thomas FitzSimons, Dominick Lynch, and Rev. Nicholas Burke of St. Peter's Church in New York City, the Catholic group emphasized the influence that Washington, by his "example as well as by vigilance," had on the "manners of our fellow-citizens." Calling attention to the progress of the United States under Washington's leadership, the address went on to say:

> From these happy events, in which none can feel a warmer interest than ourselves, we derive additional pleasure by recollecting, that you, Sir, have been the principal instrument to effect so rapid a change in our political situation. This prospect of national prosperity is peculiarly pleasing to us on another account; because whilst our country preserves her freedom and independence, we shall have a well founded title to claim from her justice equal rights of citizenship, as the price of our blood spilt under your eyes, and of our common exertions for her defense, under your auspicious conduct, rights rendered more dear to us by the remembrance of former hardships. When we pray for the preservation of them, where they have been granted; and expect the full extension of them from the justice of those States, which still restrict them; when we solicit the protection of Heaven over our common country; we neither omit nor can omit recommending your preservation to the singular care of divine providence.

Washington's reply, it has been noted, was partly addressed to "the great non-Catholic population of the nation." "As mankind become more liberal," Washington said,

> they will be more apt to allow, that all those who conduct themselves as worthy members of the community, are equally entitled to the protection of civil government. I hope ever to see America among the foremost nations in examples of justice and liberality. And I presume that your fellow-citizens will not forget the patriotic part which you took in the accomplishment of their revolution, and the establishment of their government; or the important assistance which they received from a nation in which the Roman Catholic religion is professed.

He concluded by wishing the Catholics "every temporal and spiritual felicity."

Washington's statement, according to Thomas O'Gorman, "is among the classics of the land and one of its most precious heirlooms." Peter Guilday called it "this precious document" and added, "Washington's reply has brought joy to the hearts of all American Catholics since that time; but it was especially to the Catholics of 1790 that the encomium of the first president meant much in the way of patience and encouragement." Later that year Washington's exchange with the Catholics was published in London with the prefatory comment:

> The following address from the Roman Catholics, which was copied from the American Newspapers—whilst it breathes fidelity to the States which protect them, asserts, with decency, the common-rights of mankind; and the answer of the president truly merits that esteem, which his liberal sentiments, mild administration, and prudent justice have obtained him. . . . Is this not a lesson? Britons remain intolerant and inexorable to the claims of sound policy and of nature. . . . Britons, view and blush!

DISPELLING THE CLOUD OF BIGOTRY

Like the Catholics, American Jews were also eager that the rights guaranteed all Americans under the federal Constitution be made a reality for citizens of Jewish faith. There were probably fewer than three thousand Jews in the United States when Washington became president. During the colonial period, Jewish settlers in America had at first encountered much of the same kind of discrimination and legal restrictions that they had been accustomed to in Europe for centuries past. Nevertheless, by the time of the American Revolution, as Oscar Handlin has pointed out, they had gradually won civil, political, and religious rights that far exceeded anything that their fellow religionists in Europe enjoyed, even in Holland.

Like the Catholics, American Jews realized that their future was intimately involved in the achievement of the liberal ideals proclaimed in the Declaration of Independence, and the majority gave their warm support to the revolutionary cause. They also heartily endorsed the work of the Constitutional Convention and rejoiced especially that religious tests for officeholding (which still existed in most of the thirteen states) were prohibited in the federal Constitution.

There were, at the time of the adoption of the Constitution, six Jewish congregations in the United States: Shearith Israel, the oldest, in New York City; Jeshuat Israel (now Touro Synagogue) in Newport, Rhode Island; Mikveh Israel in Philadelphia; Beth Elohim in Charleston, South Carolina; Mikveh Israel in Savannah, Georgia; and Beth Shalome in Richmond, Virginia.

Washington seems to have had few contacts with Jewish Americans before he became president. Beginning in the late nineteenth century, however, Jewish historians (like the historians of just about every other religious group in the United States) sought diligently for evidence of close association between Washington and members of the American Jewish community. Washington was said, among other things, to have been acquainted with Hezekiah Levy, a member of the Fredericksburg Masonic Lodge to which he belonged; to have eaten a kosher meal with Michael Hart of Easton, Pennsylvania, on one occasion, and to have been a guest in the home of Moses Isaacs of Newport on another; to have sent a "gracious reply" to the invitation of Jonas Phillips to attend the dedication of Mikveh Israel in Philadelphia; to have been present at the wedding of Phillips's daughter to Mordecai Manuel Noah and to have signed the *ketubah* (marriage contract); to have drawn heavily on Mosaic law in framing one of his general orders during the Revolution; to have composed one of his public addresses originally in Rabbinical Hebrew; and, finally, to have had two Jewish officers—Colonel Isaac Franks and Major Benjamin Nones—on his staff during the Revolutionary War. Colonel Franks, moreover, was variously described as "the intimate friend and companion of Washington," "Washington's right-hand man," and "one of Washington's closest friends." As for Major Nones, Washington, it was said, once "dandled" the Major's baby boy, Joseph B., on his knees.

Actually, as most Jewish scholars acknowledge today, there is as little evidence for most of these claims as there is, say, for the Baptist story that Washington was immersed by Chaplain John Gano during the Revolution; for the Presbyterian tradition that Washington asked to partake of communion at the Morristown, New Jersey, Presbyterian church in 1777; for the Catholic legend that Washington became a Catholic before he died, "or at least was thinking of taking such a step"; or for the assertion of Protestant evangelical groups generally that Washington spent most of his time during the Revolutionary War praying on his knees in the woods. About all we can say on the basis of surviving records is that (1) during the French and Indian War Washington had some correspondence with David Franks of Philadelphia, who was purveyor of supplies for the Virginia forces under Washington's command; (2) he assisted Major David Salisbury Franks (formerly on the staff of General Benedict Arnold) in his efforts to clear his name after Arnold's defection; (3) he dined with Mark Prager when he was in Philadelphia attending the Constitutional Convention; (4) he received a bottle of water from Jacob Isaacs of Newport, who was experimenting with the conversion of salt water into fresh; and (5) he rented a house in Germantown, Pennsylvania, from Isaac Franks for two months in 1793 during the yellow fever epidemic in Philadelphia, and somehow damaged "a large double Japand waiter."

This is, as Lee M. Friedman observes, a "meager list" of "attenu-
ated Jewish contacts" on Washington's part. But it was by no means
untypical of his relations with members of religious organizations other than his own. Washington was a lifelong member of the Episcopal
church, serving as vestryman and churchwarden for Truro Parish in
Virginia for many years, and he had few associations of more than a
casual nature with any religious group but his own before he became
president. Friedman is also disappointed that there are no references
to Judaism, ancient or modern, in any of Washington's writings. But
neither are there any references to Christian doctrine in any of Washington's extensive correspondence. Washington was essentially an eighteenth-century Deist, with little or no interest in the forms and creeds
of his own or any other religious body. Nevertheless, he was, as is well
known, friendly to organized religion, regarding it, as he stated more
than once, as an indispensable basis for morality and social order. He
always looked with respect upon the "different points of view" of the
religious organizations of his day, "on questions of the greatest import,
human and divine," as he once put it, even if he could not share these
points of view.

Upon his inauguration as president in April, 1789, Washington was
the recipient of a series of congratulatory letters and addresses from
the major religious congregations of his day. In his responses to these
messages, Washington took the opportunity to deplore religious intolerance and bigotry and to proclaim his own devotion and that of his
administration to the principles of religious freedom and the rights of
conscience. He assured the Baptists, for example, that the new Constitution adequately safeguarded religious liberty, explained to the Presbyterians of northern New England the advantages of the church-state
separation contemplated in the Constitution, praised the Catholics for
their services during the Revolution and called upon their non-Catholic
fellow-citizens to treat them with "justice and liberality," and expressed
to the pacifist Quakers his respect for the "conscientious scruples of all
men."

Three of the twenty-two addresses Washington received from religious groups while he was president came from Jewish congregations in
various parts of the country. In his replies to these addresses, Washington, as Harry Simonhoff points out, had occasion to state publicly, for
the first time, his attitude toward the American Jewish community "in
explicit language." His statements on these occasions have understandably been regarded by Jewish historians as "of great historic interest
as well as importance." "For a century and a half," declared Morris
Schappes in the 1950s, "these declarations have been used to confound
the enemy in the ceaseless struggle against those who would subvert

American ideals through the propagation of anti-Semitism and other doctrines of bigotry."

Early in 1790, Shearith Israel in New York began making plans for a joint address to Washington by all six congregations pledging support to the new federal government and expressing gratitude for "the Enfranchisement which is secured to us Jews by the Federal Constitution." But the slowness of communications between the six cities, together with the reluctance of the Newport congregation to participate ("as we are so small in number, it would be treating the Legislature & other large bodies in this State, with a great degree of indelicacy, for us to address the president . . . previous to any of them"), produced so many delays that the Savannah Jews finally decided to go ahead on their own. On May 6, 1790, Levi Sheftall, president of the Savannah congregation, sent a letter to Washington on behalf of Mikveh Israel, which declared in part:

> Your unexampled liberality and extensive philanthropy have dispelled that cloud of bigotry and superstition which has long, as a veil, shaded religion—unrivetted the fetters of enthusiasm—enfranchised us with all the privileges and immunities of free citizens, and initiated us into the grand mass of legislative mechanism.

"I rejoice," Washington replied, in what has been called "gracious and flowing diction,"

> that a spirit of liberality and philanthropy is much more prevalent than it formerly was among the enlightened nations of the earth; and that your brethren will benefit thereby in proportion as it shall become still more extensive. Happily the people of the United States have, in many instances, exhibited examples worthy of imitation—The salutary influence of which will doubtless extend much farther. . . . May the same wonder-working Deity, who long since delivering the Hebrews from their Egyptian oppressors planted them in the promised land . . . still continue to water them with the dews of Heaven and to make the inhabitants of every denomination participate in the temporal and spiritual blessings of that people whose God is Jehovah.

Somewhat annoyed that the Savannah congregation had acted independently ("We do not by any means, conceive ourselves well treated by the Georgians"), Shearith Israel renewed its efforts in June for united action by the other five congregations, explaining, in a circular letter, that "we are led to understand that mode will be less irksome to the president than troubling him to reply to every individual address."

This time Jeshuat Israel in Newport agreed to cooperate ("notwithstanding our reluctance of becoming the primary addressers from this State") and insisted only that Shearith Israel prepare an address in which "your sentiments will be properly express'd & *unequivocally,* relative to the Enfranchisement which is secured to us Jews by the Federal Constitution."

Beth Elohim in Charleston also approved joint action and submitted the draft of an address that it had prepared for possible use by Shearith Israel. In this address, which was never utilized, Washington was linked with "Moses, Joshua, Othniel, Gideon, Samuel, David, Maccabeus and other holy men of old, who were raised up by God, for the deliverance of our nation, His people, from their oppression."

By August, however, Shearith Israel, for some unaccountable reason, had still not acted. The Newport congregation then decided to go ahead on its own. Learning that Washington was planning a trip to Rhode Island that month and that the state legislature and King David's Lodge of Masons intended to deliver welcoming addresses, Jeshuat Israel, impatient of any further delay, composed what David de Sola Pool has called a "historic address" of its own for presentation to the president while he was in Newport. Jeshuat Israel's exchange with Washington, the most famous of the three exchanges that American Jews had with the president, took place on August 17, 1790. The Newport congregation began by formally welcoming Washington to the city and then declared:

> Deprived as we have hitherto been of the invaluable rights
> of free citizens, we now . . . behold a government which to
> bigotry gives no sanction, to persecution no assistance—but
> generously affording to All liberty of conscience, and immu-
> nities of citizenship—deeming everyone, of whatever nation,
> tongue, or language equal parts of the great governmental
> machine. . . . For all the blessings of civil and religious liberty
> which we enjoy under an equal and benign administration
> we desire to send up our thanks to the Ancient of days.

A CHAMPION OF INALIENABLE RIGHTS
In his reply, which he read in person, Washington repeated the "punch line" ("a government which to bigotry gives no sanction, to persecution no assistance") of the congregation's address, as he was accustomed to do on such occasions, but he also emphasized the important point that religious freedom is something more than mere toleration. "The Citizens of the United States of America," he told the Newport Jews,

have a right to applaud themselves for having given to
Mankind examples of an enlarged and liberal policy, a policy
worthy of imitation. All possess alike liberty of conscience
and immunities of citizenship. It is now no more that toleration is spoken of, as if it was by the indulgence of one class
of people, that another enjoyed the exercise of their inherent natural rights. For happily the government of the United
States, which gives to bigotry no sanction, to persecution no
assistance, requires only that they who live under its protection should demean themselves as good citizens, in giving it
on all occasions their effectual support. . . . May the children
of the Stock of Abraham, who dwell in this land, continue to
merit and enjoy the good will of the other inhabitants, while
every one shall sit in safety under his own vine and fig tree,
and there shall be none to make him afraid.

Washington's statement, which has been called "immortal" and "memorable," naturally delighted the Newport congregation and the Jewish
congregations elsewhere in the United States. It has, moreover, justi-
fiably been highly prized by later generations of American Jews. Dr.
Morris A. Gutstein characterized it as one of the "most outstanding
expressions on religious liberty and equality in America" and insisted
that it "will be quoted by every generation in which religious liberty is
cherished." Dr. David de Sola Pool maintained that Washington made
a "classic definition of American democracy" when he stressed the pri-
macy of "inherent natural rights" over toleration. Harry Golden said
that Washington "articulated his divine destiny" as a champion of "in-
alienable rights" in his exchange with the Newport Jews. For Harry
Simonhoff, Washington's statement "ranks with the best of Hamilton
or Jefferson." "Neither philo-Semitic nor anti-Semitic," he adds,

the "Father of his country" seeks impartially to secure for
Jews the rights of human beings. Yet he goes a step further.
The probable recollection of Jewish contributions to the war
effort causes him to show annoyance at the word toleration
when applied to freedom of worship. One cannot but detect
compassion, or even anxiety in his letter to the Newport
congregation.

Simonhoff (like Harry Golden, who says that Washington's statement
"came out of sad and solitary communion") is doubtless reading too
much into Washington's remarks on this occasion. Still, the effects of
Washington's address, as Benjamin Hartogensis remarked many years
ago, "could not have been other than to arouse strongly the feeling of

the people of Rhode Island for the Jews."

Because of the independent action taken by Mikveh Israel and Jeshuat Israel, the New York congregation's plans for a joint address of all six Jewish congregations failed of realization. But late in 1790, when the federal capital was being transferred from New York to Philadelphia, the remaining four congregations succeeded in uniting to present their compliments to Washington shortly after his arrival in the new capital.

Arranged by the Philadelphia congregation, with the concurrence of the congregations in New York, Charleston, and Richmond, the final exchange with Washington took place on December 13, 1790. Matthew Josephson, president of Mikveh Israel, presented the congratulations of the four congregations to Washington in person. The address began by expressing affection for Washington's "character and Person" and praising him for his great services to his country in "the late glorious revolution." It went on:

> But not to your sword alone is our present happiness to be
> ascribed; That indeed opened the way to the reign of free-
> dom, but never was it perfectly secure, till your hand gave
> birth to the federal constitution, and you renounced the joys
> of retirement to seal by your administration in peace, what
> you had achieved in war.

In his response, Washington again expressed his warm regard for his Jewish fellow-citizens and applauded the fact that the "liberal sentiment towards each other which marks every political and religious denomination of men in this country stands unrivaled in the history of nations." It was his last formal encounter with the American Jewish community.

Washington's replies to the three Jewish addresses have been deeply cherished by American Jews in the nineteenth and twentieth centuries. "These three letters of Washington," according to Lee M. Friedman,

> deserve to rank with the Constitutional interpretations of
> Chief Justice Marshall and of Alexander Hamilton's *Fed-
> eralist*. As if issuing an Emancipation Proclamation, Wash-
> ington rose to the opportunity which the addresses from
> these Jewish congregations afforded. He gave point to the
> theory of American democracy which, finally and expressly
> embodied in the Bill of Rights, struck from the Jews of the
> United States the shackles of disabilities, survivals of the past
> in other lands, handicapping them politically and restricting
> them in the enjoyment of their religion. Too little known to
> the general public, these letters stand enshrined in a place of

honor in American Jewish history.

In 1876, delegates to a convention of the Union of American Hebrew Congregations made a special trip to Mount Vernon to do honor to Washington's memory. Isaac M. Wise planted a tree near Washington's tomb, Lewis Abraham read the correspondence between Washington and the Jewish congregations to the assembled delegates, and Simon Wolf pointed out in his address to the group that this correspondence had been translated into Hebrew and "had aroused much interest in Europe and Asia."

Washington's Newport statement in particular, with its emphasis on "inherent natural rights" and its inclusion of the phrase, "to bigotry no sanction," has, as Friedman observes, become "famous in American Jewish history." Historians of American Judaism have uniformly regarded it as a "classic document" in the development of freedom in the United States and have praised not only its content but its "beautiful" and "impressive" style as well. Indeed, in an excess of enthusiasm, one writer even insisted that it "bears unmistakable signs of having been originally composed in Rabbinical Hebrew."

In 1824, while championing a bill in the Maryland legislature for removing all political restrictions from Jewish citizens in the state, Colonel J. W. D. Worthington read Washington's exchange with the Newport congregation *in toto* to show that "the father of his country was in favour of the political equality of the Israelites." Grover Cleveland and other notables also made extensive use of this exchange in speeches which they delivered in New York City in November 1905 in commemoration of the 250th anniversary of the settlement of Jews in America. And in 1908, when a memorial tablet was unveiled in the Newport synagogue, Leon Huhner read Washington's Newport statement at the end of his dedicatory address and voiced the hope that the first president's views "may be repeated anew in the same spirit, by the entire community, in every generation."

With the rise of the Nazi terror in the 1930s, Washington's exchange with the Newport synagogue took on renewed significance for American Jews. In August 1940, the 150th anniversary of Washington's Newport address was celebrated by Jewish congregations in Newport and in New York. In a series of nationally broadcast speeches delivered for the occasion in the Central Synagogue in New York City, Rabbi Jonah M. Wise contrasted Washington, the man of "truth, faith, and liberty," with the "leering, brutal conquerors of Europe"; Dr. Morris A. Gutstein emphasized Washington's distinction between "two types of liberty: one, mere *Toleration*, another, real *Equality*"; and Dr. David de Sola Pool called attention to Washington's "utter freedom from religious prejudice, and his conviction that in this new America all religions must stand on a footing of equality."

The following year, when the American Jewish Committee published an analysis of anti-Semitic propaganda in the United States, it reproduced Washington's Newport address on the first page of the pamphlet and entitled the report "To Bigotry No Sanction." The famous phrase—"Happily the government of the United States . . . gives to bigotry no sanction, to persecution no assistance"—was also inscribed on the pedestal of the monument erected to the memory of Haym Salomon, the Jewish financier who contributed so much to the Revolution, in Chicago in December 1941. It also appears on the tablet which was placed on the southern wall of the Newport synagogue when it became a national historic site in the summer of 1947.

REAL EQUALITY, NOT MERE TOLERATION

Two years after his exchange with the American Jewish congregations, Washington had a brief encounter with a little group of Swedenborgians in Maryland. In January 1793, when he was visiting Baltimore, the tiny New Church Society, which had been organized in the city the previous year, "boldly" (as the historian of the movement puts it) presented him with a copy of Emanuel Swedenborg's *The True Christian Religion*, together with an "energetic" address rejoicing that "Priestcraft and Kingcraft, those banes of human felicity, are hiding their diminished heads" and that "equality in State, as well as in Church, proportionately to merit, are considered the true criterion of the majesty of the people."

In what Swedenborgian writers regard as a "rational" and "manly" reply, Washington paid tribute to freedom of religion and then added significantly, "In this enlightened age & in this Land of equal liberty it is our boast, that a man's religious tenets will not forfeit the protection of the Laws, nor deprive him of the right of attaining & holding the highest offices that are known in the United States." It was Washington's final public insistence upon "real *Equality*" rather than "mere *Toleration*" for citizens of every faith in the young republic.

In September 1796, Washington issued his farewell address to the nation. The "wisdom of Providence," he declared, in a passage reminiscent of the notes he had jotted down at the beginning of his presidency, "has ordained that men, on the same subjects, shall not always think alike." Nevertheless, "charity and benevolence when they happen to differ," he continued, "may so far shed their benign influence as to banish those invectives which proceed from illiberal prejudices and jealousies."

A few months later, in responding to the address of the twenty-four Philadelphia clergymen on the occasion of his retirement from office, he expressed his "unspeakable pleasure" at viewing the harmony and brotherly love which characterize the Clergy of different denominations, as well in this, as in other parts of the United States; exhibiting to the world a new and interesting spectacle, at once the pride of our country and the surest basis of universal harmony.

The Philadelphia clergymen doubtless realized that Washington himself had played a leading role in producing this "new and interesting spectacle." He had labored hard, while he was president, as well as during the Revolution, to banish "illiberal prejudices and jealousies" in religious matters from the nation and to throw his weight against the "power of bigotry and superstition" in the young republic.

It is of course too much to say, as did the so-called "Shaker Bible," published in 1808, that "the wise and generous Washington" was solely responsible for the achievement of "civil and religious liberty" and the "rights of conscience" in the United States. Still, by the example he set, in word and deed, as Continental commander and as president, Washington unquestionably deserves major credit, along with Jefferson and Madison, for establishing the ideals of religious liberty and freedom of conscience (without which there can be no genuine cultural and intellectual freedom) for Protestants, Catholics, and Jews—and for Deists and freethinkers as well—firmly in the American tradition.

OS GUINESS, ED., *Character Counts: Leadership Qualities in Washington, Wilberforce, Lincoln, and Solzhenitsyn* (Grand Rapids, MI: Baker Books, 1999).

CHAPTER 7

The Campaign of 1852: A Civilian Beats a General

D uring the 1952 presidential campaign, when General Dwight D. Eisenhower ran for president against Adlai Stevenson, Harry Truman, the outgoing president, pointed out that a century earlier, in 1852, a military man, General Winfield Scott, ran for president against Franklin Pierce and was badly defeated. Truman's remark led me to do some research on the 1852 campaign, and I ended up writing an article on "Old Fuss & Feathers" (Scott) and "the Fainting General" (Pierce) for the Southwest Review, an excellent quarterly published at SMU, where I was on the faculty at the time. In 1952, it never occurred to me that some day I would publish an entire book on *Presidential Campaigns* (1984) for Oxford University Press that included a chapter on the campaign of 1852, about which I had learned some new things. The head of the SMU Press, Allen Maxwell, and the editor of the *Southwest Review*, Margaret Hartley, turned to me frequently for book reviews, as well as essays, and we became good friends through the years, sharing a liberal outlook on political matters. In the 1950s and 1960s that meant favoring the integration of America's schools and colleges, including SMU, and opposition to Wisconsin senator Joseph McCarthy's determined drive to destroy people he didn't like by tarnishing them with the charge of being "soft on communism."

President Eisenhower disliked McCarthy too. After the Senate voted to censure him for his recklessness, Ike told a friend with a smile, "McCarthyism has become McCarthywasm."

★ ★ ★

In response to queries about the current Eisenhower boom, President Truman recently assumed the role of history professor and, utilizing his researches, so it is said, in the many-volumed *Dictionary of Ameri-*

can Biography, lectured the press briefly on the presidential campaign of exactly a century ago. The campaign of 1852, in which a professional military man—or "military chieftain" as he was called—ran for the presidency on the Whig ticket and was ingloriously defeated by a dark horse put up by the Democrats, was, the president indicated, of special interest at the present time, and while he did not press the analogy further, the implication was clear enough. Historical analogies are, of course, among the most deceptive of all forms of intellectual exercise. Pessimists to the contrary, if there is anything we learn from history it is that history does not repeat itself, and it is obvious that the situation in America in 1852 was unique and cannot, in the nature of things, ever recur. Still, the Scott-Pierce contest of 1852, while not as boisterous as the Log Cabin campaign of 1840, or as scurrilous as the Jackson-Adams campaign of 1828, is interesting in itself. And without a doubt it does give some indication of what can happen in this country when a professional soldier aspires to the highest office in the land.

There was nothing unusual in General Winfield Scott's desire to take up residence in the White House. True, the American people from colonial days onward tended to view the military establishment with a distrust bordering at times on contempt and between wars had been quick to write off the regular army as a dispensable and somewhat irrelevant luxury. But they had always gloried in their military heroes, and they had already installed four general-presidents in the White House. Of these four, however, only Zachary Taylor, put forth successfully by the Whigs in 1848, could be considered, strictly speaking, a professional soldier.

It was argued by opponents of Scott that Washington, Jackson, and William Henry Harrison were really "citizen soldiers." Soldiering was only one of their many activities, and they had all had considerable experience in various civilian capacities before entering the White House. Zack Taylor and Winfield Scott were, by contrast, "mere military men," as their opponents charged, and their supporters felt compelled to demonstrate that they were much more than this. In 1848, the Whigs had indignantly denied the Democratic charge that they were trying to "steal into power" under the "great tail" of Taylor's "military coat." While they did not make quite clear what Taylor's other qualifications were, the American electorate, in returning the Whigs to power, apparently agreed with James Russell Lowell in the *Biglow Papers* that Taylor "hezn't told ye wut he is, an' so there ain't no know in', but wut he may turn out to be the best there is agoin'."

Taylor may not have turned out "the best there is agoin'"—he died after less than two years in office—but the Whigs had succeeded with one military hero, and in the absence of any other real campaign issues (both parties had agreed not to disagree on the touchy slavery question), perhaps another hero could lead them once again to victory. More than the Taylor-Cass campaign of 1848, the Scott-Pierce contest of 1852 came to center around the specific issue of the professional soldier versus the citizen soldier. Scott's opponent, Franklin Pierce, had been one of the "earliest volunteers" in the Mexican War—so his campaign biographer, Nathaniel Hawthorne, pointed out—and had served briefly as brigadier-general in Scott's army. Hawthorne, for one, was convinced that the American people would prefer the "chivalrous beauty" of the "devotion of the citizen soldier to his country's cause, which the man who makes arms his profession, and is but doing his regular business on the field of battle can not pretend to rival." Anyway, Hawthorne added for good measure, General Pierce, in his nine months' stint in the army, had "seen far more of actual service than many professional soldiers during their whole lives."

The Whigs found the citizen-soldier argument highly amusing, not to say hilarious. They took a closer look at Pierce's military record and came up with the delicious information that on two occasions (or was it more?) General Pierce had fainted in the heat of battle in Mexico. (In fairness to Pierce, it must be said that he had been thrown off his horse and badly injured at the beginning of one battle, and the fact that he had passed out twice thereafter is by no means evidence of faint-heartedness in battle.) Do the American people actually want a "Fainting General" in the White House? they asked jubilantly. Well, retorted the Democrats, do they want a "mere military man," a general-in-chief who has been a burden on the national treasury to the tune of more than $350,000 during his forty-four years of service and who, like Oliver Twist, is "always asking for more"? Do they want a parade-ground-minded "Old Fuss and Feathers" who struts around arrogantly in showy and expensive uniforms unworthy of a "republican soldier"?

With that, the issue was joined. The contest between the professional soldier and the citizen general had resolved itself into a contest between "Old Fuss and Feathers" and the "Fainting General" with no holds barred. To be sure the two parties did try to "smear" each other with the taint of abolitionism or—in an appeal for the Irish vote—with the charge of religious bigotry. At one point, in a manner curiously resembling the campaign of 1940, they even accused each other of intending to get the country into foreign wars. But for the most part the campaign dwelt on personalities. There is nothing new about character assassination in American history.

Unfortunately, General Scott was particularly vulnerable in this kind of campaign. For years he had been in the public eye. He had emerged from the War of 1812 as a hero—at a time when the American public badly needed heroes—and thereafter a succession of administrations had called for his services in various Indian wars and diplomatic crises. In 1841 he had achieved his long-cherished wish to become general-in-chief of the Army with headquarters in Washington, and a few years later Democratic president Polk, with great reluctance—for he feared Scott's presidential ambitions—sent him to "conquer a peace" in Mexico, which he did very thoroughly, thereby further enhancing his already great military reputation. All of these things were well known, and even his severest critics did not deny that he had served his country in various military assignments with distinction. But there was another side to Scott's career that was equally well known—or if not, the Democrats proposed to see that it was amply publicized. Scott was somewhat of a prima donna. No more, perhaps, than Andrew Jackson or Zack Taylor, but a prima donna nonetheless. He did, for one thing, love elegant uniforms. When first commissioned as a captain in 1808, he had immediately ordered a uniform from the best tailor in Richmond and spent two hours in a locked bedroom strutting about in front of a mirror. The Democrats contended that he was still strutting around, and they painted a melancholy picture of the "Reign of Epaulets" that was bound to follow his election. Furthermore, Scott had always been keenly rank-conscious, and his extreme sensitivity about the prerogatives of rank had led him into more than one quarrel with fellow officers and with various administrations in Washington. In 1828, for example, he had flatly refused to accept orders from the general-in-chief in Washington who, he felt, had been unfairly elevated over himself, and his long quarrel with President John Quincy Adams over this point makes the MacArthur-Truman controversy seem a tempest in a teapot by comparison.

Finally, Scott had a weakness for writing letters: long, angry letters, clothed in "tinsel rhetoric," as Jackson had sneered. More than once he had put his foot in his mouth in the heat of the moment. Who had not heard, for instance, of the letter he had written to the Secretary of War, with whom he was then feuding, in which he explained his absence when the Secretary sought him out by saying he had stepped out "to take a hasty plate of soup"? Or the time he had complained about a plot to "fire upon my rear" in Washington? When he was not strutting around in "unrepublican" uniforms, he was always stepping out to take "hasty plates of soup" or worrying about "*fire in his rear*," the Democrats insisted. He was "ambitious, bigoted, proscriptive"; no one could get along with him because of his "suspicious jealousy, his hasty temper, and his eagerness for personal advancement." Was this not what you would expect of a professional soldier? asked the Democrats. "The people do not like mere soldiers for presidents," they said with finality. "The regular army is not a good school for presidents."

On such points Franklin Pierce, on the other hand, was completely unassailable. He was, in fact, practically a nonentity. Many of the delegates to the Democratic convention had never heard of him until his name began appearing in the balloting. Who is Frank Pierce? was the question that echoed throughout the land after the convention had adjourned. Whigs and Democrats could not be expected, of course, to come up with the same answers, but both, it would appear, were somewhat hard put to dig up enough specific information about him to go to work on. The Whigs jeered that Pierce campaign biographies were padded with eulogies to his father, relatives, and friends because of the paucity of interesting information about the candidate himself. Even Nathaniel Hawthorne's biography (Nat had been Frank's "chum" back in college days) came in for ruthless dissection, and it must be admitted that it did, in fact, represent one of that author's less successful creative efforts. The judgment of Richard H. Dana Jr. that Pierce was "a kind of third-rate country, or at the most state politician" was certainly biased, but it could hardly be denied that Pierce's service in Congress, first as representative and then as senator from New Hampshire, had been something less than spectacular.

The Democrats, however, refused to be embarrassed by the limitations of their candidate. It was this very "negative strength"—Pierce's innocuous past record—that made them feel they had picked a sure winner. While the Whigs twitted them for advancing a candidate whose name even a supporter like the *Vincennes Sentinel* could not get straight, the Democrats went ahead confidently presenting their candidate as a modest, quiet, conscientious gentleman, who had done well in New Hampshire law and politics and in Congress, and who, as a gallant citizen soldier, had leaped to the colors upon the outbreak of the Mexican War and had served with distinction on the field of battle. The alternative, they said, was a man utterly devoid of qualifications for high civil post. Scott has "never filled any civil post and he is wholly destitute of experience in civil affairs," cried the Democratic sheet *The Campaign*. "Take away the record of his battles, and he has nothing left which would command even a passing notice." "Pure military men," said the *New York Herald*, after commenting on the Duke of Wellington's record as prime minister of Great Britain, "are the greatest bunglers at everything except fighting." Insofar as Scott had any political ideas, he was, according to the Louisiana Courier, a "blue-bellied old federalist and fogy." With what may have been possibly the greatest exaggeration of the entire campaign, the Democratic *Papers for the People* proposed the slogan: "Frank Pierce is Frank Pierce."

But what was even worse, the Democrats continued, was the prospect of introducing a "military chieftain" like Scott into the White House, a man who would "attempt to introduce the drill of the camp into the councils of the cabinet." In a speech in Richmond, Virginia, Stephen A. Douglas fairly shuddered as he contemplated the dangers of trying to convert "a good general into a bad president." He called attention to the continual turmoil which characterized South American republics because of the political ambitions of military men in those countries, and he warned ominously against importing this "Mexican policy" into the United States.

James Buchanan followed the same line of attack: "From Cæsar to Cromwell, and from Cromwell to Napoleon," he cried, "history presents the same warning—beware of elevating to the highest civil trust the commander of your victorious armies." While he did not specifically accuse Scott of Napoleonic ambitions, he insisted, "The precedent is dangerous in the extreme. . . . If the precedent can be established in the comparative infancy and purity of our institutions . . . what may be the disastrous consequences when our population shall number one hundred millions, and when our armies in time of war may be counted by the hundreds of thousands?" "Civil government," he continued, "is not a mere machine, such as a regular army. In conducting it, allowance must be made for that love of liberty and spirit of independence which characterize our people. Such allowances can never be made,—authority can never be tempered with moderation and discretion, by a professional soldier, who has been accustomed to have his military orders obeyed with the unerring certainty of despotic power." Furthermore, a military chieftain like Scott was apt, as president of the United States, to involve the country in foreign wars, and as far as Buchanan was concerned, the American people "are sufficiently prone to war without any such stimulus."

In meeting the military-chieftain argument, the Whigs took great pains to show that Scott had abundant civil qualifications for office. "His civil services," said the *Albany Journal*, "would furnish surplus capital for a dozen such statesmen as General Pierce." With pride the Whigs pointed to the skill with which Scott had restored tranquillity on the Canadian border in 1838 and the deftness with which, the following year, he had settled the Maine boundary dispute which was seriously threatening war with Great Britain. Had not the pacifist William Ellery Channing paid tribute to him as a "great pacificator" and "friend of mankind" in the preface to his *Lectures on War*? "No greater error can be committed . . . than to suppose he is a great soldier, a victorious general, and nothing else," said Congressman John Middleton Clayton. "He is a scholar, an elegant and profound scholar. He is a man, if he had never achieved a victory in battle, eminently qualified to fill the office of president because of his civil qualifications." Winfield Scott, he declared, warming to his subject, "is a man whose experience in public affairs . . . is equal to that of any member of the House of Representatives or the Senate of the United States!"

Clayton's colleague, John C. Spencer, thought it was unfair to equate Scott with the military chieftains of Europe. "Blücher and Haynan would probably disown him as a soldier of their mould." He is "simple," "natural," and "as affectionate as a child"; his "way and manners are so gentle and kind as to be almost feminine." The life of a professional soldier in the United States, Spencer explained,

> is not like that of the European officer who has spent his life in long and bloody wars, or secluded in garrisons and forts. General Scott . . . has . . . maintained for the greater part of his life an extended and various intercourse with his fellow citizens in every part of our republic, and with men of all trades, business, and professions, he has been in constant communion. The frankness and republican simplicity of his intercourse with men is the result of this extended acquaintance with their habits, views, and feelings. Strip him of his uniform and all other military trappings, and a stranger would scarcely suspect him of being a soldier. . . . No military man in this country has been called so often to the discharge of civil duties of the greatest difficulty and delicacy, and of the utmost importance, and indeed few civilians have encountered so many perplexing and sometimes repugnant occasions of public service.

It is unfortunate, but not surprising, that the discussion of the fitness of the professional soldier for high civil office was not for long sustained on this relatively lofty level of debate. Before long, the Democrats were calling Scott a "carbuncled-faced old drunkard" whose military fame rested chiefly on the valor of citizen soldiers in the ranks like Pierce, and the Whigs were accusing Pierce of having dishonored his country by cowardice in battle. With great enthusiasm, the Whigs took up the "Fainting-General" motif and published a miniature book, an inch high and a half inch wide, entitled *The Military Services of General Pierce.* Summarizing these services for its readers, the *Louisville Journal* said that Pierce "tumbled from his horse just as he was getting into one fight, that he fainted and fell in the opening of a second, that he got sick and had to go to bed on the eve of a third, and that he came pretty near to getting into the fourth, missing it only by about an hour." One devoted Whig, in a poetic mood, attempted to reduce the basic issues of the campaign to the following terms:

Two generals are in the field,
Frank Pierce and Winfield Scott, ·

Some think that Frank's a fighting man,
And some think he is not.
'Tis said that when in Mexico,
While leading on his force,
He took a sudden fainting fit,
And tumbled off his horse.
But gallant Scott has made his mark
On many a bloody plain,
And patriot hearts beat high to greet
The Chief of Lundy's Lane.
And Chippewa is classic ground,
Our British neighbors know,
And if you'd hear of later deeds,
Go ask in Mexico.

When the Whigs got tired of improvising variations on the "Fainting-General" theme, they combined it with ridicule of attempts by Pierce's supporters to dig up pertinent material from their candidate's obscure and uneventful past. Particularly amusing to them was the speech of ex-Governor Steele of New Hampshire in which he mentioned in passing that Pierce had once given a boy "a whole cent" with which to buy a stick of candy. Commenting that anyone else (presumably Whigs) would have given the lad at least a nickel, the Whigs came up with "The Ballad of the Stick of Candy" in celebration of the Democratic candidate's "reckless liberality." An anecdote to the effect that young Pierce had once corrected his aged father's spelling of the word "but" also came in for unending ridicule. Commented the *Louisville Journal*: "What political honors can be too lofty for the man who gave a cent's worth of candy to a boy who was a total stranger to him . . . and who could spell 'but' when he was only just out of college!" The *Boston Atlas* seized the opportunity to return to the subject of General Pierce in Mexico: Pierce, it said, was ordered

to proceed to a certain place, and make a feint to attract the attention of the Mexicans. . . . Now, although General Pierce had progressed far enough in the spelling book to be able to tell his illustrious father how to spell b-u-t, yet he had . . . no idea of the difference between feint and faint. Accordingly he proceeded to the spot pointed out by his superior, tumbled from his horse, and commenced to faint. A soldier, seeing the manœuver, and not understanding military tactics, asked him what he was doing. "Obeying orders," promptly replied the general.

At this point, the Springfield (Illinois) *Unionist and Statesman* finally summed up Pierce's qualifications for the presidency as follows:

1793, born.
1817, spelled "BUT."
1833–1842, voted in Congress against everything.
1842, gave a boy, who was an entire stranger to him,
 a cent to buy a stick of candy.
March 1847, appointed a brigadier-general by
 President Polk.
August 19, 1847, fell from his horse on the hard-fought
 and bloody field of Contreras.
August 20, 1847, fainted at Churubusco.
September 14, 1847, did NOT take the city of Mexico.
May 1848, came home safe.
June 5, 1852, was "astonished" by the intelligence that he
 was nominated for president.
June 6, 1852, so was everybody else!

The Whigs, to be sure, had no monopoly on such foolishness. For their part, the Democrats pounced upon every episode from Scott's long and at times stormy career that could be reduced to ridicule and made the most of them. They talked of "hasty soup clubs" and "fuss and feather societies" joining in the "Military Hurrah" for this "weak, conceited, foolish, blustering disciple of gunpowder" and predicted that the Whigs would soon be digging up "old bones from the battle fields" and running them for office. They declared that Scott had quarreled with every "great man" with whom he had ever come in contact, quoted Henry Clay as having once said there was "something rotten" about him, and Andrew Jackson as having described him as one of those "intermeddling pimps and spies of the war department in the garb of a gentleman." They pointed out that he had been suspended from the army in 1810 after a quarrel with General Wilkinson, that he had been taken a prisoner by the British in the War of 1812, and that he had mistreated Irish-Americans during the Mexican War. (Scott took the last charge seriously enough to go around the country crying "How I love to hear that rich Irish brogue!" at every conceivable opportunity.) Nor were the Democrats to be outdone by the Whigs in reducing the opposition candidate's career to an absurdity. The *Wheeling Argus* disposed of Scott in a broadside, widely reprinted in Democratic journals, which ran, in part, as follows:

After fighting through all the battles of the Revolution from
1776 to 1783 and establishing independence on a firm basis,

. . . he was born, being in the year 1786. . . . He grew up
with epaulettes on his shoulders, a canteen on his back, & a
breastplate on his rear! When a mere boy he had large com-
bativeness & evinced a desire to fight every hog, dog, cow &
horse that came within his reach. He strutted around town
like a turkey, or rode in a coach not paid for. He was fed on
hasty plates of turtle and oyster soup, which inspired him
to swim in the sea of society with plumes, lived the life of a
vain coxcomb, in all the pride and pomp of war! In 1808,
he became a soldier of fortune, snarled at patriot soldiers,
keeps their money, and is turned out of the army! was shot in
the rear at Lundy's Lane, taken prisoner at Queenstown! . . .
Drives the last nail in the coffin of federalism and gunpowder
glory!"

Whatever else one may say of the Argus broadside, it was right about
one thing: "gunpowder glory," it turned out, was not enough to carry
General Scott to victory. As election day approached, the Democrats
noted with satisfaction that the "*military madness*" for Scott seemed to
be subsiding, and that even Scott's last-minute "nonpolitical" tour of
the West, ostensibly to seek a site for a soldier's home, failed to raise
the "drum-and-fife enthusiasm" that the Whigs had counted on. With
Scott's stunning defeat—he carried only four states—the Whig party began its gradual disintegration and disappearance as a force in American
political life.

Did the military-chieftain argument emphasized by the Democrats
play any part in the outcome of the election of 1852? Most students of
the period appear to think not. James Ford Rhodes's views may be tak-
en as typical: the American people were tired of slavery agitation and
preferred Pierce to a man who appeared to have antislavery leanings
and who certainly had some support from northern antislavery Whigs.
The appeal of the military hero, which had been effective with William
Henry Harrison in 1840 and with Zachary Taylor in 1848, failed in
1852 to overcome the handicap of Scott's being a "Seward candidate
and tinctured with Free-soilism."

It is true that one Whig editor in Ohio, in a postmortem on the election, declared that it was Scott's military background that had chiefly
incapacitated him for the battle of politics: "He never had run, and he
couldn't learn how." But after the Civil War, General Grant, a greater
military chieftain than Scott and with as little experience in politics, was
to ride triumphantly into the White House, and citizen generals like
James A. Garfield and Benjamin Harrison were to find their baptism
of fire on Civil War battlefields enormously effective in their bid for
votes. On the other hand, it is also true that the argument against the

professional soldier in the White House was raised again when Grant ran for office, and there is little doubt that it will always be raised when a military man seeks high office in this country.

Would Scott have made a good president? Irving Stone, in his survey of defeated presidential candidates (*They Also Ran*), concludes that he would have. His honesty, integrity, courage, and diplomatic skill, Stone believes, would have stood the country in good stead. Scott's sympathetic biographer, Charles Winslow Elliott, however, believes that the general's weaknesses—his acute sensitivity to criticism, his vanity, and his love of ostentation—would have led him into indiscretions which would have served neither himself nor the country well. Still, it is difficult to work up much enthusiasm for the man who did win. A contemporary of Pierce's, Gideon Welles, found that the new president was a "vain, showy, and pliant man" who "by his errors and weakness broke down his Administration, and his party throughout the land," and Roy F. Nichols, authority on Pierce, does not dissent in general from this judgment.

It is impossible not to conclude after an impartial weighing of the evidence that Scott, for all his vagaries, was by far the abler man of the two. But it is also impossible to deny that Scott was temperamentally unsuited to the give-and-take of political life and that a Scott administration would probably have degenerated into a series of personal quarrels over relatively unimportant issues. Scott would not necessarily have tried to introduce "the drill of the camp into the councils of the cabinet," but there certainly would have been endless bickering over the various rights and duties of his civilian associates. It would all have been very colorful, far more colorful certainly than the administration which did materialize, but whether the country could have afforded the luxury of a prima donna in office in those critical times is another question.

As a case study of the professional soldier in politics, the campaign of 1852, while not conclusive, does lead us to certain observations. For one thing, it would appear that a military reputation per se is not enough to carry a man into the White House. The Whigs worked long and hard to prove that Scott was not a "mere military man"—the phrase recurs constantly—and that he possessed in abundance those civil qualifications which are deemed essential for the office of president of the United States. They were throughout the campaign confronted with the difficult task of trying to capitalize on Scott's military fame at the same time that they were attempting to convince the American voter that it was, after all, not this, but his civilian aptitudes that fitted him for the presidency. There is no reason to believe that this problem will not have to be faced by every professional soldier who enters the American political arena.

Secondly, it seems clear that no military man, whatever glory he has gathered about him in the past, can expect to be exempt from the bitter criticism, ridicule, and mudslinging that any man exposes himself to when he enters the presidential lists. Scott was called a "charlatan in politics" whose brains, such as they were, resided in his epaulettes; he was declared to be as "shallow as a sophomore and as conceited as a pedagogue"; and his intelligence was said to "disgrace a schoolboy and do honor to Dogberry." One Democratic publication found him down-right "repulsive." These things are hard to take, and while modern campaigns are generally more dignified and gentlemanly than the boisterous contests of the nineteenth century, politics is still a rough game and the professional soldier with political ambitions might as well realize it.

Finally, although the argument against the "military chieftain" as president is often used as a red herring by the opposition—no one honestly believed that Scott had the slightest intention of following in the footsteps of Caesar or Cromwell—it did play an important part in this campaign. The effectiveness of the argument may be difficult to assess, but it will doubtless be important for any professional soldier aspiring to the presidency to demonstrate to the American electorate that he is not bound by the limitations of what is called the "military mind." This may seem unfair to the professional soldier. With justice, he may ask why, after devoting himself conscientiously to the defense and security of his country, he should always be dismissed, between wars, as a "mere military man," his "military mind" spoken of with suspicion and disparagement. Perhaps it is unfair. Perhaps, with their ambivalent attitude toward war and the military establishment, the American people are somewhat in the position of the Quaker schoolteacher who told Scott after the War of 1812: "Friend Winfield, I always told thee not to fight, but since thou wouldst fight, I am glad that thou wast not beaten!"

But this is the American tradition: civilian supremacy over the military. "Government of, by, and for civilians," as Curtis Nettels recently expressed it in his superb little book, *George Washington and American Independence*, was the basic objective of the American Revolutionary leaders, and from the Revolutionary period onward, the military branch of government has always been considered subordinate to the civilian branch, not an end in itself. With this, of course, has gone the idea that the military man, however indispensable to the safety of the nation, is, in the last analysis, somewhat inferior in status to the civilians making up the American nation. For the reverse, one can turn to the tragic history of such countries as Japan and Germany to see what happens when the military profession is glorified at the expense of civilian government.

In America, fortunately, the professional soldier has not dissented from this basic American tradition. Thus General Scott, astonished and grief-stricken as he was over the results of the election, went quietly back to work at army headquarters (and, incidentally, to a new quarrel with the incoming Secretary of War); there was never any fear that he would do otherwise. Commented Horace Greeley after the election: "His proud form was never more erect, nor his eagle eye brighter than it is today. He stands alone amid the wreck, grand and unconcerned, like a lighthouse after a dreadful storm." It had indeed been a "dreadful storm" for a man like Scott; to say that he was "unconcerned" about the outcome is not quite accurate. But before long he had recovered from his disappointment and was absorbed again in the duties of the job that he knew and loved best, confident that the American people, if they did not want him in the White House, would some day call upon him again for his services as "military chieftain."

Southwest Review, Spring 1952.

CHAPTER 8

Professional Soldiers in the White House

In 1952, when Dwight D. Eisenhower, one of our leading generals during World War II, ran for president as a Republican against Adlai Stevenson, the Democratic nominee, there was some discussion about whether a professional soldier could be a satisfactory president of a democratic country. Years before, when the candidates were professionals—Zachary Taylor (1848) and Ulysses Grant (1868)—much was made of the military issue, though it didn't prevent them from winning the elections and serving as presidents well aware of the superiority of civilian power over the military in the American system.

In my essay on military professionals who became presidents, I took a look at General Eisenhower's views on civil-military relations and was convinced that his respect for civil supremacy was as deep-seated as that of Taylor and Grant. He believed deeply in what he called "the necessary and wise subordination of the military to the civil power" in the American system.

Some of my Adlai Stevenson friends were disappointed that I came to friendly conclusions about Ike. But I hoped that he would make a good president, even though I voted for Stevenson in 1952. Ike's eight years as president showed that he was far from being hawkish. "We should be keeping our boys at home," he declared, "and not be preparing them to serve in uniform across the seas." He also insisted that "we must guard against the acquisition of unwarranted influence, whether sought or unsought, by the military-industrial complex."

Ike was convinced that people "who know war, those who have experienced it," were "the most earnest advocates of peace in the world." Ike may well have been directing his remarks to the heads of the Central Intelligence Agency (CIA) and the Strategic Air Command (SAC), who had arranged to overthrow the democratically elected heads of Iran (1953) and Guatemala (1954) and replaced them with dictatorial rulers friendly to America's economic interests.

While Eisenhower was president, the size of the armed service declined by nearly half. In other respects, though, the military power increased steadily during his presidency. With John Foster Dulles as Secretary of State ("a grim cold Warrior," historian Eric Foner called him), "Massive Retaliation" became the heart of American foreign policy, and the number of America's nuclear warheads increased from one thousand in 1953 to eighteen thousand in 1961.

No doubt Eisenhower regretted the steady militarization of the United States while he was chief executive. No one knew as well as he did the threat to American civilization it posed. "Every gun that is made," he said, "every warship launched, every rocket fired signifies, in the final sense, a theft from those who hunger and are not fed, those who are cold and not clothed." And: "The cost of one modern heavy bomber is this: a modern brick school in more than 30 cities. . . . We pay for a single fighter with a half million bushels of wheat. We pay for a single destroyer with new homes that could have housed more than 8,000 people." He avoided sending American troops to Vietnam, where a civil war broke out between Communists and non-Communists after the French left their former colony, and he was proud of his abstention, upon the advice of General Ridgway.

★ ★ ★

No sooner had General of the Army Dwight D. Eisenhower indicated his willingness to accept the Republican nomination in the 1952 "presidentiad" than an old question, analyzed, discussed, and debated in a series of presidential campaigns during the nineteenth century, was raised once again: is it expedient for a democratic republic, with traditions of civilian supremacy over the military, to entrust its highest civilian office to a professional military man?

The reaction to Eisenhower's announcement was almost immediate. President Truman made cryptic references at a press conference to the campaign of 1852 in which professional soldier Winfield Scott was ingloriously defeated in his bid for the presidency. *New York Post* columnist Max Lerner, while not seeing any intrinsic danger in having a general in the White House, was nevertheless eager that Eisenhower at once assume civilian garb:

We live surrounded by a landscape dotted with soldiers
enough. If Ike really means to be something other than a gen-

eral, it is time he donned civilian attitudes when confronted by the high chance of becoming a civilian president. Military dedication, military language, and military ways of thought are fine in their place, but their place is not the presidential campaign.

The liberal Nation went beyond Lerner in finding the prospect of a professional soldier in the White House "disturbing." Although conceding that Eisenhower lacked the "mannerisms" and "arrogance" of the "man on horseback," it insisted:

> Eisenhower is not only a general; he belongs to the military. He was trained at West Point, and his entire career, with the exception of the brief interlude at Columbia University, has been spent in uniform. He was a tactful commander of a coalition of armed forces, but he has had no experience with political parties or political administration. The Eisenhower jacket may be less brassy than the gold braid on Mac-Arthur's cap, but it is still part of a uniform. . . . General Eisenhower may not want to represent the Pentagon in the White House, but how can he help it? The circumstances of the time . . . tend to make any president, even a civilian and a democrat, a tool of the military. If there was reason, as we believed and stated, to be concerned about the appointment of General Marshall as Secretary of State, there is much more reason to be concerned about the presence today of a regular Army officer in the White House.

John M. Swomley Jr., writing for the *Christian Century*, expressed similar fears that an Eisenhower in the White House might become the "spokesman" for the army philosophy: "When General Eisenhower speaks, he will speak not so much as a Republican but as the army's 'elder statesman.'" The *Chicago Tribune*, in a rare burst of scholarly activity, dug up a quotation from Morison and Commager's *Growth of the American Republic* for editorial use to the effect that our general-presidents since Andrew Jackson have generally been undistinguished. By the time an Eisenhower rally was held at Madison Square Garden in New York in February, an organization calling itself the "Non-Partisan Committee against a Military President" was ready to go into action on a picket line. Meanwhile, General of the Army Douglas MacArthur, in what Senator Tobey of New Hampshire termed a "left-handed slap" at Eisenhower (but what others named a "Doug-in-the-manger" attitude), raised his dramatic voice to call for a leader skilled in "the science of civil government." In another slap, not so left-handed, the former pro-consul in Japan warned ominously: "It would be a tragic development indeed if this generation were forced to look to a rigidity of military dominance and discipline to redeem it from the tragic failure of a civilian administration. It might well destroy our historic and wise concept which holds to the supremacy of civil power."

Supporters of Eisenhower's candidacy naturally found all of this extremely irritating. Certainly it would not be difficult for them to demonstrate that many of those expressing apprehensions about a professional soldier in the White House were motivated by reasons less exalted than steadfast devotion to the abstract principle of civilian supremacy. Opponents of Eisenhower's candidacy within the Republican party before the July convention were, of course, bound to take this line of approach at some point, and it is entirely fair to ask what page in Morison and Commager the editors of the *Chicago Tribune* would have turned to had Douglas MacArthur been the general in question. It could also be argued, perhaps not conclusively, that the *Nation's* lack of enthusiasm for our present foreign policy (a policy generally endorsed by General Eisenhower) and its sharp disapproval of the general's ultraconservative position on most domestic issues were more influential in shaping its attitude than any simple dedication to civilian supremacy over the military in our national government. It is clear, too, that the pacifist-anarchist philosophy motivating Mr. Swomley and the "Non-Partisan Committee against a Military President" would apply with equal force against anyone, even a simon-pure civilian, who was ever likely to receive a presidential nomination in this admittedly un-Gandhian nation. General MacArthur's oblique attack does not, of course, require any further comment, and President Truman's position is clear enough: he is a Democrat.

Greatly exasperated by the "yatter against a military man in the White House" that followed Eisenhower's bid for the Republican nomination, *Time* announced in what I take to be an editorial (it is difficult at times to know what is and what is not editorial material in most of our hebdomadal news magazines) that the "supposed American tradition" against generals in the White House "is not a tradition":

> The U.S. has always been and is now strongly anti-militaristic, in the sense that it is against a military state. This has never been taken to mean that military men are barred or tainted as candidates for political office. Americans are aware of defects in "the military mind" just as they are of "the legal mind" and "the political mind." What matters is the individual, not his profession.

The "tradition," if there was one, *Time* declared—with a frown at President Truman, whose remarks about the 1852 campaign had set off the discussion—had been as conspicuous in the breach as in the observance: no less than nine of the thirty-two men thus far elected to the White House were generals.

It is perfectly true, as *Time* points out, that nine of our presidents have been generals. Strictly speaking, however, only two of these— Zachary Taylor and Ulysses Grant—were professional soldiers who went directly from the regular army into presidential politics, and Grant is our sole example of a West Pointer in the White House. To be sure, three of the other general-presidents cited by Time—Washington, Jackson, and William Henry Harrison—had achieved considerable military fame before entering the White House, particularly Washington; however, their contemporaries were doubtless correct in viewing them as citizen soldiers, not professionals, since they had spent many years in civilian pursuits and displayed their talents in a variety of nonmilitary posts before being elevated to the presidency. The other four general-presidents mentioned by *Time*—Pierce, Hayes, Garfield, and Benjamin Harrison—are still less pertinent to any fruitful study of "the military mind" in the White House, for although all of them served long enough in the army to rise at least to the rank of brigadier general, soldiering played only a minor part in their careers and they were first and foremost politicians when they entered the presidential lists. At any rate, this is the way nineteenth-century Americans viewed their candidacies. In the campaign orations of the last century a sharp distinction was invariably made between citizen soldiers like Washington and Jackson and professionals like Taylor and Grant.

Daniel Webster, for example, saw something unprecedented in his party's choice of a professional soldier for the political battle of 1848. As a Whig he had no alternative but to support General Taylor, hero of the Mexican War, but he did so with no great enthusiasm. "General Taylor," he declared,

> is a military man—and a military man merely. He has had
> no training in civil affairs; he has performed no functions of
> a civil nature, under the constitution of his country; he has
> been known,—and is known,—only by his brilliant achieve-
> ments at the head of an Army. . . . It is the first instance in
> our history, in which any man of mere military character has
> been proposed for that high office.

After contrasting Taylor's "professionalism" with the careers of Washington and William Henry Harrison (he could not bring himself to mention his old enemy General Jackson), Webster concluded regretfully that Taylor's nomination was "not fit to be made"; it "stands by itself,— without precedent, and without justification from anything in our previous history." Supporters of Lewis Cass, the Democratic nominee, were of course delighted to have Webster provide them with ammunition to use against his own party's candidate, and they gleefully took up the phrase "nomination not fit to be made" and made it the point of departure for numerous campaign speeches and pamphlets.

Twenty years later when another military hero, General Grant, received the presidential nomination on the Republican ticket, it was no longer possible to contend that a professional soldier in the White House was "without precedent." It was still possible, however, to say that it was "without justification," and Grant's opponents were not long in reviving the old arguments against a military candidate that had played so conspicuous a part in the "campaign oratory" of 1848. There is surprisingly little in the current military argument against General Eisenhower that was not stated in greater detail and with more warmth in the campaigns of 1848 and 1868.

The principal objections to Taylor and Grant as military candidates fell into three categories. First, there was the apprehension that a victorious general, once comfortably established in the White House, might follow in the footsteps of Caesar (or Cromwell or Napoleon) and set himself up as military dictator of the land. The fear of military dictatorship was an old one in the United States. Partly it grew out of the English experience during the civil wars of the seventeenth century, and partly out of American experience with British military rule in Boston in the days before the American Revolution. This fear hardened into a kind of doctrine during the Revolution when, at times, members of the Continental Congress appeared to fear their own army as much as, if not more than, the British redcoats. That there was a genuine danger of some sort of military coup in the chaotic months following the victory at Yorktown has been amply demonstrated by historians of the period, and it was naturally very much in the minds of the Founding Fathers as they met in 1787 to draw up a constitution for the new nation. One can learn a lot about a people from the political abuse it indulges in—perhaps as much as from its laws and songs—and during the first part of the nineteenth century no word occupied a higher place in the litany of political invective than the word "Caesar."

Thus, Taylor was a "military autocrat," according to a frenetic pamphlet entitled *A Northern No!*, published very early in the 1848 campaign, and the Whigs were exposing the American republic to frightful dangers by putting forth such a candidate: "You are responsible to your successors, to posterity, to the world. By nominating Gen. Taylor, you are debauching the popular mind. You are leading this people to their political destruction." There was something ominous in the fact that Taylor had not "feigned a little modesty, and, like Caesar and Cromwell, affected to put away the crown he secretly resolved to clutch."

Similar concerns were raised during Grant's campaign in 1868. Even before his nomination, the *New York Nation* was warning the Republicans against turning to the "man on horseback," and once the campaign actually got under way, the favorite argument of Grant's opponents was that once in the White House, he would proclaim himself "uncrowned emperor" and lead the republic to its ruin. Amusingly, Grant's wife had fallen into the habit of calling her husband "Caesar" after Appomattox, but so unpopular was this word in 1868 that she soon found it expedient to substitute the more innocuous "Victor." Unfortunately for Grant, his opponents refused to follow Mrs. Grant's example, and throughout his two administrations they continued to hurl this epithet at him. When it looked as if he might try for a third term, the cries of "Caesar" became clamorous indeed, varied with such synonyms as "military despot" and "Kaiser Ulysses." "Upon what meat doth this our Caesar feed that he should assume so much?" cried Senator Sumner on the Senate floor in 1872. "Grant is a military man," stated an anti–third term pamphlet in 1875, "and he hopes to derive from war the perpetuation of his ill-omened rule. He knows that the republics of antiquity—of medieval Italy and modern France were subverted by successful soldiers. He cherishes the idea which Voltaire has so well expressed: *Le Premier qui fut roi, fut un soldat heureux.*"

It is impossible today to take seriously the "man on horseback" arguments against Taylor and Grant. Simple, honest, unassuming, both were far removed from the military monster conjured up by their political enemies. So loyal were they to the American civilian tradition that both had, before receiving their nominations, expressed grave doubts (as did Eisenhower in 1948) about the wisdom of having regular army officers mingle in politics, and their respect for the principle of civilian supremacy over the military in this country was as deeply ingrained in their thinking as that of their most severe civilian critics. Horace Greeley, no great enthusiast for soldiers in the White House, remarked after Taylor's death that "few trained and polished statesmen have proved fitter depositories of civil power than this rough soldier," and as far as Grant is concerned, there is no reason to believe that his remarks to Bismarck, later in his life, were not characteristic of the man: "The truth is, I am more of a farmer than a soldier. I take little or no interest in military affairs; and although I entered the army thirty-five years ago, and have been in two wars,—in Mexico as a young lieutenant, and later,—I never went into the army without regret, and never retired without pleasure." This from the "Greatest Soldier of the Age"! As John Lathrop Motley said during the 1868 campaign: "As long as the republic breeds such citizens, her destiny is safe. Such soldiers are not dangerous."

A second objection to military candidates, growing out of the first, was that Taylor and Grant, as ambitious soldiers, would adopt aggressive, bellicose foreign policies, designed to involve this country in foreign wars in order to enhance their personal power and gratify their lust for martial glory. Both the Whigs in 1848 and the Republicans in 1868 were compelled to go to great lengths to demonstrate that their candidates were not warmongers. Taylor was eminently a *"man of peace,"* insisted the Whigs; he had opposed aggression against Mexico and had taken part in the Mexican War simply as a loyal, patriotic soldier, subject to the orders of his civilian superiors in Washington. "Having witnessed the devastation and horrors of war, he has pledged himself, if elected, to cultivate friendly relations with all nations." The Democrats, in point of fact, were the warmongers, said the Whigs; their candidate, Lewis Cass, was a "warm advocate" of war and conquest. Taylor, on the other hand, would "arrest this mad career of conquest" and divert the American people into the gentler channels of peace. According to one Taylor supporter, "No man is better qualified than Gen. Taylor to seize with a firm grasp the spirit of war which unhappily infests the American people (the great besetting sin of all republics) and to hold it effectually in peace." Grant, too, was presented to the American electorate as a man of peace, and the famous phrase in his letter accepting the Republican nomination, "Let us have peace," became an important slogan during the 1868 campaign.

If the absence of war during the Taylor and Grant administrations is any criterion, then it can be said that our two professional soldier–presidents were, as their supporters contended, men of peace. Taylor's foreign policy was the traditional one: neutrality, no entangling alliances, and the settling of disputes, as he put it, by "wise negotiation." As a vigorous nationalist, he took a strong stand in a conflict with Portugal, and he followed European maneuvers in the Caribbean with watchful eyes. At one point, he worked hard to quell a conspiracy, involving American adventurers, to invade Cuba—a conspiracy which threatened treaty obligations and friendly relations with Spain.

In the case of Grant, it could be argued that his obsessive desire to annex Santo Domingo was an expression of his martial spirit, yet he was neither the first nor the last American to cast annexationist eyes upon the Caribbean. Taken as a whole, there is little in his two administrations to substantiate the claims of his opponents in 1868 that he was fired with military ambitions. On the contrary, as his biographer William B. Hesseltine points out, the Treaty of Washington settling the Alabama claims with Great Britain arising out of the Civil War was "a sufficient denial that Grant was a bloodthirsty and martial president, and showed that the 'Greatest Soldier of the Age' was essentially a man of peace." Actually, American opinion after the Civil War would have supported a war with Great Britain on almost any pretext. "Had Grant been so inclined," state Hacker and Kendrick in *The United States since 1865,* "he could have seized the opportunity to add further laurels to his martial fame by involving the nation in a costly and sanguinary conflict." The peaceable resolution of the difficulties with England and Spain, in the opinion of these two historians, "brought to the Grant administrations their only honorable distinction."

The third objection to Taylor and Grant—the one which, in retrospect, appears most compelling—was that they were "mere military men," utterly lacking in experience in civilian affairs, who would make a complete botch of things as political leaders of the nation. As a sarcastic pamphlet by Charles Stearns expressed it:

> The most prominent acts of Taylor's life are those relating to his glorious feats in Mexico. It is there, it appears, that he *studied* politics, there that he learned the art of governing nations, there that he finished the education necessary to obtain, before being presented as a candidate for the presidency of the United States. . . . What a school for a statesman to graduate from!

But the Whigs insisted that it was not "military greatness alone" that commended Taylor to the electorate; it was his "vigorous intellect," his "sound judgment," "warm patriotism," "incorruptible integrity," and "active benevolence"—a group of "moral virtues and intellectual powers," as Senator Rives of Virginia explained, that constituted the "highest qualifications" for the presidency.

No doubt these are high qualifications and no doubt Taylor possessed all of them in varying degrees—along with unquestioned devotion to mother, home, and God. Still, it would be a bold person indeed who would contend that his record during sixteen months in the White House—he died of acute gastroenteritis in July 1850—showed any unusual exercise of the talents enumerated by Senator Rives. Historians generally rate Taylor's administration as below average, and while his most recent biographer, Holman Hamilton, disputes this low estimate, it would take a great deal of generosity to rate Taylor much higher than average. Was this mediocrity due to his lack of political experience before entering the White House? Certainly we have had undistinguished men with civilian backgrounds in the White House, and it is only fair to raise the question whether any civilian could have done better than Taylor during the troublous days of 1849 and 1850. It would seem to be a truism, however, that, other things being equal, a man with insight into the political complexities of the day should be able to do the job better than one with no such insight. Still, there have been worse presidents. Unfortunately for supporters of professional soldiers in politics, General Grant was one of these.

The period of Grant's second administration, 1872–1876, has been called "The Nadir of National Disgrace," and the word "Grantism" came to denote the moral degradation into which politics had fallen during his tenure of office. A poll of fifty-five authorities in American history conducted in 1948 by Professor Arthur Schlesinger of Harvard places Grant at the bottom of a list rating our presidents. Along with Harding, he is judged a "failure" as president. The argument of the Rochester Union, to pick one example from many during the 1868 campaign, that Grant "is not fitted by either education or taste for a political station," would appear to have had melancholy substantiation in the years that followed. "It was my fortune, or misfortune," Grant admitted before leaving the White House, "to be called to the office of Chief Executive without any previous political training. . . . Under such circumstances it is but reasonable to suppose that errors of judgment must have occurred."

On the other hand Warren Harding, a politician par excellence, was as egregious a failure in the White House as General Grant, and such presidents as Tyler, Pierce, Fillmore, Buchanan, and Coolidge are usually rated below average along with General Taylor. If neither of the professional soldiers thus far to serve as chief executive has done so with distinction, it can most assuredly not be said that they had any monopoly on mediocrity in the White House. Furthermore, although our experience with regular army officers as presidents has so far not been particularly encouraging, one would have to have a completely doctrinaire turn of mind to refuse to entertain the possibility that our experience in the future might be different. *Time* is certainly partly right: it is not always a man's profession, military or otherwise, but his own personal qualities and capabilities (plus the circumstances of the time) which in the long run determine whether he will be a competent president or not.

What, then, can be said of General Eisenhower? To begin with, it is clear that the first traditional objection to professional soldiers in the White House—the "Caesar" argument—is as inapplicable to Eisenhower as it was to Generals Taylor and Grant. This argument is, in any case, largely *démodé* today, for the obvious reason that in over a century and a half of American history none of our professional soldiers, in or out of the White House, has ever shown the slightest inclination to seize power by military force. It is interesting to note, however, that one of Eisenhower's supporters, Paul G. Hoffman, felt compelled to acknowledge the old fear and to reassure the American people. "Concern about military people is understandable," he declared,

> because we know that power corrupts and, since military
> power is absolute, it can corrupt absolutely. But Eisenhower

> is a humble man. The question is whether a military man
> or a man of any other training would become arrogant. I
> have known men who have operated peanut stands and have
> become a little more successful than other peanut vendors to
> become arrogant. It is a question of arrogance. Eisenhower
> has no arrogance in his make-up; no inclination to abuse of
> power.

No one who observed the general on the television screen during his acceptance speech after the nomination on July 11—the tense expression, punctuated with broad smiles, during the ovation that greeted him as he mounted the rostrum, the obvious awkwardness until he got under way, the lack of timing in his address, the momentary bewilderment whenever the audience responded in unexpected places—can doubt that Hoffman's statement of the case disposes of this question once and for all.

It is also clear that the second campaign argument against Generals Taylor and Grant—the "warmongering" argument—would make no more sense if leveled against Eisenhower than it did in the campaigns of 1848 and 1868. His public addresses since World War II (and long before the present campaign) have been filled with antiwar sentiments; more than once he has commented on the brutality, futility, and stupidity of modern war, which he has called "the least acceptable solution of our problems." "Your business," he told a graduating class of civilians some time ago, "is to put me out of business." He has also emphatically rejected the notion of a "preventive war"—shooting our way into utopia—advocated by some of our romantic hotheads as a solution to the Russian problem. "When people speak to you about a preventive war, you tell them to go and fight it," he said sarcastically on one occasion; "in my opinion, there is no such thing as a preventive war. Although this suggestion is repeatedly made, no one has yet explained how war prevents war. Nor has anyone been able to explain away the fact that war begets conditions that beget further war."

It is simply not true that professional soldiers in the United States are any more bellicose than civilians. As a matter of fact, it would not be difficult to demonstrate that on the whole they have tended to be a good deal less so. Their business is to win wars, not to start them. As Eisenhower put it once during World War II: "They use fellows like me to correct the mistakes of diplomats." It is perhaps not surprising that many of those supporting Eisenhower for president look upon him as the best hope of peace. As Anne O'Hare McCormick observes in the *New York Times*:

> The idea that Eisenhower is a man who can make nations
> work as a team, can compromise differences, win friends and
> influence people is a powerful element in his appeal. It is a
> real tribute to his character that not even his enemies . . . have
> suggested that he is a war leader. He is almost universally
> regarded as a man of peace, even a potential peace-maker for
> a world at war.

The final objection to professional soldiers in the White House—that the "military mind" is unfitted by temperament and training for the give-and-take of political life—is worthy of more serious attention. *Time* to the contrary, it is no secret that there are obvious differences between the world in which the professional soldier moves and the world of most civilians in a democratic community. There is an almost monastic quality about the military world. In many respects, as J. P. Marquand points out, the professional soldier, like the college professor and the clergyman, tends to lead "an extremely sheltered life." Freed from the usual economic pressures that beset civilians, living in a world governed by definite regulations and well ordered by the omnipresent chain of command, and relying on the simple virtues of loyalty, character, and obedience, the professional soldier often has difficulty understanding the complexities of civilian government, the intricacies of civilian law, and the perpetual conflicts and readjustments of economic groups—labor, management, agriculture—that are an inescapable part of a civilian democracy. Moving in a restricted circle and isolated by a "khaki curtain," he is apt to be puzzled by some aspects of civilian life, impatient of others. Though it is not necessarily typical, Lieutenant General Albert C. Wedemeyer's announcement after the Republican convention that the "discoveries of political methods and procedures" he had made while campaigning for Senator Taft had "disillusioned" him is perhaps characteristic of the professional soldier's impatience with what is standard operating procedure in American politics.

Is there any likelihood that Dwight Eisenhower in the White House would be handicapped by the limitations of the "military mind"? And is there a further danger that he would become a prisoner of the Pentagon, a spokesman for the army philosophy?

As to the first question, his supporters are probably correct in insisting that he has broken through the "West Point mold." His extraordinary talents as a diplomat, his ability to get along with all kinds of people, his tact and skill in dealing with important military and political leaders of various nationalities and in reconciling diverse points of view during World War II and during his recent European assignment—all these are a matter of record. According to a British critic, "the personal and political integrity of the man was more important than the professional ability of the soldier" in the last war. Furthermore, most observers, including Eisenhower's critics, agree that since his return to this country in June 1952, he has done a good job of "demilitarizing" himself. As Anne O'Hare McCormick remarked of his nomination on July 11: "A professional soldier, he overrides so easily the deep national prejudice against military men in the White House that his military character hardly figured in the decision." He has much yet to learn; the disarming confession of ignorance about specific problems on the American domestic scene which characterized his preconvention strategy will scarcely be adequate in the days to come. But he has unquestioned ability, and there is no reason to believe that he will not be able to educate himself in the political facts of life as thoroughly as he mastered the tremendous problems with which he was confronted in the past.

Would Eisenhower as president tend to enthrone the Pentagon in the White House and turn the State Department into the "diplomatic voice of the Department of Defense," as some critics have warned? Eisenhower himself has said that he thinks he would "represent enough military for any administration" with which he might be connected. This may indicate no more than that he is aware of the problem—a by no means unimportant fact—but it is worthy of note that he has vigorously condemned "military waste" in the government and indicated that he does not intend to "go easy" on the Pentagon. His supporters, in fact, contend that he is just the man to cope with the problems posed by the increasing power of the military in this country since the last war. "The special reason why we need a military man of General Eisenhower's stature in the White House now," says John H. Crider, former editor of the *Boston Herald*, "is the very fact that our military establishment is so big, and the Pentagon such a large factor in the halls of Congress. . . . Who would be more in awe of, or less able to cope with the big brass of the Pentagon—a midwestern senator, an ex–artillery captain, or a career military man who has achieved a reputation far beyond that of the others?"

According to Douglas Larsen in the *New York World-Telegram and Sun* for June 4, there is little real enthusiasm for Eisenhower's candidacy among Pentagon officials:

They realize that Gen. Ike knows too much about their business and that the chances of pulling the wool over his eyes are pretty slim. . . . The brass knows just how frosty an eye Gen. Eisenhower is capable of turning on padded requests

for funds, and waste and extravagance. . . . And what
Pentagon officer has the gall to suggest that he is more of a
military expert than Gen. Ike?

This is a fair enough statement and doubtless the most "exploit-able" answer at the present time to the argument that a military man should not be president.

It is not likely, however, that the military issue will play an important role in the outcome of this year's election. It will continue, of course, to be discussed; at the time this was written (shortly after the Republican convention) there were indications that the Democrats planned to make much of the fact that the Republican nominee is not a civilian. Immediately after Eisenhower's nomination, Vice-President Alben W. Barkley noted that Americans have "reservations" about having a military man in the White House, and Senator Richard B. Russell of Georgia declared that it was "a curious commentary on Republican thinking" for the party to nominate a military man "in this time of world tension." "We are seeking a way to peace," said Russell,

and the military mind approaches even the most common-place problems differently than does the civilian mind. . . .
The soldier is familiar with the procedures and environment of his own tight, little system. The civilian, not bound by the inhibitions of military discipline and caste, views the government as it should be viewed—as an operation for all the people.

His views were echoed in the Democratic convention a few days later by several of the speakers, including the keynoter, Governor Paul Dever of Massachusetts; Senator Walter George, in his nominating speech for Senator Russell, was particularly insistent that "a military man in a civilian office tends to lead to dictatorship."

There will be much more of this kind of talk, and the issue will doubtless be thoroughly aired, as it was in the Taylor and Grant campaigns, before the polls close in November. At best, however, it is only a peripheral argument; there are too many other vital issues—economic, social, international—of primary interest to the various social, regional, religious, and ethnic groups making up the Republican and Democratic coalitions for the military argument to be decisive. There is little doubt that the American electorate, as in 1848 and 1868 (and in 1852 and 1880 when professional soldier–candidates went down to defeat), will make its final decision on grounds entirely unrelated to this issue. Still, despite the probable irrelevance of the military issue to the outcome of the election, and despite *Time's* indignation over the fact that it is discussed at all, it is probably a healthy sign that the "yatter" against a professional soldier in the White House has once again risen in this country. It reminds us again, all of us—soldiers and civilians, Republicans and Democrats—at a time when we particularly need to be reminded of it, that what General Eisenhower has called "the necessary and wise subordination of the military to the civil power" is one of the keystones of our American democracy.

Southwest Review, Autumn 1952.

CHAPTER 9

Religion in American Presidential Campaigns

I n 1992, soon after the Republicans, meeting in Houston, nominated George H. W. Bush for a second term, the president spoke to a convention of evangelical leaders in Dallas, Texas. In his talk President Bush said much about God, country, and prayer in the public schools. And then he added: "I note that the other party took words to put together their platform and left out three simple letters: G.O.D."

For a day or so it looked as if religion was going to be one of the issues of the 1992 presidential campaign. It would have been a pity. The Founding Fathers, whom many American politicians like to quote, would have been dismayed to see politics and religion being mixed at election time. They deliberately left God out of the US Constitution because they feared that mingling religion and politics would be detrimental to both; engaging in "religioneering," that is, using religion for political purposes, they thought, would produce rancor, spite, prejudice, and intolerance, not enlightenment. Their fears were justified. Whenever religion has been injected into American presidential contests, it has always brought out the worst side of the American character.

Religioneering appeared, for the first time, in 1800, when John Adams was running for reelection and Thomas Jefferson was challenging him for office. Neither Adams nor Jefferson was an orthodox Christian. Adams regarded himself as a Christian, but his leaning was toward Unitarianism. Jefferson was a Deist; he believed in a Grand Architect, a Great Creator who had designed the universe. He admired Christian ethics and even wrote a book about it, but he was not a church member and he detested orthodox Calvinism, which he considered narrow, dogmatic, and intolerant.

Jefferson was more of a freethinker than Adams, and during the campaign of 1800, he became a prime target of the Federalists, who were backing Adams for the presidency. Backed by the New England Calvinists, the Federalists dismissed Jefferson as "a howling atheist." During the campaign, John Mason, a New York preacher, published a pamphlet entitled *The Voice of Warning to Christians on the Ensuing Election.* Jefferson, he wrote, was an infidel "who writes against the truths of God's word; who makes not even a profession of Christianity; who is without Sabbaths; without the sanctuary, without so much as a decent external respect for the faith and worship of Christians."

Mason and the Calvinists warned that if Jefferson became president, one of the first things he would do would be to confiscate all the Bibles in the country and have them burned. Some Americans took this charge seriously. In a little town in Connecticut, a woman backing Adams was so afraid of what would happen to her Bible if Jefferson won election that she took it to the only Jeffersonian she knew and begged him to keep the Bible for her. The Jeffersonian tried to convince her that her fears about Jefferson were unfounded, but she remained unconvinced. "My good woman," he finally told her, "if all the Bibles are to be destroyed, what is the use of bringing yours to me? That will not save it when it is found." "I'm sure it will," insisted the woman. "It will be perfectly safe with you. They'll never think of looking in the house of a Democrat for a Bible!"

Destroying Bibles was bad enough. The enemies of Jefferson charged that if he became president he would do even worse things to religion than destroy Bibles. Having disposed of the Bibles, they said, he would next proceed to have all the churches in the United States torn down. After that, he would go after what today we call "family values." He would dissolve the marriage institution, and throw all the women of the country into houses of prostitution. As a leading Calvinist put it in one of his sermons, Jefferson would make "our wives and daughters the victims of legal prostitution, soberly dishonored, speciously polluted, the outcast of all delicacy and virtue."

In the fall of 1800, a writer for the *Connecticut Courant* summed up the case against Jefferson:

> Look at your houses, your parents, your wives, and your
> children. Are you prepared to see your dwellings in flames,
> hoary hairs bathed in blood, female chastity violated, or chil-
> dren writhing on the pike and the halbert. . . . Look at every
> leading Jacobin (Radical Jeffersonian) as at a ravening wolf,
> preparing to enter your peaceful fold, and glut his deadly ap-
> petite on the vitals of your country. . . . *Great God of Com-*
> *passion and Justice, Shield My Country from Destruction.*

In the end, of course, Jefferson won the election after some difficulty, became president, and the Bibles, churches, and women survived. Perhaps because of the excesses of the Calvinists in 1800, religion did not play a major role in presidential contests for a long time afterwards. But some religioneering took place in several other campaigns during the nineteenth century. During the 1828 campaign, John Quincy Adams was attacked for his Unitarianism and Andrew Jackson was called a Deist. In 1836, Martin Van Buren was accused of being soft on Catholicism, and in 1844, James K. Polk was accused of being a tool of the Jesuits. And in 1856, when the Republicans held their first presidential campaign, they nominated John C. Fremont as their candidate. Some of his political enemies attacked him as a Catholic, even though he was an Episcopalian, but had been married in a convent. Fremont lost the election to James Buchanan, but religion played little part in the campaign.

Not until the election of 1884 did religion play a crucial role in another presidential contest. This time, though, playing the religous card actually backfired. Grover Cleveland, former governor of New York, ran for president on the Democratic ticket that year, and the Republicans nominated James C. Blaine, the popular senator from Maine, as their candidate. Blaine needed to carry New York state to win. And to carry New York, he needed the votes of the Irish-Americans in New York City, who usually voted Democratic. But they leaned toward Blaine in 1884 because he had some Irish in his own background. The Blaine people spread rumors that Cleveland, a Presbyterian, hated Catholics, and they also played up the fact that Blaine's mother was an Irish Catholic.

The Blaine people had high hopes about the election. Then, Rev. Samuel Burchard, a Presbyterian minister, unexpectedly spoiled things for Blaine. Shortly before election day, Blaine met with some Protestant ministers in New York City who were supporting him in the election, and Rev. Mr. Burchard, spokesman for the group, greeted Blaine on behalf of the ministers and announced: "We expect to vote for you next Tuesday. We are Republicans and don't propose to leave our party and identify ourselves with the party whose antecedents have been Rum, Romanism, and Rebellion." The Democrats at once recognized the blunder that Burchard had made for the Republicans, and they flooded New York City with leaflets quoting the Rum, Romanism, Rebellion remark. Contemporary observers were convinced that Blaine lost thousands of Catholic votes as a result. In the end, he failed to take New York City, and with it, the election. Burchard's prejudiced remark helped Cleveland win the presidency, the first Democrat to become president since before the Civil War.

Religion played a minor role in 1908, when William Howard Taft, a Unitarian, ran for president as a Republican. Some of his political enemies threatened to make his Unitarianism, considered unorthodox, as an issue in the race. But "Big Bill" refused to be intimidated. He was sorry, he said, if his enemies wanted to use his religion against him in the campaign, but he was not going to pretend to be anything but a Unitarian. In the end, Taft's Unitarianism failed to become much of an issue, and he won the election. And to the joy of some religious people, he added the words "So help me God" to the secular presidential oath provided for by the US Constitution. He was the first president since Chester A. Arthur to use the words, and some of his followers were beside themselves with joy during the inaugural ceremony.

It wasn't until 1928, twenty years later, that religion played a major role in a presidential campaign again. The Republicans were running Herbert Hoover, with a Quaker background, as their candidate, and the Democrats, for the first time in American history, picked Alfred E. Smith ("Al Smith"), a Roman Catholic, as their candidate. Smith had served as a popular governor of New York state, and he was a likable speaker who possessed sympathies with the average American. To his dismay, however, his religion soon became the leading issue in the 1928 contest. After his nomination, the Republicans spread millions of hand-bills, leaflets, and posters around the country, with angry titles: "Popery in the Public Schools," "Convent Life Unveiled," and "Crimes of the Pope."

Religion didn't decide the election of 1928, but it was a major issue throughout the campaign. Even before Smith became a candidate for the presidency, he made clear his belief in "the absolute separation of church and state in America." He put it this way: "I have taken an oath of office nineteen times. Each time I swore to defend and and main-tain the Constitution of the United States. . . . I have never known any conflict between my official duties and my religious beliefs." Still, the whispers and rumors about his religion were persistent and pernicious. There were rumors that the pope had his bags packed and ready to move to Washington once Smith won the election. There were rumors, too, that if Smith became president he would have Protestant marriages annulled and Protestant children declared bastards. There were even stories that Smith, if he became president, planned to extend Manhat-tan's new Holland Tunnel to the basement of the Vatican, so he could keep in close touch with the pope.

In addition to the anti-Catholic rumors floating around the coun-try, many Protestant ministers preached strong sermons against Smith. "If you vote for Al Smith," cried one preacher, "you're voting against Christ and you'll be damned." A "vote for Al Smith is a vote for the Pope," thundered a spokesman for the Ku Klux Klan; a Smith triumph meant "Rum, Romanism, and Ruin!"

Smith was so infuriated by the anti-Catholic slurs hurled at him that he insisted on fighting back. On September 29, 1928, he went to

Oklahoma City to make a major speech on religious intolerance. But he was greeted with fiery K.K.K. crosses en route and implacable hostility in the auditorium where he spoke. The next evening, popular Evangelist John Roach Straton thrilled thousand of people in the same auditorium with a speech on "Al Smith and the Forces of Hell."

In his acceptance speech after he was chosen as the Republican candidate, Herbert Hoover carefully came out against religious bigotry, and a little later he dissociated himself from one of the most outrageous attacks on Smith's religion. In the end, though, Hoover swept the nation, with 58 percent of the popular votes to Smith's 41 percent. Hoover also carried forty states, including Smith's own state, New York, all the border states, and five states in the "Solid [Democratic] South."

Smith felt his defeat keenly. "Well," he is supposed to have remarked after the returns were in, "the time hasn't come yet when a man can say his beads in the White House." A postelection joke had it that after the election, Smith wired the pope in Italy: "Unpack!" Smith was convinced that his religion had done him in during the campaign. He was partly right; unquestionably bigotry cost him many votes. But his opposition to prohibition also hurt him, as well as his association with Tammany Hall, a shady Democratic organization in New York. Hoover himself was probably closer to the mark when he remarked that "General prosperity was on my side."

In 1960, more than thirty years later, another Catholic, John F. Kennedy, ran as the Democratic candidate for president, and though religion played some part in the campaign, he narrowly won the election against Richard Nixon, the Republican candidate. Like Al Smith, Kennedy made clear his devotion to separation of church and state. He also declared that federal aid to parochial schools was unconstituitonal and opposed the appointment of an ambassador to the Vatican. Time and again, during the campaign, he said he would make decisions as president on the basis of the public interest rather than on the basis of his religious views. He was so emphatic about this that some Catholics complained that he was becoming more Protestant than the Protestants themselves.

Kennedy's meeting with Protestant clergymen in Houston in September 1960 and his forthright answers to their questions reassured many people:

I am not the Catholic candidate for president," he told them. "I am the Democratic Party's candidate for president who happens also to be a Catholic. I do not speak for my church on public matters; and the church does not speak for me. Whatever issue may come before me as president, if I should be elected—on birth control, divorce, censorship, gambling or any other subject—I will make my decision in accordance with what my conscience tells me to be in the national interest, and without regard to outside religious pressure or dictates.

Kennedy not only faced squarely the question of church-state separation under the Constitution. With his sense of humor, he could joke about it too. At a New York dinner during the campaign, he claimed that he had asked Cardinal Spellman what he should say when people asked him whether he believed that the Pope was infallible, and the Cardinal replied, "I don't know, Senator—all I know is he keeps calling me 'Spillman.'"

Though Kennedy won by only a small margin in popular votes, his election in 1960 was a landmark. As one of JFK's supporters put it: Catholicism has "finally joined the American culture."

2011

CHAPTER 10

George Washington and Civil Supremacy

The article on "Professional Soldiers in the White House," published in 1954, led me to look into George Washington's devotion to the principle of civil supremacy over the military during the American Revolution and afterwards. I learned that, during the Revolutionary War, no matter how sloppy and irritating the Continental Congress could be at times, Washington always looked with respect to it as his superior. He set a fine example for his successors. In the twenty-first century, unfortunately, it began to look as though one could say of the United States what years ago was said of Prussia: it is "a state owned by its army."

In May 2011, *Harper's Magazine* published an article by Jonathan Stevenson entitled, "Owned by the Army: Has the President Lost Control of His Generals?" According to Stevenson, one of the Founding Fathers' basic principles—civil supremacy over the military—was increasingly being ignored by military officials in the early years of the twenty-first century. Military leaders began announcing their own policies—the way General Douglas MacArthur did in 1950—and Republican leaders like Senator John McCain began insisting that the armed forces should dictate Congress's decisions in certain matters. "I cannot think of a single precedent in American history," President Obama's Secretary of Defense, Robert Gates, reminded the senators, "of doing a referendum of the armed forces on a policy issue. Are you going to ask them if they want fifteen-month tours? Are you going to ask them if they want to be part of the surge in Iraq? That's not the way our civilian-led military has ever worked in our entire history."

Washington would have heartily approved Secretary Gates's statement. In the essay here, published in 1954, the importance of our first president's loyalty to the principle of supremacy is impressive.

★ ★ ★

For most Americans it would be unthinkable to view the Father of Our Country otherwise than as a man worthy to take his place beside the other great figures of world history. Beginning in his own generation and continuing on down to our own, biographers, historians, poets, journalists, politicians, and Washington's-birthday orators have united to shower him with honors which they have not always been willing to bestow upon other American folk heroes. There have, to be sure, been occasional dissenters. In his own day, there was the anti-Washington clique in the army and in the Continental Congress—the so-called "Conway Cabal"—which took a dim view of his competence as commander in chief. But in the end the "cabal," if such it was, fell ingloriously apart, most of those associated with it hastening to jump on the Washington bandwagon. And more recently William E. Woodward, that supreme master of the art of debunking, after striving valiantly in *Washington: The Image and the Man* to reduce the Washington reputation to mincemeat, capitulated toward the end of the book and conceded somewhat ruefully that the man as well as the image was undeniably great. As Calvin Coolidge said when asked about the debunkers: "Well, I see the Washington Monument is still there."

What has not been so clear, however, is just why Washington was great. For the early filial pietists—the cherry-tree historians—the explanation was simple enough: he was a demigod. As Mason Locke ("Parson") Weems put it, he was "pious as Numa; just as Aristides; temperate as Epictetus; patriotic as Regulus; in giving public trusts, impartial as Severus; in victory, modest as Scipio; prudent as Fabius; rapid as Marcellus; undaunted as Hannibal; as Cincinnatus disinterested; to liberty firm as Cato; as respectful of the laws as Socrates. Or, to speak in plainer terms . . ."

But why go on? How could a man uniting in himself all the virtues customarily distributed by Providence with great economy throughout long history be other than great? Or, to invert the essentially circular reasoning of the filial pietists, how could anyone—particularly an American—be great and not possess all these virtues? But in an age like our own, which is more inclined to believe in demi-devils than in demigods, such answers are hardly satisfactory—if, indeed, they do not drive us to seek refuge with Woodward. Furthermore, we might as well face the awful truth: critical historiography has pretty well disposed of the myth of Washington's infallibility as a man, as a military leader, and as a statesman. It is perfectly proper today, for example, to state that

Washington was not a military commander of the first rank and to question whether his insistence on molding the Continental Army into European forms rather than adapting it to American conditions was not itself
a huge blunder that prolonged the Revolutionary War unduly. And to a
generation of Americans which can apparently take atomic warfare in
its stride and still be moved by individual tragedies, Washington's insistence on flogging in the army seems inordinately hardhearted. We also
know that he was far from being a "democrat" in the modern meaning
of the term and that he probably shared his wife's aristocratic disgust
at the spot of dirt which a "dirty democrat" left in his house. In addition, it has been perfectly safe—to cite another example of our modern
broad-mindedness—for a former chief executive, whose inclination to
discharge his aggressions in public brought on more than one tempest,
to remark in 1951 that the father of our country was too stingy to have
thrown a coin across the river, without having the nation descend upon
him in wrath.

It is possible, in other words, to de-apotheosize Washington, to
view him as a human being with all the limitations of his personality, intellect, and background, without denying that he possessed the
essentials of greatness. But once the reservations are made about his
abilities—and they certainly do have to be made—then the problem of
his greatness becomes indeed a difficult one. More than one writer has
grappled with the problem and ended in generalities. The late Douglas
Southall Freeman, who spent the last years of his life surveying Washington's career in painstaking detail, cautiously ventured in the fourth
volume of his biography that by the spring of 1778 Washington had
the "seeds of greatness" in him. These "seeds" consisted of the "innate
spirit of freedom" that led him to join the American resistance movement at the outset of the conflict with Britain, and the magnificent patience and determination he displayed as commander in chief of the
Revolutionary forces in the face of a series of maddening difficulties
that would have broken the spirit of most men. But may I suggest that
there is one reason, apart from all others, why Washington deserves
to be considered one of the outstanding figures in the long, toilsome
course of human history: his unwavering devotion, at every stage of a
long and difficult war, to the civilian purposes for which the Revolution was being waged and the important role he played in helping to
establish the principle of civilian supremacy over the military firmly
in our American system of government. For this, if for no other reason, Washington deserves our highest respect. Some of the most dramatic episodes in Washington's life—and, indeed, in our national history—have to do with his tireless efforts to uphold the supremacy of
"government of, by, and for civilians" during the Revolutionary War.
The story, curiously overlooked in most high school and college American history courses, is worth retelling.

The deep-seated respect for civil authority which Washington brought to his position as commander in chief of the Revolutionary forces was due in part, no doubt, to his long experience with the procedures of civilian government prior to taking command. For all his military experience, he was not exactly what we would call a professional soldier. He did have military ambitions in his youth, and he served as an officer during the French and Indian War. Yet his dissatisfaction with the position of colonial officers vis-à-vis the British regulars led him to abandon the military profession before the end of the war and return to Mount Vernon, where for the next seventeen years he devoted himself to the building up of his plantation and—as vestryman, county justice, and member of the House of Burgesses—became completely engrossed in civilian pursuits. When the "cold war" with Britain followed fast on the heels of French defeat in the New World in 1763, Washington immediately joined the anti-British movement and was elected as a matter of course to the First and Second Continental Congresses, where he gained further familiarity with the processes of deliberative assemblies. When, therefore, he was elected commander in chief of the Revolutionary armies on June 15, 1775, it is not too much to say that his experience as a citizen far outweighed his experience as a soldier. He had much to learn as a soldier when he started north to assume command of the forces at Cambridge, but he was thoroughly conversant with the procedures of civilian government. Even before reaching Cambridge, he had occasion publicly to state his conception of the role to which Congress had assigned him. "When we assumed the soldier," he told the provincial congress of New York, "we did not lay aside the citizen; and we shall most sincerely rejoice with you in that happy hour when the establishment of American liberty, upon the most firm and solid foundation, shall enable us to return to our private stations in the bosom of a free, peaceful, and happy country." To the end of the war, he remained loyal to this declaration, and the fears of some Americans that he might overstep his bounds proved completely unfounded.

But there were fears. Provincial leaders, as well as members of the Continental Congress, were extremely "jealous" of the army throughout the Revolution. One of the charges against the British before the war was that Britain was plotting to establish a military despotism in America, and the Declaration of Independence specifically accused George III of stationing an army in the colonies in order "to render the Military independent of and superior to the Civil power." The British occupation of Boston, 1768–70, and the establishment of military rule over Massachusetts under General Gage following the Boston Tea Party, had made the threat of military tyranny one of the important rallying cries for the patriots. No doubt the patriots exaggerated this threat. It is difficult to believe that the British, with their own constitutional traditions, had any intention of proclaiming a military dictatorship over the colonies. Still, the fear of military domination was very real to eighteenth-century Americans, and once the Revolution commenced, they began eyeing their own army with the same kind of suspicion they had previously directed toward the British army. At times they even appeared to fear their own army more than they did the British, although in emergencies they usually relaxed these fears.

Occasionally this suspicion was extended by some of the congressional delegates to Washington himself, despite his absolutely correct behavior toward Congress and toward the various provincial officials with whom he had to deal. As his prestige mounted throughout the land after the British evacuation of Boston, there was grumbling in Congress that too many Americans were forgetting that the army and its commander were, after all, creatures of Congress. John Adams complained more than once of the "superstitious veneration" paid to Washington: "Although I honor him for his good qualities, yet in this house I feel myself his superior. In private life I shall always acknowledge that he is mine. It becomes us to attend early to the restraining our army." As he told General Gates, "We don't choose to trust you generals, with too much power, for too long time." And Richard Henry Lee, a perpetual worrier about Washington's "infallible divinity," questioned whether it was not dangerous "to inculcate and encourage in the people, an idea, that their welfare, safety, and glory depend on one man."

Most delegates in Congress, however, had complete confidence in Washington. They realized that he was no Caesar, lusting to take over. Few would have disagreed with the entry Landon Carter made in his diary in May 1776: "I never knew but one man who resolved not to forget the citizen in the soldier or ruler and that was G. W., and I am afraid I shall not know another." Washington did have occasional brushes with provincial authorities. In December 1775, for example, there were complaints that his treatment of Massachusetts officials left something to be desired. "I cannot charge myself with incivility . . . to the gentlemen of this Colony," declared Washington when he heard of the criticism, "but if such my conduct appears, I will endeavor at a reformation, as I assure you . . . that I wish to walk in such a line as will give most general satisfaction." Apparently in the end he did give "general satisfaction," for before he left Boston, Massachusetts officials made a special point of praising him for the respect he had shown the civil constitution of the colony.

A similar respect characterized Washington in all his dealings with the Continental Congress. He was in constant correspondence with Congress, and numerous congressional committees—many of them set up at his own suggestion—conferred with him on policies throughout the war. Invariably he sought the advice of the delegates on major decisions, and when he had to act on his own in emergencies, he always promptly reported on what he had done and requested congressional approval. "I am not fond of stretching my powers," he explained, "and if the Congress will say, 'Thus far and no farther you shall go,' I will promise not to offend whilst I continue in their service."

In the crisis of December 1776 he was forced to take measures for recruiting without first clearing through Congress. In reporting to Philadelphia, he outlined the desperate situation that had forced him to act without prior consultation. Then he added:

> It may be said that this is an application for powers that are too dangerous to be In trusted. I can only add, that desparate diseases require desparate Remedies; and with truth declare, that I have no lust after power but wish with as much fervency as any man upon this wide and extended Continent, for an opportunity of turning the Sword into a plow share.

Congress did more than authorize the steps he had taken. About to flee Philadelphia in anticipation of the arrival of British troops, it quickly passed a resolution granting him "full, ample, and complete powers" for six months to meet the emergency. In granting these extraordinary powers—powers which Lord George Germain declared made Washington the "dictator of America"—Congress stated: "Happy it is for this country that the general of their forces can safely be entrusted with the most unlimited power, and neither personal security, liberty or property be in the least endangered thereby." Washington's response was characteristic:

> Instead of thinking myself freed from all civil obligations by this mark of confidence, I shall constantly bear in mind that as the sword was the last resort for the preservation of our liberties, so it ought to be the first to be laid aside when those liberties are firmly established.

Ironically, Congress felt compelled at one point to administer a gentle rebuke to Washington for his "delicacy" in the use of the powers granted him. At the end of 1777 a series of resolves was passed in Congress expressing "deep concern" over the breakdown in the army supply system. After referring to Washington's restraint in exercising the powers vested in him earlier that year, Congress went on to attribute the supply crisis in part "to a delicacy in exerting the military authority on the citizens of these states; a delicacy, which though highly laudable in general, may, on critical exigencies, prove destructive to the army and prejudicial to the general liberties of America." James Lovell, an indefatigable sniper at Washington, was delighted with the reprimand.

"You could not expect more smartness in a Resolve which was meant to rap a Demi-G over the knuckles," he told Samuel Adams. Washington accepted the rap with good grace. Apologizing for his "delicacy," he explained, with a trace of irony:

> I confess I have felt myself greatly embarrassed with respect to a vigorous exercise of Military power. An ill-placed humanity perhaps and a reluctance to give distress may have restrained me too far. But these were not all. I have been aware of the prevalent jealousy of military power, and that this has been considered an Evil much to be apprehended even by the best and most sensible among us. Under this idea, I have been cautious and wished to avoid as much as possible any Act that might improve it.

Was Washington too cautious? And was the "prevalent jealousy of military power" by civilian officials carried too far? Was Samuel Adams being ridiculous when he warned in 1776 that a "standing army, however it may be at sometimes, is always dangerous to the liberties of the people" and that it should be "watched with a jealous eye"? Or Benjamin Rush when he asked whether there were not "Caesars" and "Cromwells" in the country? James Lovell's sarcastic proposal that Washington be given a blank check to do anything he pleased is unquestionably unfair to the commander in chief. It is also difficult not to marvel at John Adams's glee over the fact that Washington had not taken part in the victory at Saratoga: if he had, "idolatry and adulation would have been unbounded: so excessive as to endanger our liberties, for what I know." Was this fear of military tyranny simply a bogey conjured up by small-minded men, motivated more by sectional prejudices and jealousies than by a sincere devotion to the revolutionary cause? It is clear that there was nothing to fear from Washington. Would it not have been wiser for Congress to put aside its distrust of the army and concentrate solely on winning the war?

It is, of course, impossible to know what the upshot would have been had Washington and Congress followed a different course from that which they did follow. To the end of the war, the "best and most sensible" of the patriots, to use Washington's words, remained eternally vigilant over the military. In the end their vigilance was fully justified. For the time finally came when Washington's "delicacy" and congressional "jealousy" were put to a severe test.

The Revolution, it is too often forgotten, was far from being an easy war. The American colonies, without an effective central government, without a well-organized army or treasury, had taken on the strongest power in the world when they resorted to arms in 1775. The Continental Army, because of short-term enlistments, was perpetually on the brink of disintegration. The supply problem was baffling throughout the war, and Valley Forge, familiar to every schoolboy, appears to have been the rule rather than the exception. Provincial jealousies weakened the authority of Congress, and the gradual decline in the caliber of the delegates brought its prestige to an increasingly low level as the war went on. By the end of the war the national treasury was bankrupt, inflation was rampant, the army was unpaid, and Congress was helpless to raise enough funds even to disband the army. There were, in other words, fertile grounds for a surge toward dictatorship as a means of bringing order out of chaos. The period between the defeat of Cornwallis at Yorktown in 1781 and the final conclusion of peace with Britain in 1783 was especially dangerous. In many respects it was the truly "critical period" of American history. Amid the confusions and uncertainties of this period, men like General James Varnum began to suggest that only an "absolute Monarchy, or a military State" could save the country. And there were others fully prepared to translate these words into a plan of action.

No doubt the best known of these plans—or "schemes," as Washington called them—occurs in the letter which Colonel Lewis Nicola of Pennsylvania wrote Washington on May 22, 1782, proposing that the commander in chief, with army backing, seize power and establish a strong, stable government with himself as king. Though it is extremely misleading to apply contemporary concepts to past historical situations, it seems fair to say that what Nicola was actually proposing was essentially a kind of fascist coup akin to Mussolini's march on Rome. Doubtless it would be inaccurate to call the colonel the prototype of the modern fascist, though his lack of faith in civilian procedures is clear enough. Eminently respectable, so far as we know, he was neither fanatic nor demagogue, and he appears to have had no lust for sharing in the power which he wanted Washington to seize. Rather he appears to have been the kind of timid citizen who has existed at every stage of American history and who is always ready to scuttle constitutional processes at the first sign of an emergency.

Conditions in America at the time he wrote Washington were certainly far from reassuring, and the grievances of the army, foremost in his mind, were impressive enough. Army pay was months in arrears, and since Congress seemed incapable of meeting its financial obligations, Nicola, like many others, felt that he was confronted with the "dismal prospect" of returning to civilian life, upon the disbanding of the army, in a state of "beggary." A man of sixty-five with a family to support, he reflected the growing unrest in the army during the "critical period" after Yorktown when the issue of war or peace still hung in the balance. Apparently on his own—though his views were shared by many of his fellow officers—he composed for Washington's consideration a scheme by which the army might get its just dues and the government of the country be placed on a firm foundation. In a seven-page document, he reviewed the grievances of the army and warned that there was a growing sentiment "not to separate, after the peace, 'till all grievances are redressed, engagements & promises fulfilled." Aside from army pay, one of the "engagements" Congress made in 1780 and showed signs of welshing on was the promise of half-pay for life on retirement to all officers enlisting for the duration of the war. But even apart from these considerations, Nicola judged Congress a miserable failure. After all, the army hadn't been consulted on the kind of government under which they were living, he told Washington. Was it not time for army men, under Washington, to take a hand in devising measures for governing the country?

"I own I am not that violent admirer of a republican form of government that numbers in this country are," Nicola confessed. Even absolute monarchy was "more beneficial to the existence of a nation," although there was something to be said for the "mixed government" of England. Perhaps the best solution to the difficulties confronting the country would be the establishment of a western colony under army auspices, "to be formed into a distinct State under such mode of government as those military who choose to remove to it may agree on." In any case, the "war must have shewn to all, and to military men in particular, the weakness of republicks, and the exertions the army has been able to make by being under a proper head." Nicola finally got to the heart of the matter: Washington, victor in war, should "conduct and direct us in the smoother paths of peace." It may be expedient for Washington to refrain from calling himself king, because many Americans find it difficult to "seperate" the ideas of tyranny and monarchy; at any rate, Washington should lead the army in a movement to reconstitute the government of the land under any title he might choose to assume. "Republican bigots," concluded Nicola, would undoubtedly consider his plan as "meriting fire and fagots" if they got wind of it, but he trusted Washington to keep it in strict confidence until the time came to act.

One would like to have seen Washington's face as he read this communication at his headquarters in Newburgh. Nicola had misread his man completely. None of the "delicacy" with which Washington dealt with civilian authorities was present in his response to Nicola's scheme. If he did not at once consign Nicola to "fire and fagots," he reacted in a tone of anger and disdain that would have warmed the hearts of "Republican bigots" throughout the land. Shocked that such ideas as Nicola outlined should be circulating in the army, Washington replied immediately and also took the unusual precaution of having his two aides countersign the file draft of his letter. His reply is, according to the historian Channing, "possibly, the grandest single thing in his whole career," and it deserves to be quoted in full:

> With a mixture of great surprise and astonishment, I read with attention the sentiments you have submitted to my perusal. Be assured Sir, no occurrence in the course of the War, has given me more painful sensations than your information of there being such ideas existing in the Army as you have expressed, and I must view with abhorrence and reprehend with severity. For the present the communication of them will rest in my own bosom, unless some further agitation of the matter, shall make a disclosure necessary.
>
> I am much at a loss to conceive what part of my conduct could have given encouragement to an address which to me seems big with the greatest mischiefs that can befall my Country. If I am not deceived in myself, you could not have found a person to whom your schemes were more disagreeable; at the same time in justice to my own feelings I must add that no Man possesses a more sincere wish to see ample justice done to the Army than I do, and as far as my powers and influence in a constitutional way may extend, they shall be employed to the utmost of my abilities to effect, should there be any occasion.
>
> Let me conjure you then, if you have any regard for your Country, for yourself or posterity, or respect for me, to banish these thoughts from your Mind, and never communicate, as from yourself, or any one else, a sentiment of like nature.

Nicola did indeed communicate with Washington again. But there were no further references to "sentiments of like nature." In a state of extreme agitation, he dashed off a letter of apology for having made such proposals. Then, worried lest this letter had been too confused, he sent off another imploring Washington to clear him of "every suspicion of harbouring sinister designs." Still feeling from the impact of Washington's reply, he wrote again to disavow the ideas he advanced in his original letter. At this point we can take our leave of the unhappy Colonel Nicola. He was notably absent in the crisis that developed at Newburgh, New York, a few months later.

The Newburgh crisis of March 1783 grew out of the same conditions that had impelled Nicola to broach his scheme of the previous May. The army was still unpaid, nothing had been done about the promise of half-pay to the officers, and a majority of the soldiers, with the conclusion of peace and disbanding of the army in sight, faced the prospect of returning home without money, credit, or jobs. Washington, as he reminded Nicola, was by no means insensible to the plight of the army. Again and again he wrote Congress urging prompt action, and to his brother he revealed his own growing impatience with the dilatoriness of Congress: "The army as usual is without pay, and a great part of the soldiery without shirts, and tho' the patience of them is equally threadbare, it seems to be a matter of small concern to those at a distance." Then he added somewhat bitterly, "In truth, if one was to hazard an opinion on this subject, it would be, that the army having contracted a habit of encountering distress and difficulties, and of living without money, it would be injurious to it, to introduce other customs." Tension mounted at Newburgh on the Hudson, where Washington's main forces had been stationed after Yorktown, and so alarmed was Washington at the restlessness of his men that he stayed at Newburgh that winter instead of going to Mount Vernon as he had planned.

On Monday, March 10, 1783, the crisis finally came to a head. On that day an anonymous circular appeared in the Newburgh camp summoning the officers to a meeting the following day to consider measures "to obtain that redress of grievances which they seem to have solicited in vain." At the same time, an unsigned address to the officers started circulating in the camp urging the army to take forceful action. It was an eloquent address; Washington later admitted that "in point of composition, in elegance and force of expression" it had "rarely been equalled in the English language," and Timothy Pickering called it "so truly *Junian* a composition."

The writer began by describing himself as a "fellow-soldier" whose "past sufferings have been as great, and whose future fortunes may be as desperate" as those of the rest of the army. Until lately, he had "believed in the justice of his country":

> But faith has its limits as well as temper; and there are
> points, beyond which neither can be stretched without sink-
> ing into cowardice or plunging into credulity. To be tame
> and unprovoked, when injuries press hard upon you, is more
> than weakness; but to look up for kinder usage, without
> one manly effort of your own, would fix your character, and
> show the world how richly you deserve those chains you
> broke.

Has not the army begged Congress "in the meek language of entreating memorials" long enough? If this is the way you are treated now, how will it be "when those very swords, the instruments and companions of your glory, shall be taken from your sides?" The hour has arrived to abandon the "milk-and-water" style and carry your appeal "from the justice to the fears of government." "Assume a bolder tone, and suspect the man"—Washington—"who would advise to more moderation and longer forbearance." It is time to draw up your *"last remonstrance"* and inform Congress that the army has its alternatives: "If peace, that nothing shall separate you from your arms but death. If war, that courting the auspices and inviting the direction of your illustrious leader, you will retire to some unsettled country, smile in your turn, 'and mock when their fear cometh on.'"

The appeal of the address was tremendous. Timothy Pickering observed that it was read throughout the camp "with admiration, and talked of with rapture!" But in a letter to his wife he added, "Should rashness govern the proceedings, the consequences may be such as are dreadful even in idea. God forbid the event should be so calamitous."

It is difficult to say with certainty who were the leaders in the movement to stir up the army at Newburgh. By his own admission many years later, Major John Armstrong, aide-de-camp to General Horatio Gates, was the author of the call for a "last remonstrance." It is obvious, however, that more important figures were lurking in the background. It is possible that General Gates was at the head of the movement. Washington himself was convinced that the "old leaven"—the "Conway Cabal" that had attempted to replace him with Gates early in the war—was at work again. But he also suspected that the conspiracy originated in Philadelphia. It was significant to him that the trouble began shortly after the arrival of a "certain gentleman"—Colonel Walter Stewart—from Philadelphia. It is "generally believed," Washington wrote a friend, that "the Scheme was not only planned, but also digested and matured in Philadelphia," and he referred to rumors that public creditors were looking to the army to use its influence "in order to compel the Public, particularly the delinquent States, to do justice to creditors" both within and outside of the army. In a letter to Hamilton, he repeated his suspicion that the plot had been hatched in Philadelphia, and he commented that there was "something very misterious, in this business."

There was nothing very "misterious" in the desire of public creditors generally to have their accounts settled by Congress. How far they were willing to go in utilizing the army to frighten the states and Congress into taking action will perhaps never be known. It is clear that some members of Congress were aware of the possibilities. Shortly before the anonymous address was issued in Newburgh, Alexander Hamilton had written Washington to say that the situation was a "very interesting one." "I need not observe how far the temper and situation of the army may make it so," he added. Congress, he went on to say, was not governed by "reason or foresight" and was not likely to take "proper measures." An "embarrassing scene" was bound to eventuate in which it would be difficult to keep the army "within the bounds of moderation." What, then, to do? Washington should use his influence, not to check the army, "but rather, by the intervention of confidential and prudent persons, *to take the direction of them.*" But this should not be done openly. Like Congress some years before, Hamilton adverted to Washington's "delicacy" in such matters; carried to extremes, it prevented his espousing the army's interests "with sufficient warmth." The great "desideratum," he concluded, was the establishment of general funds for paying off public creditors, including the army, and "in this, the influence of the army, properly directed, may co-operate."

How far Hamilton was prepared to go in uniting public creditors with the army in order to bring pressure on Congress it is impossible to say. It is worth noting, however, that even after the Newburgh crisis had passed, Hamilton told Washington: "I confess, could force avail, I should almost wish to see it employed. I have an indifferent opinion of the honesty of this country, and ill forebodings as to its future system." If Washington suspected that Hamilton was involved in the Newburgh scheme, he gave no sign of it. In replying to Hamilton's earlier communication, he admitted that the "predicament, in which I stand as a citizen and soldier, is as critical and delicate as can well be conceived," but he insisted that he was under "no great apprehension" that the army would exceed "the bounds of moderation."

If Hamilton's intentions at the time of the Newburgh crisis are unclear, there is no mistaking the sentiments of Gouverneur Morris, assistant superintendent of finance, at this time. In a letter to John Jay in January 1783 he said frankly:

> The army have swords in their hands. You know enough of
> the history of mankind to know much more than I have said,
> and possibly much more than they themselves yet think of. I
> will add, however, that I am glad to see things in their pres-
> ent train. Depend on it, good will arise from the situation
> to which we are hastening. And this you may rely on, that
> my efforts will not be wanting. I pledge myself to you on the
> present occasion, and although I think it probable that much
> of convulsion will ensue, yet it must terminate in giving to
> government that power, without which government is but a
> name.

To General Nathanael Greene, then stationed in the South, Morris was even more frank. There was no likelihood, he told Greene, that the states would make the requisite grants of funds to Congress for paying off its debts *"unless the army be united and determined in the pursuit of it; and unless they be firmly supported, and as firmly support the other public creditors.*" To General Henry Knox he wrote in a similar vein. Fortunately, neither Knox nor Greene was willing to follow the dangerous course indicated by the assistant superintendent of finance. "As the present constitution is so defective," responded Knox, "why do not you great men call the people together, and tell them so? That is, to have a convention of the States to form a better constitution? This appears to us, who have a superficial view only, to be the most efficacious remedy." And Greene pointed out what should have been obvious to Morris: "When soldiers advance without authority, who can halt them?" Whether Hamilton and Morris were directly involved in the crisis that developed at Newburgh it is impossible to say on the basis of existing records. Certainly they were aware of the ominous unrest in the army, and they were at least willing to contemplate the possibility of exploiting it in the interest of strong government. What they failed to realize was that they were playing with fire.

Washington, usually ranked several pegs below Hamilton in intellectual capacity, sized up the situation at once. Thoroughly alarmed at the anonymous papers of March 10, he acted without delay. In his general orders for March 11, he characterized the call for an officers' meeting as "irregular and disorderly"; he did not, however, cancel the meeting. Realizing, as he said afterward, that it was easier "to divert from a wrong to a right path, than it is to recall the hasty and fatal steps which have already been taken," he simply postponed it until Saturday. At noon on that day, the officers were to hear the report of a committee which had returned from a conference with Congress and, "after mature deliberation," decide what further measures should be taken. Reporting the situation to Congress with "inexpressible concern," Washington explained what he had done "to rescue the foot, that stood wavering on the precipice of despair, from taking those steps, which would have led to the abyss of misery." Following Washington's general order of March 11, a second anonymous address to the officers appeared in which the writer noted that Washington's order sanctioned the meeting called for in the original address. Until now, the writer said with some bitterness, Washington has given the army "good wishes alone." Now, at long last, his general order gives "system to your proceedings, and stability to your resolves."

At noon on March 15, 1783, was enacted one of the most memorable scenes in American history. At the appointed hour the officers, their patience with Congress worn "threadbare," their minds still inflamed with the appeal of the Newburgh addresses, assembled in Newburgh "New Building" to hear their commander in chief. Washington began somewhat uncertainly—"his anxiety," he had told one of his staff, "prevented him from sleeping one moment the preceding night"—by apologizing for his presence at the meeting. It was necessary, however, for him to say something to the officers about the anonymous papers circulating in the camp. In order to do this "with greater perspicuity," he had committed his thoughts to writing and "with the indulgence of his brother officers" he would take the liberty of reading from a prepared text. Taking a manuscript out of his pocket, he began reading: "Gentlemen, by an anonymous summons, an attempt has been made to convene you together. How inconsistent with the rules of propriety, how unmilitary and how subversive to all order and discipline, let the good sense of the army decide."

At this point—although observers are not in complete agreement as to exactly when this happened—he paused for a moment, as though he were having difficulty with the manuscript, then reached into his pocket and drew out his spectacles. Apologizing for the interruption, he remarked quietly: "I have already grown gray in the service of my country. I am now going blind." The room became deathly still as he resumed. "My God!" he cried. "What can this writer have in view by recommending such measures? Can he be a friend to the army? Can he be a friend to this country? Rather is he not an insidious foe . . . plotting the ruin of both by sowing the seeds of discord and separation between the civil and military powers of this continent?" After pointing out the "physical impossibility" of carrying out either alternative suggested by the anonymous writer—marching on Congress or withdrawing to the West—Washington turned angrily to the advice of the writer "to suspect the man, who shall recommend moderate measures and longer forbearance":

> I spurn it, as every man who regards that liberty, and reveres
> that justice for which we contend, undoubtedly must. For,
> if men are to be precluded from offering their sentiments on
> a matter, which may involve the most serious and alarming
> consequences, that can invite the consideration of mankind,
> reason is of no use to us; the freedom of speech may be taken
> away, and, numb and silent, we may be led away like sheep
> to the slaughter.

Congress, Washington insisted, would eventually see that "complete justice'" was done the army. Its efforts to raise funds "have been unwearied, and will not cease" until they are successful. Furthermore, Washington himself would do everything he could "so far as may be done consistently with the great duty I owe to my country, and those powers we are bound to respect," to see that the army received its just dues. In return, the army was requested to "rely on the plighted faith" of the country and "place a full confidence in the purity of the intentions of Congress":

> By thus determining and thus acting, you will pursue the
> plain and direct road to the attainment of your wishes; you
> will defeat the insidious designs of our enemies, who are
> compelled to resort from open force to secret artifice; you
> will give one more distinguished proof of unexampled patrio-
> tism and patient virtue, rising superior to the pressure of the
> most complicated sufferings; and you will, by the dignity
> of your conduct, afford occasion for posterity to say, when
> speaking of the glorious example you have exhibited to man-
> kind, "Had this day been wanting, the world had never seen
> the last stage of perfection to which human nature is capable
> of attaining."

According to David Humphreys, it was a "proud day for the army."
Washington appeared "unspeakably greater" on this occasion "than
ever he did before." "Never, through all the war, did his Excellency
achieve a greater victory than on this occasion," said General Schuy-
ler afterward. "The whole assembly were in tears at the conclusion of
his address. I rode with General Knox to his quarters in absolute silence, because of the solemn impression on our minds." "It is needless
for me to say any thing of this production," commented Major Shaw;
"*it speaks for itself.*" Like Humphreys, Shaw thought Washington had
never seemed more impressive than on this occasion:

> On other occasions he has been supported by the exertions
> of an army and the countenance of his friends; but in this he
> stood single and alone. There was no saying where the pas-
> sions of an army, which were not a little inflamed might lead.
> . . . Under these circumstances, he appeared, not at the head
> of his troops, but as it were in opposition to them; and for
> a dreadful moment the interests of the army and its general
> seemed to be in competition! He spoke—every doubt was
> dispelled, and the tide of patriotism rolled again in its wont-
> ed course. Illustrious man! What he says of the army may
> with equal justice be applied to his own character, "Had this
> day been wanting, the world had never seen the last stage of
> perfection to which human nature is capable of attaining."

After Washington had withdrawn, the officers proceeded to adopt a series of resolutions expressing their "unshaken confidence" in Congress
and rejecting with "abhorrence" and "disdain" the "infamous proposi-
tions" contained in the anonymous addresses. "I have ever considered,"

wrote David Cobb, one of Washington's aides, many years later, "that the United States are indebted for their republican form of government solely to the firm and determined republicanism of General Washington at this time."

A few weeks later, the end of the war was officially proclaimed, and the army began to disband. After delivering his farewell address to the principal officers still remaining at headquarters, Washington set out for Annapolis to surrender the commission he had accepted from Congress eight years before. The ceremony, as worked out by a congressional committee of three, was to be a formal demonstration of the supremacy of civil authority over the military in the newly independent nation.

With this plan Washington was, of course, in full accord.

At noon on December 23, 1783, Washington entered the Hall of Congress, crowded with spectators, civilian and military, and took the place assigned him. After a brief pause, Thomas Mifflin, president of Congress, announced that Congress was ready to receive his communication. Washington thereupon rose and began reading his prepared address: "The great events on which my resignation depended, having at length taken place, I now have the honor of offering my sincere congratulations to Congress, and of presenting myself before them, to surrender into their hands the trust committed to me, and to claim the indulgence of retiring from the service of my country." With increasing emotion, he continued for a few brief paragraphs, paused for a moment to regain his composure, then concluded simply: "Having now finished the work assigned me, I retire from the great theatre of action; and, bidding an affectionate farewell to this august body, under whose orders I have long acted, I here offer my commission, and take my leave of all the employments of public life."

Delivering his commission to the president, he returned to his place and received, standing, the response of Congress, delivered by the president, who remained seated:

> Sir: the United States in Congress assembled receive with emotions too affecting for utterance the solemn resignation of the authorities under which you have led their troops with success through a perilous and doubtful war. Called upon to defend its invaded rights, you accepted the sacred charge before it had formed alliances, and while it was without funds or a government to support you. You have conducted the great military contest with wisdom and fortitude, invariably regarding the rights of the civil power through all disaster and change.

The secretary of Congress then delivered a copy of the president's address to Washington, who then took his leave. The next morning he left Annapolis and hastened down to Mount Vernon. "The scene is at last closed," he wrote Governor Clinton of New York. "I feel myself eased of a load of public care. I hope to spend the remainder of my days in cultivating the affections of good men, and in the practice of the domestic virtues."

As we know, the "load of public care" was to be placed on his shoulders again before long, and he was to render further services to his country as head of the new government inaugurated in 1789. But without a doubt his most important work had been accomplished before he became president of the United States. By his unwavering loyalty to the revolutionary cause, his judicious use of the powers granted him by Congress during the war, by his response to Nicola and his handling of the Newburgh crisis—in short, by his constant regard for the "rights of the civil power through all disaster and changes"—Washington had, with his immense prestige, helped establish constitutional processes firmly in the American system and had advanced the cause of "government of, by, and for civilians" to which the Revolution was dedicated. People who like to generalize about revolutions in history often call attention to the fact that the Puritan Revolution in England had its Cromwell, the French Revolution its Napoleon, and the Russian Revolution its Lenin and Stalin. The American Revolution, fortunately, had its Washington.

Southwest Review, Winter 1954.

CHAPTER 11

George Washington and the Quakers

While doing some research on George Washington's religious views, I spent some time examining the relations between soldier Washington and the pacifist Quakers in Pennsylvania and elsewhere. During the American Revolution, I learned, Washington respected the Quakers' right of conscience, but he was disturbed by their opposition to the struggle for independence and at times thought they wanted the British to win the war. After the war, however, he was extremely pleased by their hearty support of the US Constitution, and when they sent a delegation to New York to congratulate him for his election as president, he responded with respect and affection. The Quakers were delighted by his efforts as president to avoid war with Britain by supporting the unpopular Jay's Treaty, and when he died in December 1799, one Quaker called him a "bright Occidental Star."

★ ★ ★

George Washington was a soldier and a slaveholder, and the Society of Friends was pacifist and emancipationist; it is not surprising, therefore, that the two should have clashed from time to time. Quaker historians, as well as eulogists of Washington, however, usually minimize these clashes, preferring instead to emphasize the genuine esteem which Washington and the Quakers developed for one another after the American Revolution. With Quaker writers the point has been that Washington came gradually to sympathize with Quaker views on war and slavery. Washington's admirers, for their part, have been eager to stress the first president's broad-minded, tolerant outlook and his ability to respect religious views, like those of the Quakers, which differed from his own.

Washington did indeed believe firmly in religious liberty and in the rights of conscience. Moreover, he developed a sincere dislike of both war and slavery during the Revolution. When Warner Mifflin sought him out, after he became president, to discuss slavery with him, he was treated with "kindness and respect" and reported afterwards that Washington showed some understanding of Quaker policy during the Revolutionary War. "Mr. Mifflin," Washington is reported as asking at one point, "will you please to inform me on what principle you were opposed to the revolution?" "Yes, friend Washington," replied Mifflin, "upon the same principles that I should be opposed to a change in this government—all that ever was gained by revolutions are not an adequate compensation to the poor mangled soldier for the loss of life or limb." After a moment's pause, Washington is said to have declared: "Mr. Mifflin, I honor your sentiments; there is more in that than mankind have generally considered."

While there is no reason to question the sincerity of Washington's statement on that occasion, it would be a mistake to regard it as definitive as to his attitude toward the Quakers. Even after he came to deplore both war and slavery, there remained important residual differences between his opinions on these matters and those of the Society of Friends. It is easy to accumulate an imposing list of antiwar statements from Washington's writings, as some Quakers have done; however, it is equally necessary to remember that Washington was never a pacifist and that he mildly rebuked the Quakers when he was president for "declining to share with others the burthen of the common defense." It is also not difficult to collect antislavery pronouncements from Washington's later years to show their consonance with the Quaker point of view, but it is at the same time important to realize that Washington was willing to bow to expediency in the matter, that he did not free his own slaves during his lifetime, and that he became annoyed whenever he thought the Quakers were pushing the antislavery cause too forcefully.

Washington, in short, came gradually to respect, but not to share, the deepest principles animating the Society of Friends. He was, after all, a member of the Virginia aristocracy, reared in a society that accepted the established Anglican church as an essential prop of social order, regarded the Quakers as a vexatious sectarian group, and looked upon war and slavery as inseparable parts of the natural order of things. His remark to Warner Mifflin takes on significance only if his early background is kept in mind. For it shows that Washington was capable of growth and that he was able to free himself from his earliest influences and develop respect for a religious group which rejected many of the basic institutions—the established church, war, and slavery—that he had been trained as a youth to accept.

There are no records of any contacts which Washington had with the Quakers when he was a boy, but he was probably familiar with them from an early age. His father may have told him about John Fothergill, the English Quaker who visited Virginia in 1721, who was entertained by the Washingtons, and who called Washington's father "a friendly man." And he undoubtedly told the boy about the two trips he made to England (the second when George was about four years old) to discuss business with the English Quakers who were his partners in an enterprise for developing iron deposits in Maryland and Virginia. The first Quaker of whom we have any record that Washington met personally, however, was Dr. William Hillary, an English doctor residing in the Barbados, whom his elder half-brother Lawrence consulted when the two of them went to the West Indies in 1751 for Lawrence's health. Washington did not identify Dr. Hillary as a Quaker in the journal he kept of the trip, but he was probably aware of the fact.

Washington's first important encounter with the Quakers, however, did not come until the time of the French and Indian War, when he was serving as commander of all Virginia forces, with responsibility for frontier defenses. In 1756 six Quakers were drafted into the militia and sent to Winchester to fight under Washington. The young commander was genuinely perplexed by his first confrontation with Quaker pacifism. The six Quakers, he quickly learned, would "neither bear arms, work, receive provisions or pay, or do anything that tends, in any respect, to self-defense." When Governor Dinwiddie advised him to "confine them with a short allowance of bread and water, till you bring them to reason," Washington reported that he "could by no means bring the Quakers to any terms. They chose rather to be whipped to death than bear arms, or lend us any assistance whatever upon the fort, or any thing of self-defense." The governor's final instructions were: "Use them with lenity, but as they are at their own expense, I would have them remain as long as the other Draughts." In a final reference to the problem, Washington wrote that, in compliance with these orders, the Quakers "still remain here, and shall until the other drafts are discharged."

Washington's treatment of the six Quakers has sometimes been cited as evidence of his early respect for the rights of conscience. Actually, we know too little about the episode to draw any such conclusion. In any event, if Washington is to be commended for his forbearance, the governor of Virginia must share in the commendation. Neither showed any special animus against the Quakers in their exchanges on the subject. There is, however, evidence that Virginia Quakers thought well of the young colonel. In July 1758, shortly before Washington's election to the House of Burgesses, a Friend wrote to Washington to say of another candidate: "His interest I think declines among the Quakers, where I imagine your's is pretty good." This is the last record we have of Washington's relations with the Quakers until the American Revolution.

Washington's first Revolutionary encounter with the Quakers took place during the siege of Boston. New England Quakers, assisted by donations from Quakers in Pennsylvania and New Jersey, organized a relief expedition to help the poor and needy in Boston and sent a committee of four to seek Washington's permission to enter the besieged city. Washington "received us kindly," Moses Brown, one of the chief planners of the project, said afterwards,

> but declined permitting us to go into Boston, saying he had
> made it a rule not to let any go in, unless it was a woman
> separated from her Husband or the like; but however,
> Showed a readiness, to further the designed distribution by
> proposing to send for some of our Friends to come out upon
> the lines . . . for a Conferance with them.

The committee "concluded to adopt that method." As Brown explained later: "As the Small Pox was in Town . . . our not being allowed to go in seemed a small or no disappointment." The Quakers asked Washington for permission to write letters to General Howe explaining their plan and to two Quakers in Boston, through whom they hoped to distribute the relief, "which he concented to and proposed our shewing what we wrote to General Nathanael Greene." Greene was a disowned Rhode Island Quaker whom Washington liked to tease about his pacifist background. "Sometimes," it was said, "Washington, who really loved a jest, would slyly remind him of his Quaker origin." As Brown recalled it, Washington told the committee: "Go to General Greene; he is a Quaker, and knows more about it than I do." The committee accordingly "Waited on Nathanael," wrote the letters with his assistance, and submitted them to Washington that evening. Washington approved the letters and sent the Quakers on to the British lines under a flag of truce, where they arranged with General Howe for distributing funds among the war-sufferers of Boston.

Moses Brown developed great admiration for Washington as a result of his conversations with him in December 1775. In after years he referred to him as a "great" man and spoke particularly of "his simple, easy manner." And Washington's cordial reception of Brown and his associates and his "readiness" to cooperate in their undertaking testifies to his friendliness toward the Quakers (perhaps because of General Greene) during the early months of the war and to some appreciation of their pacifist-humanitarian principles.

With the Pennsylvania Quakers, however, Washington's relations were far less friendly. When the war shifted to Pennsylvania in 1777, Washington began to share the popular feeling among patriots generally that Quaker neutralism was, in essence, pro-British Toryism. It is true that in his correspondence with the Pennsylvania Council of Safety in January 1777 regarding the recruitment of men for the defense of Philadelphia, he took for granted the exemption of the "conscientiously scrupulous" from the draft and seems to have regarded this as unexceptionable. By May 1777, however, he was identifying the Quakers with the "disaffected" generally, charging them with attempting to obstruct the operation of the militia laws, and urging that steps be taken to defeat their "evil intentions." His distrust of the Quakers reached a climax during the British occupation of Philadelphia. On two occasions at this time, in giving orders for the impressment of supplies from the countryside, he instructed his officers to bear down especially upon the "unfriendly Quakers and others notoriously disaffected to the cause of American liberty." When Quakers outside Philadelphia sought permission to send food into the city to help the needy during the British occupation, Washington flatly denied the request and refused even to see the delegation. Moreover, in March 1778, he ordered his officers to prohibit Quakers outside Philadelphia from entering the city to attend a meeting of the Society. "This is an intercourse that we should by all means endeavour to interrupt," he declared, "as the plans settled at these meetings are of the most pernicious tendency."

Still, on other occasions during the same critical period of the war, when Washington was faced with a "Quaker problem," he reacted with kindness and consideration. In the summer of 1777, for example, several Quakers in western Virginia were drafted into the militia and marched about two hundred miles with muskets tied to their backs to Washington's camp outside Philadelphia. "But on their coming to the camp," related one of the draftees, "and the state of their case being represented to General Washington, they were, by his order discharged, and liberty given them to return home." Washington's action has understandably received high praise from Quaker historians.

Washington's polite reception of six delegates from the Philadelphia Yearly Meeting a few days after the battle of Germantown has also won much praise from Quaker writers. The purpose of the delegation was twofold: to protest the exile by Pennsylvania authorities of a number of leading Philadelphia Quakers to Winchester, Virginia, and to clear the Society of charges that it was transmitting intelligence to the British. With them the delegates carried a "Testimony against War," explaining why the Quakers "are led out of all wars & Fightings," denying any "Correspondence highly prejudicial to the public Safety," and requesting that the Virginia exiles be restored "to their afflicted Families & Friends." The delegates first visited General Howe, who received them good-naturedly, and then proceeded to Washington's camp, where they "had a very full Opportunity of clearing the Society from the Aspersions, which had been invidiously raised against them, and distributed a number of the Testimonies amongst the Officers, who received and read them and made no objections."

Warner Mifflin, apparently the leader of the group, was said to have been greeted by Washington "with open arms" and "entertained and made much of by everyone around." By everyone, perhaps, but General Armstrong, who remarked waspishly the following day, "We lost a great part of yesterday with a deputation of Quakers from their yearly meeting." The delegates later reported simply that "we were kindly entertained by General Washington," but another version of the conference has it that Mifflin told Washington boldly, "I am opposed to the revolution, and to all changes of government which occasion war and bloodshed." If Mifflin said this, it seems not to have offended Washington, for, as Armstrong noted, "The General gave them dinner . . . for which they seemed very thankful." When the delegates broached the subject of the Quaker exiles, Washington explained that he had no authority to release them and suggested they get in touch with the Pennsylvania officials "who had banished their friends." In reporting to the Yearly Meeting afterwards, the delegates insisted that

> Gen. Washington and all the Officers then present, being a
> pretty many, were fully satisfied as to Friends Clearness and
> we hope and believe . . . the Opportunity we had was useful
> many ways, there having been great Openness and many
> Observations upon various subjects to Edification and tend-
> ing to remove and clear up some Prejudices which had been
> imbibed.

Isaac Sharpless singled out Washington's courtesy toward the delegation as "abundant proof" of his good will toward the Quakers during the Revolution, remarking that "many a commander would have treated them with scant forbearance."

The hospitality which Washington extended the wives of four of the exiles when they visited him in April 1778 to request his help in securing the release of the Winchester prisoners has also pleased Quaker writers. Washington had already assured the ladies of his willingness to assist them in their plan to send food, clothing, and medical supplies to the ailing prisoners, and indeed he had interceded with Governor Wharton on their behalf. But the four ladies—Mary Pemberton, Elizabeth Drinker, Susanna Jones, and Mary Pleasants—wished to discuss the plight of the prisoners with him personally, and without receiving authorization of any kind, they left occupied Philadelphia and journeyed to his headquarters at Valley Forge. "We requested an audience with the General," Mrs. Drinker noted in her diary, and sat with his wife, (a sociable, pretty kind of woman), until he came in. A number of officers were there who were very complaisant. . . . It was not long before G. Washington came, and discoursed with us freely, but not so long as we could have wished, as dinner was served, to which he invited us. . . . We had an elegant dinner, which was soon over, when we went out with ye Genls wife, up to her Chamber—and saw no more of him.

Washington explained again that he had no jurisdiction over the prisoners, but he gave the ladies a pass to Lancaster, where they could press their suit before the state authorities. "As they seem much distressed," he wrote the governor, "humanity pleads strongly in their behalf." When the ladies reached Lancaster, they learned to their joy that the prisoners had been released the day before.

Washington received many compliments, both at the time and afterwards, for "the most cordial manner" in which he entertained his unexpected visitors. His amiable reception of the "four courageous Quaker women" is commonly regarded as conclusive evidence that he did not share the animosity toward the Quakers prevailing among the patriots. Even the exiles believed that Washington's sympathies were with them. When they reached his headquarters on their way back from Virginia, late in April, and requested and received his permission to cross American lines into Philadelphia, "we esteemed it a proof," said one of the prisoners, "of the General's sense of justice and politeness." Actually, there is little evidence of any real concern for the Virginia exiles in any of this. Even General Israel Putnam, who thoroughly disliked the Quakers, would probably have treated the ladies—certainly the seventy-five-year-old Mrs. Pemberton—courteously. As for allowing the prisoners to return to Philadelphia, what else could Washington have done once they had been released by the state? That he continued to distrust the Quakers until the end of the war is apparent in his adamant refusal in 1781 to permit a delegation of New England Friends to visit Quaker meetings on Long Island.

It is clear that Washington, as his prompt release of the Virginia draftees shows, was willing to respect the religious scruples of the Quakers against bearing arms during the Revolution. What he could not understand, however, was the insistence of Pennsylvania Quakers (who seem to have been more uncompromising than Quakers elsewhere) upon total abstention from the independence movement to which he was so firmly dedicated. They would not bear arms, of course, but neither would they hold office under the revolutionary government of Pennsylvania, affirm allegiance to it, pay its taxes, or even handle its paper money. Washington, like most patriots, wrongly concluded from this that the Quakers wanted the British to win the war and perhaps were even secretly aiding them. Although, unlike many of his associates in the army and in Congress, he strove to treat them with fairness and decency, he could never quite convince himself that they were not guilty of "evil intentions" toward the American cause. Quakers have surely exaggerated his friendship for them during the Revolution.

After the Revolution, however, Washington quickly revised his opinion of the Pennsylvania Quakers, partly, no doubt, because of their hearty support of the new Federal Constitution. "No person has spoken to me with more impartiality respecting the Quakers than General Washington," declared Brissot de Warville after a conversation with him in 1788:

> He declared to me, that, in the course of the war, he had
> entertained an ill opinion of this society; he knew but little of
> them . . . and he attributed to their political sentiments, the
> effect of their religious principles. He told me, that having
> since known them better, he acquired an esteem for them;
> and that considering the simplicity of their manners, the
> purity of their morals, their exemplary economy and their
> attachment to the constitution, he considered this society as
> one of the best supports of the new government.

In October 1789, when the Philadelphia Quakers sent a delegation to New York to congratulate Washington on his elevation to the presidency and to present him with a copy of Barclay's *Apology*, Washington seized the opportunity to announce publicly both his high regard for the Quakers and his firm support of the rights of conscience:

> Government being, among other purposes, instituted to
> protect the persons and consciences of men from oppression,
> it is certainly the duty of Rulers, not only to abstain from it
> themselves, but according to their stations, to prevent it in
> others. The liberty enjoyed by the People of these States of
> worshipping Almighty God agreeable to their consciences is
> not only among the choicest of their blessings, but also of
> their *rights*. . . .

> Your principles and conduct are well known to me, and it is
> doing the People called Quakers no more than justice to say,
> that (except their declining to share with others the burthen
> of the common defence) there is no denomination among us,
> who are more exemplary and useful citizens.

I assure you very explicitly that in my opinion the conscientious scruples of all men should be treated with great delicacy and tenderness, and it is my wish and desire that the laws may always be as extensively accomodated to them, as a due regard to the Protection and essential interests of the nation may justify and permit.

While the Quakers could not agree with everything in Washington's statement, they were delighted with his concern for the "conscientious scruples of all men" and pleased that he read his reply to their address in person, "which was considered a particular mark of respect as 'tis customary for one of his secretaries to read the answers." In France, the *Patriote Français*, reporting the exchange, italicized Washington's characterization of the Quakers as "exemplary and useful citizens" and commented, "This opinion of the most impartial and best informed judge in America, will, we hope, close the mouths of the slanderers of the Quakers."

Nevertheless, even after Washington's "formal reconciliation" with the Quakers after the Revolution, he was frequently irritated by their antislavery activities. Washington had come to deplore slavery during the Revolution, and after the war he expressed more than once his conviction that the institution "by degrees assuredly ought" to be abolished "by Legislative authority." But he held more than two hundred slaves until his death (his will provided for freeing them after the death of his wife), and he firmly upheld the right of owners to their property in slaves, pending the adoption of some plan of gradual emancipation by law. He was, moreover, anxious that the union of the states effected by the Constitution not be jeopardized by a too vigorous agitation of the antislavery issue. His—what shall we say, moderate?—views on slavery inevitably clashed with those of the Quakers.

In 1786 Washington complained bitterly of the efforts of Philadelphia Quakers to liberate a slave belonging to a resident of Alexandria, Virginia, who was visiting the city. Nor did he take kindly to a petition ("a very mal-apropos one it was") which the Quakers sent Congress in 1790, urging an immediate end to the slave trade. Alarmed by the bitterness which the petition aroused in the South, he was obviously relieved when the question, after a stormy debate in Congress, was finally "put to sleep." "The introduction of the Memorial respecting Slavery," he told a Virginia friend, "was to be sure, not only an illjudged piece of business but occasioned a great waste of time." He did, however, refuse to join his friend in denouncing Congress for discussing the slavery problem and reminded him of "the great dereliction of Slavery in a large part of this Union." Furthermore, when Warner Mifflin called on him about this time to explain the views of the Quakers on slavery, he heard him out with sympathy and respect. The fact is that Washington was finding his position as slaveholder increasingly distasteful and his references to the subject in his later years reveal a feeling of embarrassment about his own personal involvement in the slave system. One can't help believing that he breathed a sigh of relief as he wrote out a provision for emancipating his slaves in his will. The Quakers were overjoyed when they learned the contents of his will; they "felt they had won a most important point in the campaign for Freedom."

If Washington was bothered by the antislavery activities of the Quakers, he seems to have looked favorably upon their efforts on behalf of the Indians. In March 1793, when he was making plans for a peace conference with the western Indians at Sandusky, seven members of the Philadelphia Meeting for Sufferings called to ask permission for a deputation of Quakers to be present at the treaty in an unofficial capacity. When the Quakers explained that they would not "interfere in any shape with the political business of the treaty, their sole end being to effect peace by impressing upon the Ind. the necessity & advantages of it," Washington told them that "the first wish of his heart in this business, being to promote peace between the Indians & the U. S. he should be very happy to give every facility in his power to whatever might tend to promote a peace upon honorable & just terms—and that he could see no impropriety in these persons attending the treaty, upon the principles mentioned."

Late the following month, three of the Quakers who were "to attend the Treaty" visited Washington a few hours before departing from Philadelphia in order to reassure him "that they shd. in no shape interfere in the political points or matters of boundary to be settled at the treaty; their sole object being to endeavour to impress [upon] the minds of the Indians the advantages of peace & the blessings of civilization.—The president approved their intentions & hoped they might be crowned with Success."

The "Sandusky Conference," as it turned out, was not "crowned with Success." In the end there was only one short, inconclusive interview with the Indians on July 31 near Detroit. Washington was disappointed but not surprised at the failure of the conference, and he continued to be friendly to the work of the Quakers among the Indians. In 1796 he approved the "object and intentions" of the Indian Committee of the Philadelphia Yearly Meeting, and shortly before retiring from office he "recommended the Indians to attend to the voice of the Quakers, who were peaceable people and friends of Indians."

Generally conservative in outlook, the Philadelphia Quakers were firm supporters of the Washington administration. Dr. George Logan of Stenton, however, disagreed violently with the political views of his fellow Quakers. An agrarian democrat of the Jeffersonian persuasion,

Logan eventually clashed both with the Philadelphia Quakers and with Washington himself. Logan had once been on good terms with Washington, and the two had spent a pleasant Sunday together at Stenton in July 1787, exchanging views on agriculture. After Washington became president, however, Logan aligned himself with the Jeffersonians, denounced the Hamiltonian policies of the Washington administration, entertained Citizen Genêt at Stenton, fumed against Jay's Treaty with England, and even voted against a congratulatory address prepared by the Pennsylvania Assembly on the occasion of Washington's retirement from office. His Quaker associates were shocked by the vehemence with which he voiced his opinions, there was a falling-out between him and his fellow Quakers, and in 1791 he was disowned for associating himself for a time with the local militia. But Logan remained a Quaker at heart (toward the end of his life he began attending Quaker meetings again), and when in 1798, following the "X Y Z" affair, the United States seemed on the verge of war with France, he journeyed to Paris to see what he could do to prevent a rupture between the two nations.

Washington would have welcomed Dr. Logan's support of his own efforts to preserve peace with England at the time of Jay's Treaty in 1794. In 1798, however, convinced of France's hostile designs on the United States, he had donned his uniform again and agreed to head the army that the Adams administration was raising in preparation for war with France. Logan returned from France in November with assurances from high French officials that they sincerely desired peace. He was coldly received by Secretary of State Pickering, and then, since President Adams was out of town, he decided to seek out Washington, who was in Philadelphia conferring with his military staff. It was an egregious blunder. Washington was outraged by Logan's cavalier disregard for normal diplomatic channels as well as by his apparent bias toward France, and he received him with a studied indifference that bordered on boorishness. Afterwards, in a rare action, he wrote out a long memorandum of his conversation with Logan, every sentence of which breathes hostility toward his former host at Stenton. President Adams, however, received Logan more cordially when he returned to Philadelphia at the end of November, and Logan's report played some part in Adams's decision to resume diplomatic relations with France.

There is something ironic in the fact that Washington's last recorded contact with a Quaker should have been so unpleasant. For in the years since the Revolution there had been a real rapprochement between Washington and the Philadelphia Quakers. When news of Washington's death in December 1799 reached Philadelphia, one of the Quakers referred to him as a "bright Occidental Star" at First Day meeting, and even Elizabeth Drinker, the only Quaker whom we know to have resented his attitude toward the Quakers during the Revolution, expressed genuine sorrow at his passing. What adds to the irony is the fact that the Quaker with whom Washington clashed in 1798, unlike the majority of Quakers, held views on war which Washington could understand. Logan "thought all war unlawful to a Christian," according to his wife, "except that which was strictly of a defensive kind." Washington's Deist views had led him to a similar position. Both were essentially men of peace, anxious that the young nation avoid embroilment in the wars of Europe. But Washington had striven courageously as president to avoid a pointless war with England by supporting the unpopular Jay's Treaty in the face of bitter opposition from Republicans like Logan. And Logan worked hard to prevent an equally needless war with France amid angry hostility from Federalists like Washington. Politics seems to have overwhelmed principle in each instance. To cap the irony, John Adams, who had little liking for either the Quakers or France (and who later signed the "Logan Act"), listened to what Logan had to say and decided to risk a split in his party by renewing efforts for peace with France.

The Logan episode aside, Washington's associations with the Quakers from the French and Indian War onward were, on the whole, remarkably pleasant. What is noteworthy, in fact, is not that relations between them should have been frequently strained, but that they should have been as agreeable, by and large, as they were. There is much in the attitude of Washington, the slaveowner and military leader, toward this pacifist and abolitionist group that does him credit. Although, as he admitted, he had "an ill opinion" of the Quakers during the Revolution, this did not prevent him from treating them in most instances with courtesy and consideration. And after the war he learned, as he told them, that pacifists could be "exemplary and useful citizens." It was as good citizens that Washington seems chiefly to have admired the Quakers. As he told Brissot de Warville, he was impressed by "the simplicity of their manners, the purity of their morals, their exemplary economy and their attachment to the constitution." Not all Americans were disposed to be as kindly toward the Quakers after the Revolution. As late as 1833 one writer was still denouncing the "twistical proceedings" of the Quakers during the Revolution and heaping ridicule on their friendly exchange of addresses with Washington in 1789. But Washington looked upon them as "one of the best supports of the new government." And by the example he set in his respect for the "conscientious scruples" of the Society of Friends, he undoubtedly helped, with his immense prestige, to "close the mouths of the slanderers of the Quakers," as the *Patriote Français* put it, during the early years of the republic.

The Bulletin of Friends Historical Association, Autumn 1960.

CHAPTER 12

John Adams's
Marginal Comments

John Adams, the second president of the United States, was forever writing: letters, speeches, articles, and books, and he was certainly a stimulating writer. The multiplicity of nouns and adjectives that he piled up in his sentences, when he felt strongly about things, are a delight to read (and count). "In Congress," he once complained, "Nibbling and quibbling—as usual. There is no greater Mortification than to sit with half a dozen Witts, deliberating upon a Petition, Address or Memorial. These great Witts, these subtle Criticks, these refined Geniuses, these learned Lawyers, these wise Statesmen, are so fond of showing their Parts and Powers, as to make their Consultations very tedious."

When Adams was reading books, he did more writing. His favorite books were written by the *philosophes* of the Enlightenment, and he wrote comments in the margins of the pages he was turning, making it quite clear what he thought about the points being made by the author. Fortunately, Zoltan Haraszti, Keeper of Rare Books and Editor of Publications at the Boston Public Library, made Adams's marginal reactions to the ideas of the *philosophes* available to the public. The publisher thought the Adams book would be "fascinating reading for anyone." Not necessarily. But for people who wanted to understand Adams's strong feelings about life, his side-swipes in this book are indispensable.

★ ★ ★

Of the four leading philosopher-statesmen of the early republic—Jefferson, Madison, Hamilton, and Adams—John Adams has been least known, least liked. Jefferson has been cherished as a symbol of the American democratic faith, Madison admired as the "Father of the Constitution," and Hamilton respected for his realistic grasp of the economic forces that indicated the future development of the new nation. Adams alone has been claimed by no political party, invoked in no great cause, rarely quoted, and never apotheosized for the purposes of American folk hero–worship. Yet Vernon Parrington, whose own liberal predilections led him to class the conservative New Englander with the famous English Tory, Dr. Johnson, considered him the most notable political thinker, with the possible exception of Calhoun, among American statesmen; the late Harold Laski deemed him "the greatest political thinker whom America has yet produced"; and the violently anti-usurocratic poet Ezra Pound, for reasons best known to himself, called him the "Father of the Nation." Nevertheless he is seldom read today, his definitive biography still remains to be written, and his political thought, except for Correa Walsh's brilliant analysis, thirty-seven years ago, in *The Political Science of John Adams*, has never received extensive treatment by students of American intellectual history. Zoltán Haraszti, Keeper of Rare Books and Editor of Publications at the Boston Public Library, is therefore to be commended for calling our attention again to this unjustly neglected figure in the history of American thought in his excellent volume, *John Adams and the Prophets of Progress*.

While it is doubtful whether Haraszti's presentation of Adams's reactions to the ideas of the leading *philosophes* of the eighteenth-century Enlightenment will make "fascinating reading for anyone," as the publishers claim on the book jacket, for one interested in doing any primary thinking about the Enlightenment worldview, still so important for Western and particularly American thought, this collection of marginal comments by Adams in the pages of the Great Books of his age will unquestionably make stimulating reading. After brief introductory chapters on the second president's lack of popularity, on his library, and on his political philosophy, Haraszti gets down to the main business at hand: Adams's notes, presented with excerpts from the passages he was commenting upon, on his readings and rereadings in Bolingbroke, Rousseau, Frederick the Great, d'Alembert, Mably, Turgot, Mary Wollstonecraft, Condorcet, d'Hauterive, Priestley, and several other less familiar writers. As one follows Adams's arguments with the *philosophes*—earnest, witty, at times angry—he will doubtless register his own dissents to Adams's dissents, add marginalia of his own to Adams's marginalia. But he will not fail to be impressed with Adams's tough-mindedness, dogged honesty, and determination to probe to the very roots of the "divine science," as he called political philosophy, in his efforts to formulate the system of government offering the best hope to mankind.

Actually, Adams thought well of the *philosophes*. The eighteenth century, he told Jefferson, "notwithstanding all its errors and vices, has been, of all that are past, the most honorable to human nature." He also shared their generous aspirations for the future: "The way to improve society and reform the world," he wrote after a passage in Turgot, "is to enlighten men, spread knowledge, and convince the multitude that they have, or may have, sense, knowledge, and virtue." But farther than this he could not go. Moderately pessimistic, he simply could not bring himself to accept the view of the *philosophes* that human nature was fundamentally good, and that once the unenlightened feudalistic institutions of the past had been replaced by a simple form of representative government, liberty, equality, and fraternity would flourish, unhampered, indefinitely into the future. For Adams, human beings were selfish, contentious, economically aggressive by nature; furthermore, inequality in birth, wealth, and talents, not equality, was the natural law of society. From this it followed that the social order—even that of the noble savages described by that "eloquent coxcomb," Rousseau—will always divide itself into classes, continually engaged in the struggle for power. To refuse to face these facts, as the *philosophes* did with their visionary dream of human perfectibility, will, and in fact, as the French Revolution demonstrated, did lead to anarchy, bloodshed, terror, and finally dictatorship. The solution, in Adams's opinion, lay in devising a "mixed" government, representing rival interests in society, in which, by an elaborate system of checks and balances, the selfishness of one group would be neutralized by the countervailing power of other groups. In other words, as he told Mary Wollstonecraft: recognize the factor of human selfishness and prepare "bridles" for it. Only in this way could human passions be directed into peaceful, constructive channels; only in this way could the extremes of anarchy and tyranny be avoided.

It is easy enough to point out the errors and miscalculations in Adams's own specific recommendations. In his own day, the British Constitution, the model for his "mixed" government of aristocratic and democratic elements, was already beginning its gradual evolution toward legislative supremacy in one house—the "unicameral" system which he thought so dangerous. And in the United States, the distinction between an aristocratic Senate and a democratic House of Representatives has long since ceased to be a reality. But Adams's main point—that it is both impractical and dangerous to draw up systems of national (and, one may add, international) government without taking human frailties and the existence of power factors in human affairs into account—is as pertinent today as it was in the eighteenth century. His basic insight, though expressed in terms of eighteenth-century notions of aristocratic republicanism, is not unlike that of our own Reinhold Niebuhr: "Man's capacity for justice makes democracy possible; but man's inclination to injustice makes democracy necessary."

REVIEW OF ZOLTAN HARASZTI, *John Adams and the Prophets of Progress* (1952), *Southwest Review, Summer* 1952.

CHAPTER 13

Jefferson's Dreams
for the Future

know a lot more about Thomas Jefferson today than I did when I
wrote this article about him, and though I'm still impressed with
his thinking and writing, I'm disappointed that his dislike of slavery
was more in the abstract than deeply felt. He was in debt much of the
time, to be sure, but couldn't he have saved money, as George Washington did, for his slaves' ultimate freedom?

★ ★ ★

Thomas Jefferson once admitted to John Adams that he liked "the
dreams of the future better than the history of the past." "Your taste is
judicious," was Adams's amused reply. It was a revealing exchange. For
while Jefferson, like Adams, was widely read in history and painfully
conscious of the grievous shortcomings which humanity had displayed
in the "history of the past," he preferred, unlike his New England
friend, to emphasize the better side of human nature. "We believed," he
said, "that man was a rational animal, endowed by nature with rights,
and with an innate sense of justice; and that he could be restrained from
wrong and protected in right by moderate powers." It was Jefferson's
deep-seated faith in man's basic capacity for wisdom and goodness that
led him to formulate "dreams of the future."

Jefferson believed that the American people had an unprecedented
opportunity, after the American Revolution, to devise the kind of political and social system in which human potentialities for good could be
realized. As he saw it, it would have to be a system based upon freedom
rather than coercion, on merit rather than privilege, and upon informed
intelligence rather than blind prejudice. If, as Adams insisted, the history of the past had been so largely the story of folly, greed, and cruelty,
this was precisely because force, entrenched privilege, and superstition
had governed the lives of men. But a system in which liberty flourished,

talent and virtue were honored, and the pursuit of knowledge was encouraged would, Jefferson thought, release the finest qualities in the human character. Jefferson's dreams of the future centered around the achievement of such a system. What we call "Jeffersonian Democracy" consisted, in essence, of a set of principles designed to develop an open society whose chief features would be freedom, opportunity, justice, and enlightenment. These principles are deceptively simple.

The first principle of Jeffersonian Democracy was majority rule: that is, government resting on the freely given consent of the people. Jefferson had enough faith in the American people to believe that they could govern themselves wisely. His Federalist opponents said that it was dangerous to entrust the majority with political power. Jefferson insisted that the alternative—government by a privileged minority—was far more dangerous. When the Federalists declared that "man cannot be trusted with the government of himself," Jefferson retorted, "Can he, then, be trusted with the government of others?"

The history of the past, in Jefferson's opinion, was conclusive on this point: whenever one man or a small group of men held a monopoly on the powers of government, the inevitable result was tyranny and oppression. Majority rule, in short, was for Jefferson the only safeguard against despotic government. It would undoubtedly be far from perfect, given the frailties of human nature, but it was far preferable to rule by kings, nobles, and privileged classes. "While in Europe," Jefferson once wrote,

> I often amused myself with contemplating the characters of
> the then reigning sovereigns of Europe. Louis the XVI was
> a fool, of my own knowledge. . . . The King of Spain was a
> fool; and of Naples, the same. . . . The King of Sardinia was
> a fool. . . . The Queen of Portugal . . . was an idiot by nature;
> and so was the King of Denmark. . . . The King of Prussia
> . . . was a mere hog in body as well as in mind. Gustavus
> of Sweden, and Joseph of Austria, were really crazy; and
> George of England, you know was in a strait waistcoat.

It did not seem conceivable to Jefferson that government by the people could be more incompetent than government by such as these. He was, of course, firmly convinced that it would be infinitely better.

Jefferson's faith in the people was neither sentimental nor utopian. He was fully aware of human fallibilities, and he acknowledged that the people, through passion or shortsightedness, frequently make mistakes. But he was convinced that the mistakes of the people were less harmful, on the whole, than the selfish and arrogant policies of power elites. Moreover, he believed that the errors likely to be made by the people under a system of majority rule could be considerably reduced if the people were well informed about social and political issues. The second principle of Jeffersonian Democracy, therefore, was educational democracy. The American people must have opportunities for education if they were to learn how to govern themselves intelligently. "A system of education," said Jefferson, "which shall reach every description of citizen from the richest to the poorest, as it was the earliest, so will it be the latest of all public concerns in which I shall permit myself to take an interest." He considered the democratization of education to be an indispensable concomitant of majority rule. He also believed that newspapers, guided by a high sense of public responsibility, could be a potent educative and informative agency in a democratic society. Schools and colleges would develop the natural talents of the common people, and a free press would keep them informed about public questions.

Jefferson's third principle was what he called an "aristocracy of virtue and talent," which he distinguished sharply from an aristocracy founded upon wealth and birth. It was closely linked to his second principle since it depended for its development upon the availability of educational advantages to all classes of citizens. The Hamiltonians insisted that society must be managed by an aristocracy of the "rich and wellborn," but Jefferson regarded this kind of aristocracy as "artificial" since it was based upon inherited advantages and accident of status rather than upon intrinsic worth. He refused, in other words, to equate intelligence and character with social position and property, though he did not deny, of course, that men of talent are sometimes found among the rich and wellborn, and that such persons qualified for inclusion in his aristocracy of virtue and talent. An aristocracy of wealth, he declared, was likely to be "of more harm and danger than benefit to society." He looked upon political and social power and influence growing out of morally and intellectually unlegitimated privilege as a perennial source of mischief. "The artificial aristocracy," he told Adams, "is a mischievous ingredient in government and provision should be made to prevent its ascendancy." What he wanted, instead, was an aristocracy based upon genuine merit—a kind of "meritocracy"; such would be a "natural" aristocracy, composed of the "really wise and good," drawn from all ranks of society. "The natural aristocracy," he declared, "I consider as the most precious gift of nature, for the instruction, the trusts, and government of society. . . . May we not even say, that that form of government is the best, which provides the most effectually for a pure selection of these natural aristoi into the offices of government?" Mass education would be the means of discovering and developing the "precious gifts" latent in the American people, and a majoritarian political system would, he hoped, provide "most effectually" for the elevation of true excellence to high office. "Worth and genius would thus have been sought out from every condition of life," Jefferson concluded, "and completely prepared by education for defeating the competition of wealth and birth for public trusts." Jefferson's first three principles were closely knit together; to isolate one from the other is to do violence to the whole Jeffersonian system.

The fourth principle which Jefferson emphasized centered around the protection of minority rights. "All too will bear in mind this sacred principle," he announced in his First Inaugural Address, "that though the will of the majority is in all cases to prevail, that will, to be rightful, must be reasonable; that the minority possess their equal rights, which equal laws must protect, and to violate would be oppression."

He was thinking of the civil liberties and legal rights guaranteed all citizens—whether of the majority or of the minority—by the Federal Bill of Rights. Fresh in his mind, also, was undoubtedly the recent effort of the Federalists to suppress all criticism of the policies of the Adams administration, by means of the Alien and Sedition Acts, during the cold war with revolutionary France. Jefferson was understandably enraged that the Federalists had made his followers the chief target of their conspiracy-hunting in 1798. But insistence upon minority rights was a principle, not partisan politics, with him. He recognized the obligation of his own party, when in power, to bear patiently with the attacks of the Federalists. There were plenty of attacks, but there were no alien and sedition laws while he was president.

Jefferson was a shy and sensitive person who hated controversy, and he was shocked and distressed by the violence with which his administration was denounced. He was especially discouraged by the irresponsibility of the press attacks upon him, and he once suggested that American editors divide their newspapers into four sections and label them plainly for what they were: Truth, Probability, Possibility, and Lies. The last two sections, he explained, "should be professedly for those readers who would rather have lies for their money than the blank paper they would occupy." But though he was disappointed in his expectations for the American press as a civilizing force (a "polluted vehicle," he came to call it), it never occurred to him to follow the Federalist precedent of trying to silence his opponents. On one occasion Baron Alexander von Humboldt, the distinguished German scientist, was visiting Jefferson and noticed a newspaper on the table in Jefferson's study containing a bitter attack on Jefferson. "Why are these libels allowed?" exclaimed the Baron, indignantly. "Why is not this libelous journal suppressed or its editor at least fined or imprisoned?" "Put that paper in your pocket, Baron," said Jefferson, "and should you hear the reality of our liberty, the freedom of the press questioned, show them this paper—*and tell them where you found it.*"

Encompassing all of Jefferson's political principles, then, was a final principle: freedom. Without freedom, Jefferson's dreams of the future would very likely become nightmares. There is no theme on which Jefferson expressed himself in more inspired language. It is only partially and superficially true to say, as a congressman did many years ago, that Jefferson's words can be used "every which-a-way; he writ so much." Jefferson lived a long and busy life, and he revised his opinions—though not his basic principles—from time to time in response to the changing times. Some of the things he said, wrenched from their context and divorced from his fundamental goals, can doubtless be used to support causes that would have filled him with dismay. His pronouncements on the subject of intellectual and cultural freedom, however, are uniformly clear, consistent, and unequivocal. Time and again he asserted that self-government could work only if the American people were able to think, question, inquire, discuss, argue, criticize, and express themselves freely in all fields of human endeavor. "If this avenue [free speech] be shut to the call of sufferance," he warned, "it will make itself heard through that of force, and we shall go on, as other nations are going, in the endless circle of oppression, rebellion, reformation; and oppression, rebellion, and reformation again, and so on forever."

Jefferson favored adding a Bill of Rights to the Constitution, partly, he told Madison, because of "the legal check which it puts into the hands of the judiciary." When federal justices placed no "legal check" on Federalist prosecutions under the Alien and Sedition Acts but, instead, cooperated zealously with the Federalists in the campaign of suppression, Jefferson, along with Madison (who had played a leading role in drafting the Bill of Rights in the first Congress), looked to the states for leadership in the defense of free speech and issued a vigorous protest against Federalist tyranny in the Virginia and Kentucky Resolutions. To charge Jefferson with inconsistency because he was friendly to the federal courts on one occasion and hostile later on is to miss the point. And to say, as many have said, that Jefferson placed states' rights above all other rights is a gross misunderstanding of Jefferson's principles. Had the federal courts defended the First Amendment freedoms during the Adams administration, as Jefferson thought they should have, there would have been no Virginia and Kentucky Resolutions. It should never be forgotten that one of the amendments which Jefferson and Madison wanted to include in the Bill of Rights (but which the Senate rejected) expressly prohibited the states from infringing on personal rights. It is futile to try to make a "statist" out of Jefferson. Like Madison, he placed human rights above states' rights.

Jefferson's insistence upon freedom was grounded firmly in "philosophical anthropology." In his generalizations about the nature and destiny of man, Jefferson emphasized both unity and diversity. When he stated in the Declaration of Independence that "all men are created equal," he was not, of course, asserting the identity of all men (George of England and George of America were surely not identical!); he was referring to the unity of all men in the human species. All men, he pointed out, have a common source of descent, possess similar physical characteristics, are endowed with reason and a moral sense, and have a capacity for communal life. They all belong, in other words, to the human species, and a just and rational society will therefore provide them with equal rights and opportunities. Within the human species, however, there exists great diversity among individual men. Each person is unique; he differs, to some extent, physically and mentally, from every other person. His perception of reality and thus his opinions will necessarily be somewhat different from those of his fellow men. But differences of opinion, "like differences of face, are a law of our nature," said Jefferson, "and should be viewed with the same tolerance." Moreover, "Difference of opinion leads to inquiry and inquiry to truth." No single person, by himself, can penetrate all the mysteries of creation; a variety of persons, however, with different talents and interests, can, by working peacefully together, explore different aspects of reality and thus endlessly advance mankind's insight into the nature of things. This cooperative pursuit of truth was, in Jefferson's opinion, the highest destiny of the human species and it depended for its realization upon freedom.

It is not difficult to detect ambiguities and uncertainties in Jefferson's thinking. He idealized rural living, regarded the small, independent farmers of America as "the chosen people of God," and feared that the democratic system he envisaged might be incompatible with an urban, industrial economy. And while his equalitarian faith led him to oppose slavery, he could never quite make up his mind about the innate capacities of the American Negro. In applying his principles to his own time and place, he was limited, in other words, by his position and outlook as a Virginia planter living in a slave-owning society. Yet he strove always to rise above these parochial limitations. When it became clear, in his later years, that the United States was destined for an industrial future, he revised his agrarian doctrines and expressed confidence that democracy could be made to work in an industrial as well as in an agricultural civilization. And he sought eagerly for empirical evidence that the Negro was equal in natural ability to other races and that "the want of talents" which he observed in Negro slaves "is merely the effect of their degraded condition, and not proceeding from any difference in the structure of the parts on which intellect depends." Principles, in short, took precedence over prejudices. It was principles that formed the substance of his dreams of the future. Southern slavery apologists knew exactly what they were doing when they repudiated Jefferson's philosophy. It is beyond dispute that Jefferson would have rejoiced if the later scientific confirmation of his presuppositions regarding the races of man had been made during his lifetime.

On several occasions in recent years Bertrand Russell has remarked that no one dares to mention the name of Jefferson in public in the United States any more. This is not, of course, strictly true. Jefferson's words, as the congressman said, are still used "every which-a-way": to support repressive and dictatorial policies on the part of state governments; to uphold restrictions of educational opportunities; to throw an aura of respectability around corrupt newspapers; to legitimate a self-serving elite of wealth, power, and status; and to justify a brazen disregard for the Bill of Rights and an obscene vilification of its champions. Had Jefferson been able to foresee this perversion of his principles, he might have felt, as William James did in similar circumstances, like "cursing God and dying." The name of Jefferson, turned upside down, is, unfortunately, all too frequently invoked in public. With his principles, however, it is quite otherwise. Bertrand Russell was surely right in sensing the existence at the present time of widespread indifference or even outright hostility to Jefferson's most cherished ideas. Every opinion poll involving basic Jeffersonian ideas and key phrases conducted in this country during the past few years has met with annoyance, indignation, and, at times, bitter resentment.

It would be easy under these circumstances to join Adams in jeering at Jefferson for having counted more on the dreams of the future than on the history of the past. Yet to do so would be to abandon the field to the debasers of the Jeffersonian heritage. Adams himself, as a matter of fact, came, in the course of his long exchange with Jefferson, to respect and even in part to share Jefferson's dreams. And Jefferson, while he experienced many great disappointments and disillusionments during his lifetime, never wavered in his serene faith. "I shall not die," he told Adams toward the end of his life, "without a hope that light and liberty are on a steady advance." "All eyes are opened, or opening," he wrote, "to the rights of man. The general spread of the light of science has already laid open to every view the palpable truth, that the mass of mankind has not been born with saddles on their backs, a favored few booted and spurred, ready to ride them legitimately, by the grace of God."

On July 4, 1826, the fiftieth anniversary of the Declaration of Independence, Adams and Jefferson both departed from the American scene. Jefferson was the first to die that day in Monticello, and Adams, far off in Quincy, was unaware of the fact. Shortly before he passed away, a few hours later, Adams cried out, "Thomas Jefferson still survives." One likes to think that his words are still symbolically true.

Southwest Review, Spring 1959.

CHAPTER 14

Thomas Jefferson and Tom Paine: Aristocrat and Democrat

Thomas Jefferson, according to Richard Hofstadter, was "the Aristocrat as Democrat," while Tom Paine was the "Democrat as Democrat." The two shared democratic values but came from quite different backgrounds and behaved quite differently. They liked each other but simply didn't move in the same circles. John Adams disagreed with Jefferson on many issues, but held him in real respect, and he loathed Paine. For Adams, Paine was "a mongrel between pig and puppy, begotten by a wild boar on a bitch wolfe," and his popular and influential *Common Sense*, a "poor, ignorant, malicious, short-sighted, crapulous mass." It is not known whether Adams had heard the rumors about Jefferson's supposed affair with Sally Hemings, his slave. In her book on Jefferson, Fawn M. Brodie insists the affair brought both of them a secret happiness for thirty-eight years. Though Dumas Malone, Jefferson expert, denied there was any such affair, it has become politically correct to accept Brodie's view.

★ ★ ★

Fawn M. Brodie's "intimate history" of Thomas Jefferson is likely to be the most controversial book of the year, at least among people interested in American history. Garry Wills has blasted it in the *New York Review* (April 18, 1974) for finding sexual significance in trivial passages in Jefferson's writings, and Dumas Malone (the fifth volume of whose definitive biography of Jefferson has just appeared) recently released to the *New York Times* a previously unpublished letter (which Professor Brodie had seen but was permitted to quote only in part) written by

Ellen Randolph Coolidge, Jefferson's granddaughter, on October 24, 1858, in which she vigorously denied one of the major points Brodie makes in her biography: that Jefferson had a slave mistress for many years.

Brodie undoubtedly overpsychologizes and occasionally she reads too much between lines and forgets that sometimes, with people, there is less (rather than more) there than meets the eye. Still, her accomplishments are considerable all the same. She has loosened up our thinking about the third president and breathed life and spirit into a man who has for many people seemed cold, aloof, elusive, and impenetrable. Her success in making Jefferson a warm and interesting figure rests largely on her readiness to discuss frankly and in depth his racial views, his sex life, and his emotional involvements with other people. She makes no secret of what she is up to, and we are free to accept or reject the interpretations which she places on the evidence which she presents for all to see.

Brodie's Jefferson is both a racist (like most whites of his day) and an emancipationist (unlike most southern whites in the first part of the nineteenth century). As a monogenist, he thought blacks deserved the rights belonging to all humans which he wrote into the Declaration of Independence, and he sponsored measures for facilitating the emancipation of slaves in Virginia, for banning slavery in the West, and for ending the Atlantic slave trade. In 1770 he undertook the defense of a Virginia mulatto who was seeking freedom and argued that "under the law of nature, all men are born free, and every one comes into the world with a right to his own person, which includes the liberty of moving and using it at his own will." (He lost the case.)

At the same time, however, he favored colonizing free blacks and had serious doubts about the intellectual capacities of black people. Somewhat like William Shockley today, he thought blacks were inferior to whites in reason and imagination though equal to whites in memory. When Benjamin Banneker, Negro mathematician, sent him a copy of his almanac to show him what blacks could do, Jefferson assured him of his eagerness to accumulate evidence of black talent, but to a friend afterward he belittled Banneker's work.

Still, it is impossible to put Jefferson's views on race into any neat little categories. He seesawed back and forth on the issue all his life, and though he became increasingly conservative with age, he seems never to have abandoned either his deep-seated faith in the right of people of all races to freedom and self-determination, or his conviction that the blacks both deserved and were destined to be free. His reluctance to free many of his own slaves during his lifetime may have grown out of the fact that Virginia law forced free blacks to leave the state, and his failure to free more than a handful of slaves in his will was probably due to his hopeless indebtedness. He did, though, permit several slaves who could pass for white to leave his plantation quietly and without any interference.

If Brodie's Jefferson is a mass of contradictions when it comes to race, he is no puzzle at all when it comes to sex. He tried as a young bachelor to seduce the wife of a friend, became intimate with a married Englishwoman in Paris a few years after the death of his wife Martha in 1782, and when this passion subsided took a young slave girl, Sally Hemings (the half-sister of his wife), as his mistress and had several children by her. Jefferson's relations with Hemings, Brodie contends, were tender and deeply satisfying and brought the two of them much secret happiness for thirty-eight years. Her evidence for Jefferson's miscegenation: James T. Callender's allegations, published while Jefferson was president, based on stories circulating among Jefferson's neighbors in Virginia; the fact that Jefferson and Hemings were in the same places (Paris and Monticello) nine months before the births of each of Hemings's seven children; and the memoirs of two former Monticello slaves, Madison Hemings (Sally's son) and Israel Jefferson, appearing in the *Pike County* (Ohio) *Republican* in 1873.

Jefferson scholars like Merrill Peterson and Winthrop Jordan are inclined to accept Jefferson's liaison with Hemings as a fact, though Dumas Malone is not. The evidence is of course purely hearsay and circumstantial, and, as Jefferson's granddaughter pointed out in the letter which Malone published in the Times on May 18, 1974, it is always difficult, if not impossible, to get negative evidence. The reader will have to examine Brodie's evidence and decide for himself how convincingly she has made her point. She makes the strongest case that has yet been made for Jefferson's illicit love life, but it is important to remember that her evidence would scarcely hold up in a court of law. For the tenderness of Jefferson's relations with Hemings she has of course no evidence whatsoever.

Less controversial, perhaps, but more solidly grounded is the Jefferson whom Brodie portrays as a family man and as a friend and associate. Brodie examines with sympathy and skill the tensions between Jefferson and his mother, wife, daughters, and in-laws, his fluctuating relations with people like George Washington and John Adams, and his hostile encounters with Alexander Hamilton and Aaron Burr. (Unlike Gore Vidal, she does not admire the latter.) Brodie's Jefferson is more temperamental (even neurotic) than the Jefferson of tradition, but more admirable, too, for the remarkable serenity he achieved in his public life despite an enormous amount of pain, grief, loneliness, and frustration in his private life. Professor Brodie, in short, has done a fine job of disproving the charge that Jefferson's "blood is very snow-broth" without slighting in the least his great achievements as a statesman, scientist, architect, educationalist, writer, thinker, and political organizer. But in discussing the British attack on the US frigate Chesapeake in June, 1807, she makes one serious error. "Had Jefferson chosen to declare war at that moment," she writes, "he could have had the whole nation behind him." The US Constitution, it is too often forgotten, gives Congress, not the president, the power to declare war.

In *Thomas Jefferson: The Man . . . His World . . . His Influence*, Lally Weymouth has assembled a fine group of essays discussing Jefferson's legacy to the nation in a dozen fields. Merrill Peterson takes an overview of Jefferson; Henry Steele Commager discusses Jefferson as a man of the Enlightenment and analyzes the Declaration of Independence; Garry Wills does a linguistic study of the Declaration; Richard E. Ellis examines Jefferson's economic views; Kenneth Clark studies his relation to the Italian Renaissance; William Goetzmann concentrates on Jefferson's program for exploring and settling the West; James R. Wiggins focuses on his relations with the press; Walter Muir Whitehill evaluates him as an architect; Leonard Levy has a critical essay pointing out Jefferson's shortcomings as well as strengths in the field of civil liberties; and Christopher Lasch ends the book with an analysis of Jeffersonian democracy (agrarian, mercantile, and populistic) and glumly concludes that Jeffersonian traditions—commitment to equality, suspicion of centralized power, and insistence on free speech and inquiry—seem quaint if not outmoded to the rulers of America today.

The essays are all of a high intellectual order, but the illustrations for the book, some of them published here for the first time, are magnificent: maps, portraits, sketches, designs, photographs, and architectural plans having to do with just about every phase of Jefferson's remarkably rich life. If President Kennedy was correct when he told the Nobel Prize winners in 1962 that Jefferson all by himself was perhaps "the most extraordinary collection of talent" ever gathered in the White House, Lally Weymouth's book is a handsome tribute to that talent. You don't have to be a Jeffersonian to enjoy it.

You don't have to be a Jeffersonian, either, to enjoy Samuel Edwards's breezy little *Rebel! A Biography of Tom Paine*, but it helps a lot if you are. For it is a fact that Paine, both in his own day and afterward, had a way of arousing intense dislike among people not sharing his political, social, and religious predilections. Richard Hofstadter called Jefferson "the aristocrat as democrat." Paine was the "democrat as democrat." Jefferson and Paine saw eye to eye, as Edwards shows, on most abstract issues: on the folly of monarchy and hereditary institutions generally, on the sovereignty of the people, on the natural rights of all individuals, on government by popular consent, on the necessity of good constitutions for good government, on the importance of science and invention for social advance, and on the superiority of deism to

Christianity. But as concrete human beings, no two men could have diverged more widely. Paine's origin, educational background, social experience, and personal style and manners were utterly at variance with those of the reserved and dignified aristocrat of Monticello. Paine came from the lower middle class in England, had only a few years of schooling, and spent his early years eking out an existence as corset-maker, apprentice seaman, exciseman, teacher, itinerant preacher, and shopkeeper with little or no promise of things to come. No one would have been more astonished than Paine himself had he been told in November 1774, when he arrived in America at the age of thirty-seven, that he was destined to become famous throughout the Western world and to walk some day among the great in America, England, and France. Paine was not a "dirty little atheist," as Theodore Roosevelt charged, but, as Edwards acknowledges, he was careless about his personal appearance, sometimes neglected bathing, drank too much on occasion (though Edwards denies he ever became an alcoholic), and after the failure of his second marriage was in the habit of consorting with teenage harlots, occasionally two at a time. TR would not have approved. Edwards thinks Paine was emotionally immature.

Unlike Jefferson, Paine was blunt, forthright, and uncompromising in the expression of opinions (and also more consistent when it came to such issues as slavery, which he strongly opposed and helped end in Pennsylvania); he had a massive ego and a deep love of controversy and accumulated enemies wherever he went without even half trying. One shudders at his errors and misjudgments: the venomous and unjustified attack on George Washington, the apparent blindness to the nature of Napoleon's dictatorship, the failure to realize that the values he cherished had their roots in British traditions, the repeated calls for a French invasion of England, and the petty quarrels, particularly toward the end of his life, with people hardly worth his bother. Yet he was high-minded and disinterested on most major issues, and Edwards is able to cite example after example of his generosity, humanity, courage, and compassion as well as instances of vulgarity and pettiness. He refused to accept royalties for such widely circulated books as *Common Sense, The American Crisis, and The Rights of Man*, insisting that profits on sales go to the causes he was defending. He argued and voted against the execution of Louis XVI in the French National Assembly when it was not easy to do so. He also saved two British Tories, both of whom loathed his ideas, from the guillotine during the French Terror. And of course one cannot fail to be impressed with the lucidity, forcefulness, and charm with which he could present abstract ideas to the general public; his remarkable insights into some of the tangled issues of his day; and his enormous contributions, through his marvelous journalistic talents, to the advance of democratic values in the Western world.

Edwards has written a critical but friendly biography of Paine, and it is as pleasantly written and as enjoyable to read as Paine's own prose pieces. One regrets only the absence of footnotes and a critical discussion of resources.

REVIEWS OF FAWN M. BRODIE, *Thomas Jefferson: An Intimate History* (1974); Lally Weymouth, ed., *Thomas Jefferson: The Man . . . His World . . . His Influence* (1974); Samuel Edwards, *Rebel! A Biography of Tom Paine* (1974); *Southwest Review*, Summer 1974.

CHAPTER 15

The Madisons:
James and Dolley

Virginia Moore's biography of James and Dolley would have been unusual—even impossible—in the old days. With most biographers, the presidents' wives were given short shrift. There were a few books devoted to the wives themselves, but the conventional books about the presidents contained only a page of two about their wives.

Moore's "dual biography" showed how important James and Dolley were for each other. During the War of 1812, James went off to the front, and Dolley rescued a famous Gilbert Stuart painting of George Washington from the White House when the British began burning the Federal buildings in the nation's capital. Today, no one would write the biography of a president without including many pages on the part his wife played in his life and work.

★ ★ ★

In *The Madisons: A Biography*, Virginia Moore, author of books on Emily Brontë and William Butler Yeats, presents a biographical study of James Madison, the "least known of the founding fathers," and his charming wife Dolley. There have been numerous biographies of Madison (notably Irving Brandt's), and there have also been several books about his wife, but this is the first "dual biography." Moore's aim is twofold: to "put blood back into the veins" of both Jemmy (as he was called) and Dolley, and to examine their "reciprocal relationship." There are difficulties involved in this approach, and Moore has not surmounted all of them. Still, she writes in a sprightly fashion, knows her material well, likes her protagonists very much, and by following closely the leading events, public and private, in their lives, convinces us that a marriage which began somewhat inauspiciously ended by being almost ideal in the eyes of all their friends and associates.

Moore begins her book with the Madisons' marriage in 1794, and then pauses to recount first Dolley's background and then Jemmy's. Even within this framework she utilizes flashbacks from time to time, and it isn't really until Madison becomes secretary of state for Thomas Jefferson in 1801 and then president himself in 1809 that the narrative begins to move ahead in a straightforward fashion. The marriage, Moore tells us, was one of opposites: "The groom was forty-three, the bride twenty-six; the groom an intellectual, the bride a woman who ran largely on her feelings; the groom a bachelor, the bride a widow with a little boy two and a half years old." In a letter to her best friend right after the wedding, the bride signed her name "Dolley Payne Todd"; then she corrected herself and wrote, "Dolley Madison; Alas! Alas!" But despite Dolley's misgivings at first, the marriage turned out to be a good one both for her and for Jemmy. Dolley became Jemmy's "anchor in the storm": she took charge of his social life, planned official dinners, decided which invitations to accept and which to reject, saw that their clothes and living quarters were kept in order, and arranged her Wednesday evening levees (which were the talk of the town) so that he could slip out any time duty called him. At official dinners she eased her husband's burdens by placing him at the side of the table while she sat at the head and took the lead in the conversation herself. Sometimes Madison would sit with her for an hour or so before these dinners and then tell her, "My dear, you have rested me and helped me to go on."

But Dolley did more than assume responsibility for her husband's social life. She also familiarized herself with the problems he faced as a public official and came to identify herself strongly with his positions on various political and social issues. One of the best chapters in the book, dealing with the War of 1812, describes Dolley's conscientious efforts to rescue the famous Gilbert Stuart portrait of George Washington before the British, who were invading the Capital City, got to the president's mansion. Madison himself was in the field with American forces at the time. He took his duties as commander in chief more literally than our other presidents have done.

In 1817, when James Monroe succeeded Madison as Chief Executive, the Madisons left Washington and retired to Montpelier, Virginia, where Madison, with Dolley's help, managed a fairly sizable plantation and assumed the role of elder statesman for the nation he had helped create. Visiting them in 1819, Eliza Collins Lee exclaimed, "They look like Adam and Eve in Paradise."

There was, to be sure, a snake in the garden: John Payne Todd, Dolley's son, a spendthrift and a wastrel, whom Madison had tried to raise as a son and whose debts he paid off time and again. But John Payne Todd never came between Dolley and Jemmy. The Madisons shared their hopes, fears, and disappointments and together did their best by him. In the spring of 1835, the famous English economist and sociologist Harriet Martineau visited the Madisons at Montpelier and after observing them for three days decided that they were remarkably well matched. Dolley, she wrote afterward, was "a strong-minded woman, fully capable of entering into her husband's occupations and cares; and there is little doubt that he owed much to her intellectual companionship." By this time, according to Moore, Jemmy and Dolley were "warp and woof of the same cloth, white and yolk of the same egg, two eyes focusing for vision."

REVIEW OF VIRGINIA MOORE, *The Madisons: A Biography* (1980),
Southwest Review, Spring 1980.

CHAPTER 16

The Gifted Abraham Lincoln

A braham Lincoln was the only president of the United States who was both a humorist and a literary artist. His amusing stories not only entertained people, they also enabled him to make serious points about his policies that impressed his associates. He possessed a melancholy streak that was exacerbated by the cruel crises he faced during the Civil War. But a pun, a joke, a hilarious story usually made him forget his troubles.

Lincoln was utterly without malice in his relations with other people, including his enemies. But he was probably the most vilified of all our presidents. From the day of his inauguration in 1861 to the day of his assassination in 1865, his haters seem to have searched dictionaries to find invectives to hurl at him: ape, baboon, idiot, clown, traitor, demagogue, tyrant, eunuch, lunatic, monster, charlatan. But Lincoln's sense of humor helped him brush aside these assaults and lifted his spirits when he heard a good joke or encountered an amusing situation.

Reading poetry also helped Lincoln to put up with the tough going that faced him so frequently. He buried himself at times in the great British poets and read America's fine poets of his day with pleasure, too. He also adored Shakespeare, reading and rereading his favorite plays and seeing them performed in Washington whenever he could. There is no question but that his love of fine writing helped him develop a superior writing style of his own. He was the only president ever to be called a "literary genius." His contemporary Ralph Waldo Emerson said Lincoln's writing, particularly the Gettysburg Address, was "destined to a wide fame." And the tough twentieth-century critic H. L. Mencken called the Gettysburg Address "genuinely stupendous."

★ ★ ★

Abraham Lincoln was the first humorist to occupy the White House. "He could make a cat laugh!" exclaimed Bill Green. "It was as a humorist that he towered above all other men it was ever my lot to meet," said another friend from Lincoln's youth. H. C. Whitney, a lawyer who rode the circuit with Lincoln in Illinois, was struck by Lincoln's keen sense of the absurd: "He saw the ludicrous in an assemblage of fowls, in a man spading his garden, in a clothesline full of clothes, in a group of boys, in a lot of pigs rooting at a mill door, in a mother duck teaching her brood to swim—in everything and anything." During the Civil War, London's *Saturday Review* told its readers, "One advantage the Americans have is the possession of a president who is not only the First Magistrate, but the Chief Joker of the Land." By the middle of 1863, several joke books—with titles like *Old Abe's Jokes, Abe's Jokes—Fresh from Abraham's Bosom*, and *Old Abe's Jokes, or, Wit at the White House*—were circulating in the North and spreading Lincoln stories, many of them spurious, far and wide, and there have been collections of Lincoln anecdotes in print ever since.

Humor was unquestionably a psychological necessity for Lincoln, though being a serious, not a solemn, man, he wouldn't have put it quite that way. He once called laughter "the joyous, beautiful, universal evergreen of life," and he enjoyed droll stories the way some people enjoy detective stories. But both as a lawyer and as a politician he also found amusing stories enormously helpful in putting across important points he wanted to make. And as president he used his gift as a storyteller to put people at ease, to win them over to his point of view, or simply to get them off the point and out of his office without having to deny their requests in so many words. Humor, he once said, was "an emollient" that "saves me much friction and distress." A group of people who had gone to the White House seeking government jobs reported resignedly afterward that "the president treated us to four anecdotes." But humor was also important for Lincoln during the Civil War as a means of relaxing, getting away from his troubles for a moment, and refreshing his spirit. Once, when a congressman came to see him to complain about something, Lincoln said, "Well, that reminds me of a story." Outraged, the congressman told him he had not come to the White House to hear a joke. "Now, you sit down!" exclaimed Lincoln. "If I couldn't tell these stories I would die." On another occasion, Ohio's Senator Benjamin Wade called to demand that

> General Grant, who was not doing very well before Vicksburg at the time, be fired at once. "Senator," said Lincoln, "that reminds me of a story." "Yes, yes," said Wade impa-

tiently, "that is the way it is with you, Sir, all *story, story!* You are the father of every military blunder that has been made during the war. You are on the road to hell, Sir, with this government, by your obstinacy, and you are not a mile off this minute!" "Senator," said Lincoln gently, "that is just about the distance from here to the Capitol, is it not?"

Lincoln's taste in jokes ran all the way from the lowly pun to the satirical anecdote. Like all lovers of the English language, he took keen pleasure in plays upon words. Once he was looking out of the window of his law office in Springfield, Illinois, and saw a stately matron, wearing a many-plumed hat, picking her way gingerly across the muddy street. Suddenly she slipped and fell. "Reminds me of a duck," said Lincoln. "Why is that?" asked a friend. "Feathers on her head and down on her behind," said Lincoln. On another occasion he was taking a walk in Washington with his secretary of state, William H. Seward, and they passed a store with the name of the proprietor, T. R. Strong, in bold letters on a sign in front of the store. "T. R. Strong," said Lincoln, "but coffee are stronger." Seward smiled but made no reply. "We don't see how he could reply after so atrocious a thing as that," commented the newspaper which reported the story.

But Lincoln's humor ordinarily rose above the level of puns. He particularly enjoyed teasing solemn people. When a temperance committee called to tell him that Union defeats were "the curse of the Lord" on a drunken army, Lincoln (who was a teetotaler) could not resist saying that it was "rather unfair on the part of the curse, as the other side drank more and worse whiskey than ours did." He treated some Chicago ministers who came to give him advice the same way. When they told him they had come to deliver "a message to you from our Divine Master" about his slavery policy, Lincoln said it was "odd that the only channel he could send it by was the roundabout route of that awful wicked city of Chicago!" He had some fun, too, with a pompous Austrian count who wanted to obtain a position in the Union army. In making his request, the Austrian harped on the fact that his family was ancient and honorable and that he bore the title of count. With a twinkle in his eye, Lincoln finally patted him on the shoulder and said, "Never mind, you shall be treated with just as much consideration for all that. I will see to it that your bearing a title sha'n't hurt you."

Lincoln's humor was not always gentle. Sometimes he used it to point up a blunt truth. Asked once how large the Confederate army was, he said, "About 1,200,000 men," and when his questioner expressed amazement, Lincoln explained, "Well, whenever one of our generals is licked he says he was outnumbered three or four to one, and we have 400,000 men." He also could not help making wry remarks about General George B. McClellan, whose extreme caution in pushing military campaigns drove Lincoln almost crazy. Once, when a man from a Northern city asked him for a pass to Richmond, Lincoln exclaimed: "My dear sir, if I should give you one, it would do you no good. You may think it very strange, but there are a lot of fellows who either can't read or are prejudiced against every man who takes a pass from me. I have given McClellan, and more than 200,000 others, passes to Richmond, and not one of them has gotten there!" A little later, greatly irked by McClellan's inactivity, he wrote, "Dear General, if you do not want to use the army I would like to borrow it for a few days." Lincoln gave as good as he got, too, when he felt like it. When McClellan, irritated by one of Lincoln's orders requiring detailed reports to the White House, sent him a telegram saying, "We have just captured six cows. What shall we do with them?" Lincoln answered: "Milk them."

Sometimes Lincoln's humor had satirical and ironic overtones. When he was in Congress, 1847–1849, he opposed the Mexican War and in one speech he said that people who denied that it was a war of aggression reminded him of the Illinois farmer who said, "I ain't greedy 'bout land. I only want what jines mine." "Young America," he said in another speech, "is very anxious to fight for the liberation of enslaved nations and colonies, provided, always, they have land. As to those who have no land, and would be glad of help, he considers they can wait a few hundred years longer." He once told of a congressman who had opposed the War of 1812 and come under heavy attack, and who, when asked to oppose the Mexican War, exclaimed: "I opposed one war; that was enough for me. I am now perpetually in favor of war, pestilence, and famine." And he liked to tell people about the old loafer who said to him, "I feel patriotic," and when asked what he meant, cried, "Why, I feel like I want to kill somebody or steal something!" A Toledo reporter who interviewed Lincoln at the time of the Lincoln-Douglas debates decided he was "a master of satire, which was at times as blunt as a meat-ax, and at others as keen as a razor." Once a senator came to the White House, furious about what he regarded as unfair distribution of patronage, and he let loose a flood of profanity on Lincoln. When he had finished, Lincoln said calmly, "You are an Episcopalian, aren't you, Senator?" "Yes, sir, I belong to that church." "I thought so," said Lincoln. "You Episcopalians all swear alike. But Stanton [secretary of war] is a Presbyterian. You ought to hear him swear!" Lincoln, who rarely used intemperate language, was frequently criticized for not being a church member, and he was doubtless amused at hearing profanity from the orthodox.

Lincoln laughed at himself as well as at other people. When Senator Stephen A. Douglas called him a "two-faced man," Lincoln said: "I leave it to my audience. If I had another face, do you think I would wear this one?" He joked about his homely looks again when he spoke to a convention of newspaper editors in Bloomington, Illinois. Pointing out that he was not an editor and therefore felt out of place at the meeting, he said: "I feel like I once did when I met a woman riding on horseback in the woods. As I stopped to let her pass, she also stopped and looked at me intently, and said, 'I do believe you are the ugliest man I ever saw.' Said I, 'Madam, you are probably right, but I can't help it.' 'No,' said she, 'you can't help it, but you might stay at home.'" Lincoln also enjoyed telling about the grouchy old Democrat who walked up to him and said, "They say you're a self-made man," and when Lincoln nodded, he snapped, "Well, all I've got to say is that it was a damned bad job."

Lincoln came to be known as "the National Joker," but he was far more than the Chief Joker of the land. As president he showed himself to be shrewd, serious, selfless, dedicated, strong-willed, resourceful, compassionate, and extraordinarily magnanimous. The burdens he bore during the Civil War were far heavier than those of most American presidents, and he undertook his responsibilities with remarkable patience and determination. Though his critics could not always see it, he remained steadfastly true throughout the war to his basic objectives: restoration of the Union (which he regarded as a magnificent experiment in government of, by, and for the people) and the abolition of slavery (which he regarded as utterly incompatible with democracy). He was anxious to get the very best men, civilian and military, he could find to help him in realizing these objectives, and he did not mind if they personally held him in contempt. When someone told him that his secretary of war, Edwin Stanton, had called him a damned fool, he said lightly, "If Stanton said I was a damned fool, then I must be one for he is nearly always right and generally says what he means." Stanton came to hold Lincoln in high esteem. But others never did. They found it hard to understand that in pursuing his objectives—preserving the Union and emancipating the slaves—Lincoln had to proceed cautiously to avoid alienating the border slave states (and driving them to secession) and keep from offending Northern public opinion (which was by no means sympathetic to abolitionism at first). He also thought it important to synchronize his policies with progress on the battlefield (which came slowly at first) if he was to avoid making futile and perhaps even counterproductive gestures.

No president of the United States has been vilified the way Lincoln was during the Civil War. He was attacked on all sides: by abolitionists, Negrophobes, states' righters, strict constitutionalists, radicals, conservatives, armchair strategists, and by people who just did not like his looks or who resented his storytelling. From the day of his inauguration to the day of his assassination, the litany of invective was unrelenting. Among other things, Lincoln was called: an ape; a baboon; a buffoon; a low-level obscene clown; a usurper; a traitor; a tyrant; an old monster; the Great Apotheosis of the Great Hog; Fox Populi; a cross between a sand-hill crane and an Andalusian jackass; Abraham Africanus the First; a smutty joker; a third-rate country lawyer; an African gorilla; an abortion; an idiot; Simple Susan; the Abolition orangutan; the incompetent, ignorant, and desperate "Honest Abe"; a border-state eunuch; a narrow-minded bigot; an unprincipled demagogue; a drivelling, idiotic, imbecilic creature; a third-rate district politician; a lunatic; a despot; a dangerous character; the ineffable despot; a blunderer; a charlatan; a temporizer; a man who jokes when the nation mourns; a crude, illiterate, bar-room witling; an unblushingly corrupt bully; and a half-witted usurper. One New York newspaper regularly referred to him as "that hideous baboon at the other end of the avenue" and said that "Barnum should buy and exhibit him as a zoological curiosity." The *Illinois State Register* called him "the craftiest and most dishonest politician that ever disgraced an office in America." "*Honest Abe, forsooth!*" sneered one editor. "*Honest Iago! Benignant Nero! Faithful Iscariot!*" Even his hometown newspaper joined the chorus: "How the greatest butchers of antiquity sink into insignificance when their crimes are contrasted with those of Abraham Lincoln!" No wonder Lincoln said, when asked how it felt to be president, "You have heard about the man tarred and feathered and ridden out of town on a rail? A man in the crowd asked how he liked it, and his reply was that if it wasn't for the honor of the thing, he would much rather walk." But Lincoln was not thinking of the abuse heaped on him when he said this. He was thinking of the terrible loss of life on the battlefield and the heartbreakingly slow progress being made toward the achievement of his objectives. He had enjoyed politics immensely before he became president, and he had been eager, too, to hold the highest office in the land. But in the White House, he said, instead of glory he found only "ashes and blood."

Humor lightened the cares of office for Lincoln. So did the theater. He had a special fondness for Shakespeare, and he experienced exquisite pleasure one evening at seeing the veteran actor, James Hackett, perform the role of Falstaff in a Washington theater. He was so delighted with the performance that he wrote a letter of congratulation afterward and Hackett, flattered by the attention paid him by the president of the United States, turned the letter over to the *New York Herald*. For the *Herald*, Lincoln's letter provided another opportunity for ridicule, and the editor reprinted the letter and accompanied it with savage comments. Greatly embarrassed, Hackett wrote Lincoln to apologize. "Give yourself no uneasiness on the subject," Lincoln told him. "I certainly did not expect to see my note in print; yet I have not been much shocked by the comments upon it. They are a fair specimen of what has occurred to me through life. I have endured a great deal of ridicule, without much malice; and have received a great deal of kindness, not quite free from ridicule. I am used to it." For Lincoln, the pleasure of seeing Hackett do Falstaff far outweighed the pain of abuse from the *Herald*. But even this pleasure was short-lived. A little later Hackett sought a government job, and when Lincoln was unable to give him one he turned against the president and joined the ranks of the Lincoln-haters.

Lincoln's love of Shakespeare grew out of his love of fine writing. As a young man he read and reread the King James Bible, Aesop's *Fables*, Shakespeare, John Bunyan, Daniel Defoe, and Robert Burns, and he worked hard to improve his own vocabulary, grammar, and lucidity of expression. By the time he became president, he had developed a distinguished prose style of his own: simple, clear, precise, forceful, rhythmical, poetic, and at times majestic. When Vicksburg surrendered in July 1863 and the Mississippi River was open again, he told the country, "The 'Father of Waters' again goes unvexed to the sea." It is hard to imagine any other president writing such a stunning sentence, or penning such masterpieces of prose as the Gettysburg Address and the First and Second Inaugural Addresses. Thomas Jefferson and Woodrow Wilson (and to a lesser degree John Adams and Theodore Roosevelt) possessed unusual literary skills, but at his best Lincoln towered above them. He had a deep feeling for the right use of words, and he employed them lovingly both in his storytelling and in his letters and speeches. He was the only president ever to be called a "literary artist." Jacques Barzun, in fact, called him a "literary genius." "Nothing," wrote John Nicolay and John Hay, in their multivolumed biography of Lincoln (whom they knew personally), which appeared in 1894, "would have more amazed him while he lived than to hear himself called a man of letters; but this age has produced few greater writers." Ralph Waldo Emerson ranked Lincoln with Aesop in his lighter moods, but when it came to serious moments he said this of the Civil War president: "The weight and penetration of many passages in his letters, messages, and speeches, hidden now by the very closeness of their application to the moment, are destined to a wide fame. What pregnant definitions, what unerring common-sense, what foresight, and on great occasions what lofty, and more than national, what human tone! His brief speech at Gettysburg will not easily be surpassed by words on any recorded occasion."

At Gettysburg on November 19, 1864, Edward Everett, famed for his oratory, spoke close to two hours, and Lincoln took up only a few minutes. Afterwards, Everett took Lincoln's hand and said: "My speech will soon be forgotten; yours never will be. How gladly would I exchange my hundred pages for your twenty lines!"

Social Science, Spring 1980.

CHAPTER 17

Herbert Hoover and the Great Depression

Herbert Hoover never appealed much to me. With his Quaker background, it is true, he was reluctant to get into foreign wars; he preferred diplomacy. He was the first president, moreover, who took measures to cope with the deep depression that followed the crash of 1929. Previous presidents—Martin Van Buren (Panic of 1837), James Buchanan (Panic of 1857), Ulysses Grant (Panic of 1873), and Grover Cleveland (Panic of 1893)—carefully refrained from taking any action that might have helped improve conditions in the country. But Hoover's measures were mainly for the banks and corporations; he absolutely refused to do anything for the unemployed, who comprised 25 percent of the workers by the time he left office.

Hoover wasn't very friendly, at least to the White House help. He made it clear he did not want to see them when they came down the hall, so they were obliged to jump into the bathrooms and closets when they heard his footsteps. His wife Lou was also aloof. She developed a set of finger movements to use at the White House dinner table so she wouldn't have to talk to the waiters and waitresses.

★ ★ ★

In some respects this is a curious book. In his introduction, Harris Gaylord Warren, professor of history at Miami University, deplores the "customary biased, prejudiced, and grossly unfair accounts" of Herbert Hoover's efforts to combat the Great Depression, and expresses irritation at the "distorted picture of what some historians are calling 'the age of Roosevelt.'" "Forgotten," he insists,

> is the fact that what Hoover did was in a very real sense preparation for the next steps collectively known as the New Deal. Herbert Hoover was too progressive for the conservatives and too conservative for the radicals. While Mr. Hoover's rivals should be thankful that he and not one of them was president from 1929 to 1933, the country, too, should be grateful.

Yet in what follows there is really little of a fundamental nature to which Arthur Schlesinger Jr. can take serious exception and even less that is likely to please ex-President Hoover. The author does not, in fact, always appear to be especially grateful that the Great Engineer was at the helm during the early years of the Depression.

It is true that Professor Warren emphasizes Hoover's selfless devotion to what he conceived to be the public good, his firm grasp of the factual details of some of the major problems confronting his administration, and his willingness (in contrast to the Old Guard) to depart, in a limited fashion, from the economic principles which he prized so dearly. The author also regards the moratorium on intergovernmental debts in 1931, the creation of the RFC, and the Hoover Dam (together with other conservation measures) as major achievements of the Hoover administration and clear refutations of the belief that Hoover was incapable of "vigorous action." At the same time, however, he calls attention to (1) the complacency, even pride, with which Hoover contemplated the economics of normalcy ("There had been plenty of signs," insists Warren, "for the wise to heed" in the 1920s); (2) the mediocrity, except for Henry L. Stimson, of Hoover's cabinet (at best, he says, it contained one or two "Manchester liberals, or people whose ideas were a century or more behind events"); (3) the slowness with which Hoover came to realize the gravity of the situation after the Great Crash; (4) the inadequacy of his various farm, relief, and public works measures to cope with the crisis; and (5) the inexcusable blunders he committed in accepting the Hawley-Smoot Tariff and in panicking over the Bonus Army and chasing it out of Washington "at bayonet point." Moreover, in dealing with the interregnum, Professor Warren is entirely fair to Franklin Roosevelt, pointing out that Hoover was willing to cooperate with the president-elect only on his own terms, and that he "did not ask Mr. Roosevelt how the Republicans could get the New Deal started for him. Yet that, too, would have been co-operation!"

Exasperation, in other words, not gratitude, is frequently the tone of the book. For instance, in discussing Hoover's relief policy, Professor

Warren asks impatiently at one point:

> Had Hoover never seen any of the scores of Hoovervilles?
> Was he blind to the thousands and millions who had ex-
> hausted their savings, were doubling up with relatives, were
> burning their furniture because they had no other fuel? Did
> he not know that thousands of children, for whom he had
> promulgated the verbose Children's Charter, were going to
> school, if they went at all, with inadequate clothing, unat-
> tended diseases, and undernourished bodies? Did he not
> know that the fine reports of how well relief problems were
> being met ignored realities? No matter how often he denied
> it, people were starving in the midst of plenty. They were
> starving physically, and a dry rot had set in which could
> provide an excellent seed bed for communism.

His rather lame (but not necessarily incorrect) conclusion is that Hoover was "the greatest Republican of his generation," and that the major weakness of his program was "its failure to strike hard enough at the basic causes of depressions, the same failure that attended later New Deal efforts."

Professor Warren, it would seem from this, is by no means antipathic to the New Deal. On the other hand, he also gives a friendly sketch of Hoover's "individualistic" philosophy on pages 32–36. Elsewhere, however, he seems to realize that this philosophy, stripped of its rhetoric, was essentially a system of business paternalism little to his liking, and in a passage on page 187, too long to analyze here, he even seems to be warning that departure from the principles of pure competition can only lead to an inevitable "day of reckoning" for the country. Interestingly, this imprecision and apparent uncertainty in his own point of view is one of the book's chief charms. Professor Warren follows no clearly articulated line (except that of simple humanity), and he is endlessly unpredictable. The upshot is a fresh, lively, and, though not always consistent, frequently penetrating series of commentaries on the perplexities of the "greatest Republican" of the period.

....

REVIEW OF HARRIS GAYLORD WARREN, *Herbert Hoover and the Great Depression* *(1959), Journal of Southern History,* November 1959.

CHAPTER 18

Franklin D. Roosevelt and the New Deal

I n his lively study of the "New Deal" programs that Franklin Roosevelt devised, with the help of Congress, to combat the Great Depression, historian Arthur Schlesinger Jr. refers to the comment that the ninety-two-year-old Supreme Court justice Oliver Wendell Holmes Jr. is said to have made about the new president in 1933: he was a "second-clas intellect—but a first-class temperament."

There is some doubt that Justice Holmes actually said that about FDR. He only met FDR once, shortly after the inauguration, and it is unlikely that he could have come up with such a sweeping characterization of FDR after such a short meeting. He might well have made the remark about Theodore Roosevelt, who appointed him to the US Supreme Court in 1902, and whom Holmes knew well. Theodore certainly had a "first-class temperament" and, like Franklin, broke precedents and tried to regulate the big corporations. As to intellects, who is to say? Theodore was more of a reader than Franklin and knew his history and literature in a way that few presidents did. But maybe Justice Holmes was talking about common sense.

★ ★ ★

George Bancroft, it used to be said, cast a vote for Andrew Jackson on every page of his famous history of the United States. Arthur M. Schlesinger Jr., professor of history at Harvard, is in many respects Franklin Roosevelt's Bancroft. His earliest books—*The Age of Jackson* (1945) and *The Vital Center* (1949)—were shaped by the point of view of an ardent Roosevelt Democrat. And in his present ambitious undertaking, a many-volumed history of *The Age of Roosevelt*, Professor Schlesinger makes no secret of his enthusiastic admiration for Roosevelt and the New Deal. Here, at any rate, is one of our younger American historians who—*mirabile dictu*—steadfastly refuses to read the popular presuppositions of the present decade into his interpretation of the American past.

In a 1957 volume, *The Crisis of the Old Order, 1919–1933*, Schlesinger provided the background for the Roosevelt period: the "Golden Twenties," seemingly prosperous, but inherently unstable; the Great Crash of 1929; the onslaught of the Depression; the helplessness of the business community and of the Hoover administration in the face of economic crisis; and the political ascendancy of Franklin D. Roosevelt. The present volume, *The Coming of the New Deal*, second of what will surely be more than the four volumes originally planned by Schlesinger, examines in great detail the emergence and development of the various programs comprising the First New Deal, from Roosevelt's inauguration on March 4, 1933, to the Congressional elections in the fall of 1934. In a lively prologue ("The Hundred Days"), which vividly recaptures the pace, sense of urgency, confusion, and excitement of the first frantic Hundred Days of Roosevelt's administration, Schlesinger sets the stage for the unfolding of the New Deal: the president's surprisingly quick mastery (and thorough enjoyment) of his grave responsibilities; the emergency action which saved the nation's banks and ended the panic which had gripped the country; the arrival of the "bright young men," representing various classes, occupations, and philosophies (but all of them "chain talkers"), in Washington to participate in the work of national recovery; the transformation of Washington, as Ray Tucker put it, "from a placid, leisurely Southern town, with frozen faces and customs, into a gay, breezy, sophisticated and metropolitan center"; and the enactment by Congress, under the guidance of the president, of fifteen major laws designed to shore up the economy and to alleviate the widespread misery. "At the end of February," Schlesinger quotes Walter Lippmann as saying, "we were a congeries of disorderly panicstricken mobs and factions. In the hundred days from March to June we became again an organized nation confident of our power to provide for our own security and to control our destiny."

"We have had our revolution," said *Collier's* simply, "and we like it." Of Roosevelt during this hectic period, Schlesinger observes:

> Reporters took from his press conferences images of urbane
> mastery, with the president sitting easily behind his desk,
> his great head thrown back, his smile flashing or his laugh
> booming out in the pleasure of thrust and riposte. He saw
> agitated Congressmen, panicky businessmen, jealous bu-

reaucrats; he kidded the solemn, soothed the egotistical, and inspired the downhearted. There remained too a sense of ambiguity and craftiness. He could be hard and frightening when he wanted to be, and he played the political game with cold skill. Charm, humor, power, persuasion, menace, idealism—all were weapons in his armory.

And of Roosevelt's associates he says: "At his worst, the New Dealer became an arrant sentimentalist or a cynical operator. At his best he was the ablest, most intelligent, and most distinguished public servant the United States ever had." The force of these characterizations, made early in the book, becomes quite apparent in the pages that follow.

The bulk of the book is devoted to an analysis of the purposes and performances of—and the personalities involved in—the various measures undertaken by the Roosevelt administration to combat the depression and promote recovery. "Part of the New Deal impulse," says Schlesinger, "was defensive—the determination to protect the freedom and opportunity of Americans from the ravages of unemployment and despair. But part too was a desire to build a better America." Five chapters deal with the major New Deal policies: "The Fight for Agricultural Balance" (AAA), "Experiment in Industrial Planning" (NRA), "The Economics of Nationalism" (monetary and trade policies), "The Cry in the Streets" (federal relief, public works, and social security), and "The Battle for Public Development" (TVA, CCC, and the Resettlement Administration). One chapter ("The Transformation of a Labor Movement") is devoted to the administration's labor policy, the Wagner Act, and the emergence of the CIO, and one ("Resurgence on the Right") to the overwhelming popular endorsement of the New Deal at the polls despite the development of strong conservative opposition during 1934. A final chapter ("Evolution of the Presidency") contains an acute analysis of Roosevelt's philosophy of administration and an attempt to explore the mystery that lies behind the mask Roosevelt wore even in the presence of his family and his most intimate friends and advisers. While Schlesinger does not probe as deeply into the psychological sources of the Roosevelt personality as Rexford Tugwell did in *The Democratic Roosevelt* (1957), he is probably right in concluding that the key to Roosevelt lay in his "basic simplicity of mind and heart." "His complexity was infinite," says Schlesinger, "but it all pertained to tactics. On questions of essential purpose, he retained an innocence which was all the more baffling because of its luminous naïveté." And finally: "The essence of Roosevelt, the quality which fulfilled the best in him and explained the potency of his appeal, was his intrepid and passionate affirmation. He always cast his vote for life, for action, for forward motion, for the future."

Based upon massive research in the Roosevelt papers at Hyde Park, in memoirs, diaries, newspapers, magazines, and government documents, and in the records of the Oral History Research Office at Columbia University, *The Coming of the New Deal* shows an impressive grasp of the complex crosscurrents of American life and thought in the early New Deal years; it is superbly organized, written with skill and verve, and informed throughout with a sophisticated wit and irony and a talent for the appropriate word, phrase, and quotation. Among the many statements which Schlesinger has resurrected from the period, the following were among this reviewer's favorites: "It's exciting and educational to be alive and asked out in Washington these days" (Ray Tucker); "I guess at your next election we will make it unanimous" (William Randolph Hearst); "I am afraid I couldn't be trusted around Mr. Roosevelt. For the first time in my life in this business, I might find myself squabbling for a chance to carry the champion's water bucket" (Westbrook Pegler); "Turning federal funds over to the states for administration would mean more politics instead of less politics in administration" (Senator James F. Byrnes of South Carolina).

Professor Schlesinger is by no means uncritical of Roosevelt and his advisers. He detects a "thin streak of sadism" in Roosevelt's treatment of his subordinates, calls his handling of the London Economic Conference "deplorable," regards his gold-purchase program as "ineffectual" and "based on a shallow and incorrect thesis," acknowledges that Roosevelt had no "primary experience or clear-cut views" in the labor field and was inclined at first to be antilabor, and quotes without comment Justice Oliver Wendell Holmes's famous remark that the new president was a "second-class intellect—but a first-class temperament!" Cordell Hull, whom Schlesinger takes more seriously than this reviewer has ever been able to, was "a peculiar combination of evangelism and vindictiveness, of selflessness and martyrdom"; Frances Perkins was "more interested in doing things for labor than enabling labor to do things for itself"; and Harold Ickes's "egotism was so massive that he remained personally unconscious of its existence." But he is perhaps hardest of all on Henry Wallace, whose strange relationship with Dr. Nicholas Roerich, the White Russian mystic, he examines at some length. Schlesinger is generous in his acknowledgment of Wallace's undoubted abilities, but the secretary of agriculture's curious combination of misty idealism and hardheaded practicality leads him (evidently influenced in part by Dwight MacDonald's cruel dissection in *Henry Wallace: The Man and the Myth*) to say:

> But neither mysticism nor rhetoric could abolish the fissure, the emptiness, at the core of his own personality. He rarely made contact with others, perhaps because it was so hard for

him to make contact with himself. His associates speculated whether he had any capacity for human affection. At times it seemed as if he had a greater sense of intimacy with plants. . . . And in his public life his inner division led to evasiveness and vacillation. Confronted by choice, he was always inclined to cut things in half and split the difference, mistaking eclecticism for synthesis.

Despite occasional sharp criticisms, however, Professor Schlesinger casts his vote (as did the majority of Americans at the time) regularly for Roosevelt and the New Deal. Critics from the extreme right and from what remains of the extreme left in this country will, no doubt, find this extremely deplorable. But for those who, like this reviewer, regard Roosevelt, for all his vagaries (especially in the field of foreign policy), as a remarkable person, and the New Deal, for all of its undoubted shortcomings, as a common-sense, humane, and even prudent response to the collapse of the American economic system in the early thirties and to the agonies of the Great Depression, Schlesinger's masterly recreation of the hopes and fears, ideas and interests, conflicts and compromises, and actions and passions of the first two years of Roosevelt's first administration will make absorbing and, at times, exciting reading.

REVIEW OF ARTHUR M. SCHLESINGER JR., *The Age of Roosevelt: The Coming of the New Deal* (1959), *Southwest Review*, Spring 1959.

CHAPTER 19

Harry Truman in the White House

There were things I liked about President Truman: his down-to-earth frankness and his "Fair Deal" liberalism. I applauded his firing of General Douglas MacArthur for defying him, his civilian commander; his support of the Marshall Plan for helping the Western European countries out of the economic mess World War II had left them in; and his desegregation of the Armed Forces. But I was shocked and disappointed when he sent American troops to Korea, where a civil war was raging, without asking for a declaration of war by Congress. It not only set a bad precedent for his successors in the White House; it also helped transform the United States into a military state that felt obliged to station troops around the world and intervene whenever our presidents decided that other countries, miles away, were disobeying our rules.

★ ★ ★

Shortly after Harry Truman took his oath of office as president following Franklin Roosevelt's death in April 1945, he told reporters, "Boys, if you ever pray, pray for me. I don't know whether you fellows ever had a load of hay fall on you, but when they told me yesterday what happened, I felt like the moon, the stars, and all the planets had fallen on me." "Good luck, Mr. President," cried one reporter. "I wish you hadn't called me that," sighed Truman.

This plain style and utter lack of pretension were to make Truman a folk hero after his death in 1972. In 1945, though, it was hard for people to think of the folksy fellow from Missouri as president of the United States after twelve dazzling years with the breezy, self-assured, and patrician Roosevelt. Some people were never reconciled.

For a while, though, Truman, like most presidents, enjoyed a brief honeymoon with Congress, the press, and the public. He went to a Big Three conference in Potsdam in July, joining Churchill and Stalin in planning the occupation of the recently defeated Germany; reaffirming FDR's unconditional surrender policy; and best of all, he thought, committing the Soviet Union to entering the war in Asia in the near future. The Soviet Union soon came into the war, as promised, but by then Truman had authorized the dropping of atom bombs on Hiroshima and Nagasaki, and Japan had decided to throw in the towel.

The atom bombs came as a stunning surprise to most people. But America's allies, Britain and the Soviet Union, warmly approved of their use and so did most Americans. There was, to be sure, some dissent. A few pacifists, pre–Pearl Harbor anti-Interventionists, and conservatives such as Herbert Hoover and David Lawrence were appalled. But the majority of American liberals and radicals, including the Communists, hailed Truman's action with enthusiasm. It was a long time before the American Left began to have second thoughts about Hiroshima.

With the end of World War II in August 1945, there was great elation and sudden discontent. When the tumult and shouting died, everything seemed to go wrong for the new president. On the home front came mounting unemployment, skyrocketing inflation, and labor upheavals across the land. In Europe, Stalinist Russia was moving relentlessly into Poland and other countries along its eastern borders, despite Western protests. In China, Mao Tse-Tung's Communists were gradually winning the civil war against America's wartime ally Chiang Kai-Shek, and no amount of American aid to Chiang seemed to make any difference.

Americans were bewildered. What was happening? Why were the fruits of victory turning sour? The Allies had gone to war to stop Hitler's brutal aggressions. Yet with the achievement of victory, here was Poland—which Hitler had invaded in 1939—a victim of aggression again. And the United Nations, which the United States had invented to check aggression and preserve world peace, seemed helpless.

It was all very ironic. When Congress appropriated funds in 1942 to build the Pentagon, the bill authorizing the money provided that when peace came, the Pentagon would become a veterans hospital. But peace never came, and the Pentagon never hospitalized. Instead came NATO and the Truman Doctrine (military aid to other nations to "contain" Soviet aggression). The Marshall Plan for economic aid to the war-torn nations of Western Europe was also part of the plan to check Soviet expansion.

People tend to blame presidents for world problems. By 1948, Truman's standing in public opinion polls was abysmally low. Cruel quips abounded: "To err is Truman"; "I wonder what Truman would do if he were alive"; "Don't shoot our piano player; he's doing the best he can." Liberal Democrats began looking to wartime hero General Eisenhower to lead them out of the wilderness. But Ike refused to get involved in politics in 1948, and Truman was determined to get the Democratic nomination himself that year. The Democratic convention in July was lackluster and spiritless. There were signs in the auditorium: "We're just mild about Harry." When *Taps* sounded for the war dead, the bugles hit several sour notes. When Lawrence Tibbett sang *The Star Spangled Banner*, the organist gave him such a high pitch he sounded as if he were strangling. And when, at Truman's appearance, a flock of doves was released as a symbol of peace, one of them perched on the bald head of Speaker of the House Sam Rayburn, who was presiding ("funniest thing in the convention," according to Truman), and another banged into the balcony and flopped dead on the floor ("A dead pigeon," murmured one delegate, looking up at Truman). Truman's rousing acceptance speech revived the delegates' spirits only momentarily.

The Republicans chose Gov. Thomas E. Dewey of New York as their candidate in late June in a mood of euphoria. Truman is a "gone goose," Congresswoman Clare Boothe Luce told the exuberant delegates; his "time is short" and his "situation is hopeless." Truman's party indeed seemed to be falling apart. The states' rights Dixiecrats deserted the Democrats because of the president's civil rights policies and ran South Carolina's Strom Thurmond for president on their own ticket. Progressives in the Democratic Party also seceded, blaming Truman for the Cold War, and nominated former vice president Henry A. Wallace for president.

It looked as though the little man from Independence, Missouri, was doomed to inglorious defeat. Most experts—pundits, prophets, pollsters, prognosticators—predicted easy victory for Dewey. Fifty of the nation's leading political writers chose the Republican candidate as the winner, and a St. Louis betting commissioner called him a 15-to-1 favorite. "Thomas E. Dewey's election as president is a foregone conclusion," announced Leo Egan in the *New York Times*.

Truman refused to be intimidated. He took to the stump shortly after his nomination, launched an aggressive, energetic, and populistic campaign against the "do-nothing" Republican-dominated 83rd Congress, and made fun of the pollsters. "Lay it on, Harry! Give 'em hell!" people cried. "I have good news for you," he shot back gleefully. "We have the Republicans on the run. We are going to win!" From the rear platform of his train he would speak briefly about his Fair Deal program, blast the Republicans, then say, "Howja like to meet the Boss?"

and introduce wife Bess, and then "Howja like to meet the Boss's boss?" and bring out daughter Margaret. His wife and daughter didn't especially like the ritual, but the crowds loved it.

During the campaign Truman was warmly received by huge crowds wherever he went, but the experts were not impressed. People always turn out to see presidents, they explained; Dewey is still a shoo-in. In the final days of the campaign, Dewey took time out to plan his inauguration; after all, the "do-nothing" Congress had made generous appropriations for the occasion. The pollsters—Gallup, Crossley, Roper—stood firmly by their Dewey forecast. "Dewey will be in for eight years," predicted the *Kiplinger News Letter*. Just before election day *Life* carried a big picture of Dewey with the caption, "The Next President of the United States." The morning after the election, the *Chicago Tribune* had a banner headline: "Dewey defeats Truman."

Truman's victory on November 2 stunned the pollsters and stupefied the Republicans. Afterwards, Groucho Marx declared, "The only way a Republican will get into the White House is to marry Margaret Truman." Shattered by his defeat, Dewey said he felt like the man who woke up to find himself inside a coffin with a lily in his hand and thought: "If I'm alive, what am I doing here? And if I'm dead, why do I have to go to the bathroom?"

Dewey's pedestrian style undoubtedly helped do him in. But Truman's fighting spirit was primarily responsible for the victory. Truman waged the kind of campaign FDR would have waged, according to journalist I.F. Stone, and he was able to hold together the old coalition—labor, farmers, the South, blacks, and ethnic minorities—that had given FDR so many triumphs. "You've got to give the little man credit," said Republican Sen. Arthur Vandenberg of Michigan. "There he was flat on his back. Everybody had counted him out but he came up fighting and won the battle. That's the kind of courage the American people admire."

The admiration was short-lived. Truman's next four years were even stormier than the first three. In June 1950 came the Korean War. About the same time came Sen. Joseph McCarthy's demagogic assault on the Truman administration as a hotbed of subversion. Congressional investigations, too, were uncovering instances of influence-peddling in Washington. By 1952, with the Korean War in stalemate, the Republicans thought they had a sure-fire formula for success: K1C2, that is, Korea, Communism, and Corruption. And with the immensely popular Eisenhower as their standard-bearer, the GOP succeeded in riding to victory for the first time since 1928. Truman retired to Independence, wrote his memoirs, joined the college lecture circuit, and stumped for Democratic candidates with his usual zeal until his health began to fail in the 1960s.

Students of history have mixed feelings about the man from Missouri. On the left, historians give him low marks, blaming him, rather than Stalin, for the Cold War. Stalin's takeover of Eastern Europe, they contend, was defensive, not aggressive, designed to safeguard Russia from the invasions that had devastated the country in two world wars. Mainstream historians are friendlier. They insist that the Soviet Union was at least as responsible for the Cold War as the United States was (if not more so), and that Truman's response to Stalinist depredations was by and large cautious, restrained, sure-footed, and statesmanlike.

In polls taken among professional historians since the 1960s, Truman comes off well, usually ending up among the ten best presidents and sometimes receiving the rating "near-great." One fact seems undeniable: Truman continued generally in the Roosevelt tradition. On the domestic front, FDR's New Deal created the welfare state, and Truman's Fair Deal broadened it. In foreign affairs, FDR's policies transformed the United States into a superpower, and Truman accepted America's new status in the world much as his predecessor would have, had he lived to finish his fourth term. Superpowers, of course, require both Pentagons and veterans hospitals, as FDR well knew, and as Truman quickly learned.

Truman would have been surprised by his sudden rise to popularity in the 1970s and astonished to know that someday people would be celebrating the one hundredth anniversary of his birth on May 8. Once called a fool, liar, cheat, coddler of subversives, and the worst president in history, he appears in retrospect refreshingly bold, straightforward, feisty, and independent. But the plain people probably liked him all along. They enjoyed his outspokenness (the angry letter to the music critic who belittled Margaret's singing); his humility ("I wasn't one of the great presidents, but I had a good time trying to be one"); his courage (firing Gen. Douglas MacArthur in 1951 for insubordination); his decisiveness ("The buck stops here").

Truman's democratic simplicity also has been enormously appealing to many people. The White House servants adored him; he was kind and friendly to them and never was condescending. There was nothing high-falutin' about Harry. His behavior at Potsdam, as concert pianist Eugene List observed it nearly forty years ago, was characteristic.

One night, List recalled recently, he did a piano recital for the Big Three after they had had an all day conference. Churchill was bored stiff and Stalin noncommittal, but Truman was enchanted by the performance. Afterward, he asked the young man to play a Chopin rhapsody he liked the next night. The Chopin number was not in List's repertoire, but the music was flown in from Paris the following morning, and he spent the rest of the day mastering it. When it came time for the recital that evening, he announced he hadn't had time to memorize the composition, would have to use the music, and needed someone to turn pages. A White House aide offered to help, but admitted he couldn't read notes. At this point, List reports, President Truman, "with a wonderfully sweeping gesture," said: "No, I'll do it." And so, as young List played Chopin, the new superpower's new chief magistrate dutifully turned pages. The "Imperial Presidency" was to come after Truman.

Dallas Morning News, May 6, 1984.

CHAPTER 20

The Eisenhower Diaries

n both 1952 and 1956, I voted for Adlai Stevenson, the Democratic candidate for president for whom I had much admiration, but I did not despair because Dwight D. Eisenhower, the Republican candidate, won the election both times. He was friendly and likable and famous for the important part he played as an army general during World War II. Poor Stevenson hardly had a chance to beat him when running for president, and he knew it.

President Eisenhower gave us eight years of peace, and he refrained from sending American troops to Vietnam to help the non-Communists there keep Communist leader Ho Chi Minh from taking over the whole country after the French gave it up as a colony. Still our military forces grew in numbers and power, and the CIA succeeded in overthrowing the elected ruler of Iran because he nationalized the oil fields there, and then they imposed the Shah, a cruel dictator, on them. The CIA also forced a change in leaders in Guatemala to advance American interests there.

Still, Eisenhower is remembered for warning against what he called "the military-industrial complex," and against needless wars abroad. "How do we stop or avoid any further Koreas?" he asked in a speech in Rock Island, Illinois; "in short, how do we get away from the fumbling and bumbling that led us into Korea?" In Newton, Iowa, the next day, he said, "We should be keeping our boys at home and not be preparing them to serve in uniforms across the seas." And on another occasion he told Americans that each "warship launched, every rocket fired signifies, in the final sense, a theft from those who hunger and are not fed, those who are cold and not clothed." A modern bomber, he noted, cost the country a modern school in thirty cities or two state-of-the-art hospitals. "This is not a way of life at all in any true sense," he added. "Under the cloud of threatening war, it is humanity hanging from a cross of iron."Eisenhower strongly opposed what he called a "garrison state," and he urged Americans to reject dependence on military power as a guarantor of liberty and "use our power in the interests of world peace and human betterment." He knew very well, noted Nancy Gibbs in *Time* magazine on July 26, 2010, "how many times in the course of his two terms his advisers urged him to dispatch the marines, whether to Vietnam, Suez, Hungary, Quemoy and Matsu—advice he resolutely resisted in his hunt for a better way." The United States "never lost a soldier or a foot of ground in my administration," he declared in retirement. "We kept the peace. People asked how it happened. By God, it didn't just happen, I'll tell you that.".

★ ★ ★

Dwight D. Eisenhower impressed some people (especially Democrats) as being affable and well-meaning, but essentially bumbling and inarticulate. One reporter rewrote the Gettysburg Address in a parody of Ike's meandering style at press conferences. But Ike's critics got it wrong. The general-president was no Jerry Ford; he was (as Garry Wills observed years ago) shrewd, self-assured, and politically astute.

When he bumbled at meetings with the press he knew exactly what he was doing. "I'll just confuse them," he assured an aide shortly before facing journalists during a crisis he did not wish to discuss frankly.

Eisenhower's diaries, skillfully edited by Indiana University historian Robert. H. Ferrell and published now for the first time in complete form, provide ample evidence of the thirty-fourth president's professional skills. Ike began the diaries while he was aide to Gen. Douglas MacArthur in the Philippines in the mid-1930s, and he continued them, on and off, while supreme commander of the Allied Expeditionary Forces during World War II, as Army chief of staff, as president of Columbia University, as head of NATO forces after the war, as president of the United States from 1953 to 1961, and, after that, as elder statesman until his death in 1969.

From almost the beginning the diaries reveal a thoughtful, ambitious, knowledgeable, fair-minded, self-confident and public-spirited citizen-soldier. The writing is clear, concise, analytical, and, if undistinguished, unquestionably competent. Ike dictated some of the entries; he also tried typing for a time without success. But he wrote mostly by hand.

There are some lively passages in the daily jottings. Ike regarded US fleet commander Adm. Ernest R. King as "an arbitrary, stubborn type with not too much brains" and not long after Pearl Harbor exclaimed, "One thing that might help win this war is to get someone to shoot King." Of Manuel L. Quezon and MacArthur he once complained, "Both are babies." Bataan, he observed, was "made to order" for MacArthur: "It's in the public eye; it has made him a public hero." A little later: "But he's a hero! Yah."

But acerbity was not Eisenhower's mode. The private Ike, unfortunately for the reader, seems to have been as good-natured most of the time as the public Ike. He has nothing whatever to say about Harry Truman's firing of MacArthur in 1951, and very little of interest to say about Sen. Joseph McCarthy (whom he detested) or Richard M. Nixon (for whom he recorded polite praise).

Like most diarists, Ike appears to have had his eye on posterity most of the time. The notations, sprightly at first, soon take on a formal, bland, official tone. The Eisenhower diaries end by being far less revealing than, say, those of John Quincy Adams or James K. Polk, or even Rutherford B. Hayes.

When it comes to Ike's political outlook, there are few surprises in the diaries. Time and again he records his middle-of-the-road philosophy; dedication to free enterprise, willingness to have the government take some action to help the underprivileged, but implacable hostility to the welfare state.

His foreign policy views are similarly conventional. He seems from the evidence here to have been as doughty a Cold Warrior as his Secretary of State John Foster Dulles, whom he regarded highly. On the other hand, he did cast a cold eye on lavish defense spending: he simply did not believe in "throwing money" at the Pentagon to solve problems.

He also ended the Korean war, refused to get militarily involved in Vietnam, and made continual efforts to lessen the tensions between the United States and Russia. He also questioned Dulles's habit of acting like "a sort of international prosecuting attorney." Ike wanted the United States to be a powerful force in world affairs, but he was also convinced that America's ultimate survival as a free nation rested on an avoidance of nuclear holocaust.

At the present time, "Eisenhower revisionism," as it is called, is flourishing in the historical profession. Many of the younger historians in this country give Ike's foreign policy—especially when it came to preserving the peace—far higher marks than they do the policies of Truman, Kennedy, and Johnson. Curiously enough, though, what Ike says in his diaries about foreign affairs does not differ appreciably from the views of the Democratic presidents whom the revisionists are criticizing.

Yet it is a fact that Ike did give the country eight years of relative tranquility in the world of nations. It is ironic that an experienced soldier-president like Eisenhower took a far less military view of reality than his civilian successors.

....

REVIEW OF ROBERT H. FERRELL, ed., *The Eisenhower Diaries* (1981), *Fort Worth Star-Telegram*, June 28, 1981.

CHAPTER 21

The Diversions of Lyndon B. Johnson

Whether you like him or not, I've often said, Lyndon B. Johnson was one of the most interesting presidents we've ever had. He could be a dignified gentleman, a crude guy, a friendly fellow and a sadistic person, a big talker but a good absorber, too, a workaholic but also a hilarious fun-maker, and, above all, a hard-working political leader who would fight as hard as he had to in order to get legislation passed that he thought would make the United States a better country. "My father was naughty," admitted his daughter, Luci, in an interview with Ken Herman, a writer for the *Austin American Statesman,* on April 3, 2011. "I'm sure his mother sent him to the corner on more than one occasion. And for good reason, too."

★ ★ ★

Lyndon Johnson was eager to learn what people thought about the issues when he was president. Sometimes, when entertaining guests at the White House, he turned the meeting after dinner into a kind of classroom with himself as the instructor. He started things off by passing a basket around containing slips of paper marked either "speaker" or "writer" for his guests to pick out. The people who got the papers marked "speaker" were expected to tell him what was on their minds that evening. Those who happened to take out the papers marked "writer" were expected to write him letters discussing the issues that concerned them the most, to which he would respond by phone or mail. Once the papers were distributed, he called on the "speakers," from one table after another, and listened quietly to what they said about the economy, education, civil rights, medical programs, and foreign policy.

One evening, a business executive came up with some criticism of Johnson's style. "Mr. President," he said, "we've heard these briefings and we've seen the people in your cabinet. They are very talented, very bright, very wise people. But they all look very tired. Mr. President, in business in our company we require that our top executives each go away and take at least a month of vacation a year. I suggest that you insist on that for your people."

Johnson frowned fiercely as the man was talking, for he didn't like to be lectured. When the man finished giving the president his advice, the room remained quiet until Johnson motioned for the next speaker to say something. The businessman had hit a sore spot on Johnson. He was irritated when people told him that he overworked the people on his staff. He worked hard himself—he was a workaholic—and he saw no reason why the people working for him shouldn't work hard too. Zephyr Wright, his cook, once told him, "Anybody who works for you for a long time has to love you, because you kill yourself and everybody else too."

In November 1963, when Johnson became president after the assassination of President Kennedy, reporters preparing stories about Johnson for their newspapers found it almost impossible to dig up anything about his hobbies. Johnson "has no daily routine of relaxation," concluded the Associated Press, "but at the end of the day, he liked to sit and talk."

Once, when someone mentioned hobbies to Johnson, he exclaimed: "Hobbies!!! What in hell are hobbies? I've got too much work to do to have hobbies!" He did, to be sure, take time off now and then to board the presidential yacht, the *Honey Fitz*, with his wife and friends, and cruise down to Mount Vernon and back. He also liked spending vacations at the Johnson ranch in Texas. But his work as president was usually on his mind when he was supposed to be relaxing. He talked politics when he was playing golf with various Congressmen. And when he went to a baseball game, he had presidential problems on his mind so much that he hardly paid any attention to the game going on. "On such days," recalled George Reedy, one of his press secretaries, "I sat at home praying that television cameras would not catch him with his back turned to the field in deep conversation about a tax bill or an upcoming election while a triple play was in process or when a cleanup hitter had just knocked a home run with the bases loaded." One of Johnson's friends summed it all up: "Sports, entertainment, movies—he couldn't have cared less."

Until Johnson's heart attack in 1975, just after becoming the youngest Senate majority leader in history, his habits were those of a "Type A" personality. He smoked three or four packs of cigarettes a day, gulped down his food, and was always in a hurry. Once, his aides persuaded him to see someone in the oval office for a brief moment. And when the visitor ended up staying twenty minutes, Johnson was furious. "Hell," he stormed afterward, "by the time a man scratches his ass, clears his throat, and tells me how smart he is, we've already wasted fifteen minutes!" Johnson gave up smoking after his heart attack, and he slowed down for a while, but he was soon back to his breakneck speed and lengthy work days.

According to George Reedy, LBJ "knew of no innocent form of recreation": The only sanctified activity was hard work to achieve clearly defined goals; the only recreation was frenetic activity that made one forget the problems of the day; and the only true happiness was the oblivion he could find in Scotch or in sleep. The concept of reading for the sake of contemplation, of community activity for the sake of sharing joy, of conversation for the sake of human contact was totally foreign to his psyche. He did understand dimly that other people had some interests outside of their direct work, but he thought of such interests as weakness, and, if they included classical music or drama, mere snobbery practiced by "the Eastern Establishment."

Still, Johnson was no couch potato. He actually did some swimming in the White House pool, and in the outdoor pool on the ranch in Texas. But he usually had at least one person with him so he could talk politics while moving around in the water. He enjoyed horseback riding on his ranch, too, but of course he was doing his job as a ranch owner, not having fun when he made the rounds. Above all, though, Johnson liked to dance. He was a good ballroom dancer, and there's no reason to believe he talked politics with his attractive partners on the dance floor. "He had a good sense of the rhythm," observed one social columnist, "and did a smooth fox trot." He was "a marvelous dancer," said singer Edie Adams, who had been at one of the presidential parties. "You don't find dancers like that any more. Usually they're sort of milquetoast fellows, but he knew exactly where he was going. . . . I thought, 'Gee, that's good. This is the strong man we've got up here running the country. I like that!'"

When Johnson was in the Senate, he did a little golfing, but he didn't take it seriously. He was the devotee, it was said, of the "Hit-Till-You're-Happy School of Golf." He had a swing that looked like he was chopping wood or was trying to kill a rattlesnake, and he always hit as many shots as he wanted, until he made one he liked. One observer said Johnson played by his own rules: he "flattered, cajoled, needled, scolded, belittled, and sweet-talked the golf balls" the way he did his colleagues in the Senate.

In the spring of 1964, a few months after Johnson became president, Jack Valenti, one of his aides, suggested taking a little time off from work to play some golf with him. Johnson hadn't played in a long time, and he was reluctant to interrupt his work to play golf with Valenti. But when Valenti proposed inviting some senators to join him, Johnson's eyes lit up. "That's a helluva idea," he cried. "This can be a new forum for me to browbeat these guys." When a newspaper reported that LBJ liked golf because he had a zest for walking, Valenti said it was "a zest for politicking." People teased Johnson about his golfing, but he didn't seem to mind. "I don't have a handicap," he once said. "I'm all handicap." One golf pro said the president "didn't play very well, but he had a hell of a good time. He would josh around, kidding whoever was with him. He'd make comments to the other players—of a personal nature."

When the Vietnam War became increasingly unpopular with the American people, Johnson decided to give up the game. He told his aides that if people saw him on the golf links while American boys were dying in Asia, they would "eat me alive." Then, in the late summer of his last year in office, he announced, for the fun of it, at a White House dinner, that he was planning to give up alcohol and return to golf. "This is alarming, if true," wrote James Reston mischievously in his *New York Times* column, "for in the present state of the world and the presidency it really should be the other way around." Golf, Reston went on to say, was a form of self-torment, invented by the Scots, along with whiskey, to make people suffer: "To substitute golf for 'whiskey's old prophetic aid' is a puzzle and could be a calamity. And to do it as an escape from agony is the worst miscalculation since the start of the Vietnam War. Golf is not an escape from agony. It is itself an agony." Golf was never an "agony" for Johnson, but it was not a major pleasure either. Swimming and dancing were also minor indulgences. Johnson's greatest enjoyment was his 410-acre ranch outside Johnson City in South Texas. He liked to go boating on the Pedernales River, which ran in front of his ranchhouse. Sometimes he even went fishing for bass and catfish in the ponds and lakes of the surrounding area. More fun for him, though, was taking people—friends, reporters, White House aides—on tours of his ranch. Like Johnson himself, the tours were fast-paced, a bit rowdy, and at times challenging. They usually included a trip to the ramshackle cabin, which he claimed was his humble birthplace (like Lincoln's), even though he knew it wasn't. He also liked to show off the horses and cattle they encountered as he careened around the place, sometimes at ninety miles per hour.

Johnson liked to have special fun on the ranch with people on his staff, and with men he was considering for a position in his administration. In July 1965, he invited Joseph H. Califano Jr., whom he planned to make his adviser on domestic affairs, for a little visit, so he could size him up. First came a swim. After breakfast, Johnson asked Califano to join him in the pool. When Califano got in the water, Johnson asked solemnly, "Are you ready to help your president?" Replied Califano, "It would be an honor and a privilege." There was more talking than swimming after the exchange, but Califano seems to have held his own with the president.

After the pool came a drive around the ranch, followed by a car and a station wagon containing some Secret Service agents. While LBJ drove and talked, he helped himself generously to the Cutty Sark, ice, and soda in a large white foam cup, and whenever he wanted a refill, he slowed down, held his left hand out of the car window, and started shaking the cup with the ice in it. Then one of the Secret Service men rushed up, took the cup, ran back to the station wagon, asked another agent to refill it, and then took it back to Johnson as the car continued moving slowly along.

The afternoon for Califano was more vigorous. Johnson persuaded him to do some water-skiing on a nearby lake. Johnson's main objective, as he drove the speed boat up and down the lake, was to propel Califano off the skis into the water. "He drove faster and faster," Califano recalled, "zigging and zagging around the lake. . . . The faster he drove and twisted, the more I was determined to stay. He threw me once. He was going so fast that I thought I'd split in two when I flew off the skis and hit the water. Determined to prove myself, I got back up and managed not to fall again."

But Johnson wasn't through with Califano. After the skiing, Johnson took Califano for a ride around the lake in a small blue car, with his secretary, Vicky McCammon, sitting next to him in front, and Califano in the back seat. At one point, the car reached a steep incline at the edge of the lake and started rolling down toward the water. "The brakes don't work!" Johnson yelled frantically. "The brakes won't hold! We're going under!" The car then splashed into the lake, and Califano started to get out. Just then the car leveled, and he realized that they were in an amphibious car, and in no danger at all. As they putted along the lake, Johnson started teasing Califano. "Vicky," he said to his secretary, "did you see what Joe did? He didn't give a damn about his president. He just wanted to save his own skin and get out of the car."

It turned out that Johnson was fond of playing this trick on visitors. He especially enjoyed trying it out on young married couples, to see whether the husband would try to save his own life before helping his wife survive. It wasn't a very nice prank, but then Johnson's sense of humor wasn't always very nice. Still, he ended up hiring Califano to be his adviser on domestic affairs, and Califano was ready to do the president's bidding.

Many people regarded Johnson as a "Texas Hill Philistine." But he sponsored federal aid to the Arts and Humanities while he was in office. The "desire for beauty," he declared in one of his speeches in

May 1964, was as important as "the needs of the body." He may have believed this; he loved the countryside where his ranch was located. But art and literature played a small part in his life. He never read novels or poems, and he had little interest in opera, ballet, and symphonic music. He knew little about painting and sculpture, and he wasn't much of a play-goer or movie fan, either.

But he did like Western art—pictures of cowboys and scenes in the part of Texas he knew. He also liked Western music—"Wagon Wheels" and "The Yellow Rose of Texas." In the summer of 1965, he and Lady Bird hosted a festival of the arts at the White House, attended by scores of artists and writers who presented poetry readings, dance recitals, art exhibitions, and film screenings. It wasn't Johnson's domain, but, like George Washington, he thought the government ought to encourage art and literature.

FROM A LECTURE, "LYNDON JOHNSON'S DIVERSIONS," BASED ON *Presidential Diversions: Presidents at Play from George Washington to George W. Bush*, written in 2007.

CHAPTER 22

Bush-Speak

In the grand old days, the idea of teasing a president was unthinkable. Criticize, yes, making fun of him, no. George Washington received plenty of criticism from people who opposed his policies, but it never occurred to them to make fun of the way he walked, talked, and dressed. The same with Thomas Jefferson. Teasing some presidents—Andrew Jackson, for one—might have proved dangerous. Teasing Abraham Lincoln might have worked, but brickbats were better. People might not have liked Woodrow Wilson, but they didn't go in for any teasing. It wasn't until the 1970s, in fact, that the media began finding good copy in reporting the stumbles, bumbles, and gaffes our presidents produced.

Gerald Ford was the first target. When he slipped while descending the steps from a plane, with an umbrella in one hand and his wife's hand in the other, the newsmen reported it with zest and verve. Since no one was hurt in the fall, it became a legitimate show-off piece for bored reporters. After Ford's first slip, he couldn't seem to make any little misstep without having it featured on the news. Chevy Chase devoted his TV show to teasing Ford about his clumsiness, and, to calm people down, Ford deliberately appeared on the show and pretended to be awkward and clumsy every time he turned around. But Ford's little parody didn't stop the silly reporting.

Jimmy Carter, following Ford as president, became an object for laughter, too, but for quite different reasons. During the campaign of 1976, Carter emerged as something of a pious goody-goody, not a reg'lar guy, to many people, and he felt obliged to do something to appear more likable. To solve his problem, he agreed to an interview with one of the writers at *Playboy*, the sexy men's magazine. Some of the questions Carter answered were sensible enough, but when the interrogator got around to asking him about sex, he seems to have lost his head. He was a tough guy, not a softie, he wanted to prove. Although happily married, he said, he lusted in his heart for pretty women, even though the Bible condemned it. In addition, he was such a good guy that he refrained from going around denouncing regular guys who played around with women outside marriage. He even used the word "screw" at one point in the interview, leading a prominent Baptist minister to announce sternly that "screw" was not a Baptist word. The reporters had a field day with Carter's interview. They even composed a little ditty about "lusting in the heart" to sing whenever there were Carterites around.

When it came to Ronald Reagan, Carter's successor in the White House, the newsmen didn't have much about him to tease. A professional Hollywood actor, Reagan knew how to stay in control of things when he met with reporters. He happened to be the oldest president up to that time, but he did the teasing himself, about himself. Sometimes he would mention having chatted with Jefferson and some of the other Founding Fathers in the old days. With Reagan's successor, George Herbert Walker Bush, however, the fun began again. Bush lacked Reagan's panache when speaking informally on his own, and he had a way of unintentionally mangling the English language as he went along. His language trips and slips became so common that New York Times columnist Maureen Dowd began calling his utterances "Bush-Speak." Years later, his son George W. became known for his sloppy mispronunciations when he was in the White House, but his father's slips were far more entertaining.

In 1992, I gave a talk on "Presidential Prose" at the annual meeting of the Texas Institute of Letters, dealing with the best prose (Jefferson, Lincoln) and the worst (Harding, George H. W. Bush). My exposition of Papa Bush's prose produced such hilarity in the audience that I decided to write a separate piece on Bush-Speak.

★ ★ ★

"You can tell these Yale men—articulate devils, you know!"—President Bush, chatting with members of the Young Astronaut Society. Jan. 24. 1992

George Herbert Walker Bush is famous for his gaffes. But he isn't the only president of the United States to achieve such fame. Jerry Ford once referred to California's S. I. Hayakawa as "Hiawatha" in a convention speech. Jimmy Carter called Hubert Horatio Humphrey "Hubert Horatio Homblower," and Ronald Reagan called his vice president "George Bosh" on at least one occasion.

But President Bush is far better than his predecessors. "Outside the protective tutelage of his media adviser," noted *Newsweek* in May 1988, "Bush seems to be a veritable gaffe-o-matic." During the 1988 presidential campaign he denounced drug "ping-pins" (kingpins), called for increased "experts" (exports), and announced that he saw "an America in the midst of the largest peacetime explosion (expansion) ever." He also talked about the AFL-CIA.

But these are minor slips. At his best, Bush occasionally comes up with verbal gaffes that leave audiences rubbing their eyes in bewilderment. Speaking of bigotry during the 1988 campaign, he assured people that "I hope that I stand for anti-bigotry, anti-Semitism, antiracism. That is what drives me. It's one of the things I feel very, very strongly about." There was a clarifying statement afterwards, of course, but a little later, speaking about unemployment, Bush promised that if elected president he would "make sure that everyone who has a job wants a job." He fairly outdid himself, though, when bragging to voters about his close relationship to President Reagan. "For seven and half years," Bush declared, "I have worked alongside of him, and I am proud to be his partner. We have had triumphs. We have made mistakes. We have had sex . . ." There was a stunned silence in the audience, and he quickly corrected himself: "We have had setbacks."

Tongue slips, however, form only a small part of the Bush style. Bush-Speak (or Bushspeak), as the president's spoken word has come to be called, contains preppyisms (like "deep doo-doo") as well as *lapsi linguae*. Bush attended Phillips Academy in Andover, Massachusetts, before going on to Yale and becoming a member of Phi Beta Kappa, and traces of his prep-school background appear in his choice of words as well as in his occasional boyish gestures. This is something new in presidential style, and it is not without a certain goofy charm. Charged with running a negative campaign in 1988, Bush insisted he wasn't going to let the Democrats get away with it when they started pulling "that naughty stuff" on him. He also expressed great glee over the way campaign aide Lee Atwater was "getting into their knickers," that is, angering the Democrats. And along more positive lines, he promised to "hit a lick for peace" if he won the election.

Along with tongue slips and preppyisms, Bush-Speak includes a kind of goofy jocularity that goes with the president's efforts to make small talk on informal occasions. Offering a chair to a woman at a reception, he volunteered, "Chivalry is only reasonably dead." When Sen. Alan Simpson, entering a restaurant in Beeville, Texas, with the president, ordered Chablis, Bush said amiably, "Al, ya gonna have a draft?" Visiting a school in Harlem, he asked a third grader whether she was "número uno" in spelling, and when she hesitated, Bush said jovially, "Comme çi, comme ça!"

Far more striking than tongue slips, preppyisms, and goofy jocularities, however, are the amiable meanderings with which the president so frequently indulges himself when speaking off the cuff in public. With these dizzy flights of words we come to the heart of Bush-Speak. Here, for instance, is what President Bush had to say in Knoxville, Tennessee, when a high school student asked whether he planned to seek ideas overseas for improving American education:

> Well, I'm going to kick that right into the end zone of the Secretary of Education. But, yea, we have all—he travels a good deal, goes abroad. We have a lot of people in the department that does that. We're having an international—this is not as much education as dealing with the environment—a big international conference coming up. And we get it all the time—exchanges of ideas. But I think we've got—we set out there—and I want to give credit to your governor McWhetter and to your former governor, Lamar Alexander—we've gotten great ideas for a national goals program from—in the country—from the governors who were responding to maybe, the principal of your high school, for heaven's sake!

Bush's discussion of what he called "the religion thing," while campaigning for reelection in New Hampshire in February 1992, was equally flighty:

> Somebody said . . . we pray for you over there. That was not just because I threw up on the prime minister of Japan either. Where was he when I needed him? But I said, let me tell you something. And I say this—I don't know whether any ministers from the Episcopal church are here. I hope so. But I said to him this. You're on to something here. You cannot be president of the United States if you don't have faith. Remember Lincoln, going to his knees in times of trial in the Civil War and all that stuff. You can't be. And we are blessed. So don't feel sorry for—don't cry for me, Argentina."

In March, 1992, President Bush treated guests at a fundraising lunch in Tampa, Florida, to another prosaic peregrination. "Somebody—somebody asked me, what's it take to win?" he said:

> I said to them, I can't remember, what does it take to win the Super Bowl? Or maybe Steinbrenner, my friend George, can tell us what it takes for the Yanks to win—one run. But I went over to the Strawberry Festival this morning, and ate

a piece of shortcake over there—able to enjoy it right away, and once I completed it, it didn't have to be approved by Congress—I just went ahead and ate it—and that leads me into what I want to talk about today. . . ."

He then segued into some carefully scripted remarks.

Sometimes, amid all the improvisatory weirdness that makes up Bush-Speak, comes a strange rhetorical question that leaves people surprised and bewildered. Touring the Nazi death camp at Auschwitz in 1988, Bush suddenly exclaimed, "Boy, they sure were big on crematoriums, weren't they?" And at a Ford Aerospace facility in the spring of 1989, he exclaimed: "I want to give the high-five to high tech. . . . The truth is, it reminds a lot of people of the way I pitch horseshoes. Would you believe some of the people? Would you believe our dog?"

Strange answers as well as odd questions adorn the Bush repertoire. When asked (December 1987) about his experience as a fighter pilot during World War II, when he was shot down over the Pacific by Japanese gunners, Bush exclaimed: "Was I scared? Floating around in a little yellow raft off the coast of an enemy-held island, setting a world record for paddling? Of course I was. What sustains you in times like that? Well, you got back to fundamental values. I thought about Mother and Dad and the strengths I got from them—and God and faith and the separation of church and state." There is surely something intriguing in the picture of a young man contemplating disestablishmentarianism at a time when his life is hanging in the balance.

Equally strange was Bush's response to a question about whether he ever sought Ronald Reagan's advice after entering the White House: "Life its own self, as Dan Jenkins said. Life its own self. Figure that one out. But what it means is. I have a lot more to learn from President Reagan." (Reporting these remarks, *Newsweek* dubbed the president "the mysterious Easterner.") And when reporters quizzed the president about his flip-flop on taxes in June 1990, and one reporter asked whether it was naive of people to take campaign promises seriously, Bush had a puzzling answer: "I think people are smarter than a lot of us think they are, including me." Bush watchers are still trying to figure that one out.

Along with tongue slips, preppyisms, goofy jocularities, amiable meanderings, and curious questions and answers, Bush-Speak includes what might be called the "thing thing." Listening to President Bush's public ruminations, one can't help thinking of the lines from *A Child's Garden of Verses*: "The world is so full of a number of things/I'm sure we should all be happy as kings." During the 1988 campaign, Bush referred to his lack of a grand world outlook as "the vision thing." On another occasion he talked about the "blame America first crowd from the post-Vietnam thing." He asked the Atlantis astronauts about "the deployment thing," called his thyroid problem "the thyroid thing," talked about "the hostage thing" and "the Soviet thing," and once confessed: "I feel a little. I will say, uncomfortable sometimes with the elevation of the religion thing."

Bush may have a thing about things, but when it comes to what he might call "the clarity thing," he fails abysmally. At times the president has what *Texas Monthly*'s Emily Yoffe calls "Olympian moments of incomprehensibility," and in these moments come the most egregious Bushisms of all: puzzling pronouncements. Here are a few choice Bushian ineffabilities:

Drugs—In May 1988, when a reporter asked Bush how he planned to address the drug problem, he announced, "I'm going to be coming out with my own drug problem."

Iran-contra affair—When Peter Jennings asked Bush what part he had played in the Iran-contra affair, he exclaimed: "You judge the record. Are the Soviets coming out of Afghanistan? How does it look in a program he called or some one of these marvelous Boston adjectives up there and—about Angola—now we have a chance—several Bostonians don't like it, but the rest of the country will understand."

Advice—Soon after Bush became president, a reporter asked how he would do things differently in the White House, and Bush responded: "Like the old advice from Jackman—you remember, the guy that came out—character. He says, 'And then I had some advice. Be yourself.' That proved to be the worst advice I could possibly have. And I'm going to be myself. Do it that way."

Travel plans—On November 9, 1991, clarifying his travel plans for the coming year, Bush told reporters: "No, you're not going to see me stay put. I am not going to forsake my responsibilities. You may not see me put as much—I mean, un-put as much."

Endorsement—At a meeting of the National Governors' Association on February 3, 1992, Bush told Colorado Gov. Roy Romer, "All I was doing was appealing for an endorsement, not suggesting you endorse it."

Recession—Campaigning in New Hampshire in January 1992, Bush took time out to discuss the recession. Here are his lucubrations: "The guy over there at Pease—a woman, actually—she said something about a country-western song, you know, about the train, a light at the end of the tunnel. I only hope it's not a train coming the other way. Well, I said to her, well, I'm a country music fan. I love it, always have. Doesn't fit the mold of some of the columnists, I might add, but nevertheless—of what they think I ought to fit in, but I love it. . . . But nevertheless, I said to them you know there's another one the Nitty Ditty Nitty City that they did. And it says if you want to see a rainbow you've got to stand a little rain. We've had little rain. New Hampshire has had too much rain.

A lot of families are hurting."

Whence Bush-Speak? Whence the aimless clauses, awkward adverbs, dangling predicates, and jaunty jump-cuts that adorn the president's speech? Some observers attribute the verbal infelicities to the fact that Bush is left-handed, like Jerry Ford, another (but far less accomplished) gaffemeister. "Much research," writes Daniel Seligman in Fortune, "suggests lefties are indeed prone to 'language disturbances,' especially if they come from families genetically prone to leftiness." Seligman asked the White House whether there were other members of the Bush family who were left-handed and was told, "We do not give that information out."

Not genes, but misguided energies probably account in large part for Bush-Speak. In private, the president can be charming and amusing. In public, his efforts to escape his patrician background and sound like a regular fellow almost always lead him astray. "The worst thing you can do in politics," a Republican strategist once remarked, "is to try to be something you aren't." Many Bush-watchers attribute the president's linguistic awkwardness to his attempts to hide the signs of his upper-class upbringing as the son of a wealthy US senator (Connecticut's Prescott S. Bush).

The genteel president becomes particularly inarticulate whenever he tries to sound tough. Ordinarily a man of dignity, he "goes ballistic," to use his own phrase, when putting on a tough act in public; he speaks faster, with his voice climbing into the higher registers, looks increasingly frantic, and begins to sound slightly silly. Bush does not seem to realize, noted the *New Yorker*'s Elizabeth Drew, that in most cases tough equals calm (e.g., Clint Eastwood and Gary Cooper).

But even when Bush is calm, he sometimes loses control of the language. Some observers attribute this to desperate attempts to avoid taking stands on controversial public issues, or attempts to conceal the fact that he hasn't really given much thought to the subject under consideration. "His whittling of words," the *New York Times*'s Maureen Dowd explains, "is a reflection of his distaste for reflection." Elizabeth Drew concluded that Bush's "mangling of thoughts or words when on his own" bespoke "a certain sloppiness of thought processes, or some kind of short circuiting that goes on in his head."

Some critics are harsher. They attribute Bush-Speak to plain and simple insincerity, and like to quote George Orwell: "The great enemy of clear language is insincerity." Bush is invariably at his worst, writes Daniel Seligman, when he finds himself in a situation requiring "massive insincerity." *Harper's* Lewis Lapham can't help feeling that the president's smile in public is frequently fraudulent and that his sloppy way of expressing himself off the cuff comes from uneasiness about "putting his conscience in escrow."

Bush is by no means oblivious to his speech problems. "I don't always articulate," he told some New Hampshire voters in February of 1988, "but I always do feel." He was doing the best he could, he told his campaign advisers early in the 1988 presidential race, and doubted that he could do better. For him, Bush explained, public speaking was like tap dancing. Even if he spent the rest of his life trying to learn to tap dance, he said, he would never be better than merely competent. And the same was true of his public speaking. But his campaign people were not appeased. They knew he was coming across (in Dowd's words) as "goofy, ruthless, insincere, a man out of touch with the common people," and that he simply had to do better to win the election. In the end, they paid political consultant Roger Ailes $25,000 a month to serve as Bush's top media adviser and help him improve his style. Ailes at once put an end to all interviews and, through careful coaching, got Bush to pitch his voice lower, get rid of the nasal whine, and speak more slowly. Later on, the Bush people arranged for Reagan speechwriter Peggy Noonan to prepare both his 1988 acceptance speech and his inaugural address and see to it that he came across as a "quiet man" who wanted a "kinder, gentler" America.

Bush's inaugural address, written in what Dowd calls "High Noonan," came off rather well. After entering the White House, however, Bush resumed his old habit of straying from the script when speaking in public, and as a result his propensity for saying ditsy things continued to embarrass his friends and amuse his foes. And as the Bushisms multiplied during his four years in office, some observers began to wonder if there was really any "there" there and whether Bush-Speak, in the last analysis, represents absence, rather than confusion, of thought. Conservative writer Michael Novak bemoaned the lack of gravitas in the president's outlook. And George Will was convinced that the president was "on the losing side of a monologue with himself." Wrote the *Washington Post* columnist in January 1992: "Because Bush on the stump expresses synthetic sentiments in garbled syntax, Americans often wonder what he means. The answer may be that he doesn't mean very much."

Texas Observer, September 18, 1992.

CHAPTER 23

Presidential Wives:
The Quest for Identity

The history of the status of the presidents' wives in the White House is fascinating, and I prepared a lecture on the subject based on the information I gathered when working on *Presidential Wives* (1988). Some wives, like Eleanor Roosevelt, were concerned about their "identity" in the White House, and other wives took it in their stride. There were "invisible wives," I found, but also hostesses, fashion leaders, partners, and finally activists like Mrs. Roosevelt who worked busily with their husbands, both in private and public. As they achieved a higher status in American society during the twentieth century, their positions in the White House gained in importance. When Lyndon Johnson became president in 1963, his wife worked actively with him as Eleanor Roosevelt had with FDR. On his inauguration in 1965, LBJ saw to it that Lady Bird held the Bible for him as he took his oath, and that she danced with him at the inaugural balls. She was the first president's wife to do these things, and her successors all followed in her footsteps.

★ ★ ★

"The tender breasts of the ladies," Thomas Jefferson once declared, "were not formed for political convulsions." And he carefully brought up his two daughters in the women's sphere of activity. So did most Americans in Jefferson's day. There were two spheres of activity, according to convention, when the American republic was founded. The woman's sphere centered on the home; she was to be a good wife and a good mother. She was also regarded as the moral guardian of the home, for, according to the two-spheres theory, women were morally superior to men. As for the men in the family, their sphere of activity was outside the home. They worked in the great outside world; they were the providers and brought home the bacon. They also served in the professions: law, medicine, and the ministry. Naturally they lived in the world of politics. By and large, it was inconceivable that a woman should either vote or hold office, or even have political opinions worth taking seriously.

The two-spheres theory dominated American thinking from colonial times until the middle of the twentieth century and, in fact, still persists in certain circles. From the beginning, most of our early presidents' wives kept very low profiles. They rarely appeared in public and almost never made public pronouncements. Unless they wrote letters or kept diaries, it is difficult to find out much about them. They were practically anonymous and came close to being "invisible women."

Jane Pierce, wife of Franklin Pierce, who became president in 1853, was surely an "invisible woman." She almost never appeared in public. Right after her husband's inauguration, she moved into the living quarters of the President's House, and practically disappeared. She almost never went downstairs to appear at her husband's official dinners and receptions. People called her "the shadow in the White House"; she was surely one of the most invisible of all the presidents' wives.

Not all the early presidents' wives were as invisible as Mrs. Pierce. Some of them became known as good hostesses for the president, and, according to the two-spheres theory, it was a permissable part of a woman's activities. The very first woman to become a hostess for her husband in the President's House was Martha Washington, the likable first presidential wife. George Washington's wife received high praise for her amiability as hostess for official functions at the President's House, as it used to be called. Both George and Martha Washington were keenly aware of the fact that they were the first couple to occupy the President's House and would inevitably set precedents for their successors, so they took their behavior seriously.

Washington himself was known for his quiet reserve. For many people he was awe-inspiring because of his accomplishments, and they felt tongue-tied in his presence. With Martha by his side, however, things relaxed considerably, for she was good-natured, folksy, and down-to-earth, and people felt comfortable when she was around. She received a great deal of praise for her behavior as the president's wife. Usually, at evening receptions, she got up after a couple of hours and announced, "The general always retires at nine o'clock, and I usually precede him." It was a polite signal for the guests to depart.

Even more famous as a hostess in the President's House was Dolley Madison, James Madison's charming wife. Dolley was hostess for sixteen years. The third president, Thomas Jefferson, was a widower when he became president in 1801, so he asked Dolley, whose husband was his secretary of state, to help him as a hostess during his two terms as president, and then, when her husband succeeded Jefferson as chief executive in 1809, she continued her hostessing for eight more years. She soon became the most famous hostess in Washington and gradually won national fame.

Dolley did better than Mrs. Washington as a hostess for Madison. She charmed all the leading politicians of the day when her husband was entertaining them. But Dolley was not a "feminist"; she fully accepted the two-spheres theory and carefully refrained from talking politics with her husband's visitors. She loyally supported his policies, bristled in private over attacks on him by his political enemies, but refrained from talking politics. Political matters, she once said, are "always imperfectly understood by her sex." Yet she was able to carry on pleasant conversations with the leading politicians of the day—Daniel Webster, Henry Clay—and even got the lugubrious John C. Calhoun to smile, even laugh.

As the president's wife, Dolley did even more for her husband that was clearly permissible under the two-spheres rulings. She began emphasizing American cooking for the presidential dinners, soliciting recipes from women around the country so she could try out new dishes from time to time. At the same time she developed into a fashion leader for women in the United States, and even for women in Europe. She loved to try out new styles in dresses, hats, and shoes, and before long women everywhere were following her example. It got so that if Dolley discarded wigs, or wore a train in public, or put on emeralds, or acquired a parrot, or revealed a cleavage, or emphasized a certain color, other women did the same. She also made the Dolley Madison hat famous. It consisted of silk cloth coiled upward to look like a Turkish headdress, and it became the fashion for a time in Europe as well as in the United States. Sometimes she topped her turban with ostrich feathers towering to the ceiling.

What is surprising about Dolley as a fashion plate is that she had a Quaker background. Her parents were devout Quakers, and they brought her up to emphasize plain and simple living. But she had a grandmother who was an Episcopalian and taught her to like fine food and fine fabric. She was a likable hostess like Mrs. Washington but also a friendly "fashionista" without straying from the woman's sphere or, presumably, wanting to stray.

Far more common, however, were the partners—the presidents' wives who, within the privacy of the family, tried to help their husbands in their work. The women who became partners were seriously interested in politics and public issues. They discussed political problems with their husbands, talked over the appointments he had to make in the federal government, and sometimes went over speeches with him. As a partner, she was clearly intruding into the man's sphere of activity, but got away with it because it was done in the privacy of the family, and the public was not aware of it.

The first serious partnership came early, with John Adams, the second president, and his lively wife, Abigail Adams. Abigail had an intense interest in public affairs, strong opinions about many of the leading issues of the day, and she didn't hesitate to let her husband know what she thought about problems he dealt with. But John Adams didn't mind it a bit; in fact, he welcomed her advice and accepted her as an intellectual equal. He didn't always agree with her, but that didn't matter. He enjoyed talking over political issues with her. But Abigail was still bound by the woman's sphere; she never dreamed of going public. She carefully avoided public statements; her dabbling in politics was kept to her husband and herself. In the privacy of the home, she and John were real partners. For the rest, she was shocked and angered when someone at a local meeting quoted her in a political speech one evening.

There were other partners, although invisible to the public, such as James and Sarah Polk, Woodrow and Edith Wilson, and Harry and Bess Truman. The Trumans, though, are of special interest because Bess wanted to stay out of the limelight when she entered the White House, even though her immediate predecessor, Eleanor Roosevelt, had abandoned the two-spheres conventionalities and gone public. But though Mrs. Truman wanted to protect her privacy as much as she could, she also insisted on being Harry's partner without letting the public know. Mrs. Roosevelt was the first president's wife to give interviews, for women reporters first, and then for male interrogators, and they all expected Mrs. Truman to talk to them too. At first, Bess agreed to see them, and then cancelled the appointment. The reporters pled with her to reschedule the interview, but she absolutely refused to do so. Finally they asked her if she would answer some questions in writing, and when she reluctantly agreed to do so, they drew up a list of twenty-five questions and submitted them to her. Mrs. Truman answered all the questions in writing, but only briefly. Some of the answers were simply, "No comment."

Mrs. Truman didn't seem to enjoy being in the White House; she called it "the great white jail," and kept as low a profile as she could. She did only the necessary things, presiding as hostess at White House receptions and appearing at dedications and ceremonial meetings. But though she tried hard to be an invisible woman, there was one thing that she insisted on: being her husband's partner in his presidential activities. There was nothing new about it. From the very beginning of Truman's entry into politics, he had been in the habit of discussing his work with her at the end of each day. It became an essential part of his daily routine, and Mrs. Truman came to accept it as a natural part of the family relations. We don't know exactly what they talked about, but years later, Truman said that his wife had been his chief adviser, that he had talked over all his important decisions with her, and that her advice was always good because she kept the welfare of the nation in mind in the advice she gave him.

At one point, however, it looked as though the partnership of Bess and Harry was going to fall apart. When Franklin Roosevelt died in April 1945, Truman suddenly found that he was president of the United States at a momentous period in American history. The war in Europe was winding down, the war with Japan was nearing an end, and the United States was about to enter the difficult postwar period. Truman was overwhelmed by the tremendous responsibilities suddenly thrust upon him when FDR passed away. As he told reporters after becoming president, he felt as if the moon, planets, and stars had all fallen on him after his swearing in. He became so immersed in the manifold problems facing him as president that he began to neglect his wife. The daily conversations about his work at the end of the day came to an end. It looked as though the close partnership was being abandoned. We know this is so because in his letters to Bess, when he was away from Washington, a note of apology begins creeping in.

In July 1945, a couple of months after he became president, Truman flew to Potsdam, Germany, for a Big Three conference with England's Winston Churchhill and the Soviet Union's Josef Stalin. He phoned and wrote his wife every day, and in his letters he kept reminding her how overwhelmed with work he was. When he returned to Washington after the Potsdam conference ended, his neglect continued until the end of the year. Just before Christmas, 1945, Mrs. Truman flew out to Independence, Missouri, their home, with daughter Margaret, to spend the holidays there. A couple of days later, Truman flew out to join his wife and daughter, and then came what may be called the "great confrontation." There's no way we can know exactly what Bess told Harry, but it is clear that she read him the riot act for having neglected her so much after they moved into the White House. Truman flew back to Washington the next day, boiling mad at the way she had treated him, and one of the first things he did on his return was to sit down and write her a letter filled with resentment and anger at the way she had blasted him, and then mailed it, special delivery, to Independence.

Not long after Truman sent his wife the letter, he calmed down, had second thoughts, got on the phone, called Margaret, told her about the letter to her mother, and asked her to go to the post office, pick it up when it arrived, and burn it at once. Margaret did as he requested, and we'll never know what he told Bess. But he wrote another letter, which has survived, explaining that as "leader of the free world," a position he never wanted, his responsibilities were tremendous and kept him enormously busy most of the time. Still, he reminded her that her opinions were more important to him than anything else in the world, and that he had always put her on a pedestal and still did. This letter seems to have healed the breach, and before long he was taking his wife into his confidence again. After that, apparently, the Trumans lived happily ever after.

Mrs. Truman was a quiet partner. But in addition to invisible women, hostesses, fashion leaders, and family partners, there were also activists, that is, presidential wives who took an active role in political matters, both privately and in public. Florence Harding went public several times when her husband, Warren, became president in 1921, but it was Eleanor Roosevelt who broke the old rules and became a busy partner of her husband, Franklin, during his twelve years as chief executive, from 1933 to 1945. Mrs. Roosevelt was a kind of turning point in the history of presidential wives in America. After Mrs. Roosevelt, the role of the president's wife became important in a way it had never been before.

Eleanor Roosevelt was in no way a born activist. For years, in fact, she accepted the two-spheres view of things and believed that her main function as a woman was to concentrate on being a devoted wife and mother. She had narrow social sympathies as a young woman and little interest in politics, even after FDR became a member of the New York legislature. In 1921, however, when FDR contracted polio at the age of thirty-nine, life changed drastically for him and Eleanor. Roosevelt worked hard to recover the use of his limbs, but he was permanently crippled and never able to walk again without the use of braces and canes. His mother wanted him to retire from political life and settle down as a country squire at Hyde Park, but he didn't want to do that. He was anxious to continue his career in politics, despite his handicap. There was, of course, only one way he could resume his political activities: he needed the help of his wife. Before long, Eleanor, once apolitical, began boning up on politics. She became active in the League of Women Voters and joined the women's division of the Democratic Party. She also started mingling with professional politicians and learning things about the working of the American political system She even learned to speak in public. It was a terrible ordeal for her at first, for she was a rather shy woman, and her first public speeches were hesitant and awkward. Sometimes she even started giggling in the middle of a speech. But FDR's friend, Louis Howe, gave her good coaching, and gradually she developed into a pleasant speaker in public.

During the 1920s, people in New York began talking about the "Franklin and Eleanor team"; they had become known as close partners in public and private. When Roosevelt became governor of New

York in 1928, Eleanor was a major help to him. She became his "eyes and ears" when he needed it. Since it was difficult for him to travel around the state, she did the traveling for him. She visited hospitals, prisons, schools, and other state institutions and prepared reports for him to read about conditions in those places. Roosevelt always showered her with shrewd questions when she returned from her inspection tours, and she learned to keep a sharp eye for details when studying state institutions for him.

In the 1920s, though, Eleanor did more than serve as her husband's partner. She began to strike off on paths of her own. She became a teacher and did some part-time teaching. She also began writing articles for newspapers and magazines and found she enjoyed writing very much. She also began associating with other journalists and derived a great deal of satisfaction from being accepted as one of them. In other words, in addition to being her husband's partner, she had become a woman with a career of her own in the field of journalism. She was very proud of this. Right after Roosevelt was elected president in 1932, Eleanor's friends found her at one point weeping in the corner. They were astonished. Why was she weeping? She should have been celebrating her husband's victory, they told her, but she explained the tears. She was afraid that when she entered the White House, she would have to give up her work as a journalist and, as she put it, "lose her sense of identity."

But Eleanor never did lose her identity. After entering the White House, she continued writing for newspapers and magazines and even expanded her outlets. She wrote a monthly column for the *Ladies Home Journal*, acquired a daily column in the newspapers called "My Day," and in 1937 she published her autobiography, *The Story of My Life*, which was warmly received. Still, she continued to be her husband's hardworking partner. She participated in discussions of New Deal legislation and even came up with ideas of her own. Sometimes FDR accepted her suggestions, and sometimes he didn't. He liked to use her as a sounding board by trying out new ideas on her. She also became FDR's conscience when it came to people in trouble. If there were people she thought needed help, she brought their plight to the attention of FDR, and she also did what she could to advance the civil rights of black Americans. Frequently, too, she introduced her husband to experts in various fields with whom she thought it would be good for him to meet and discuss ideas. There were times when a person who sought an appointment with the president, but failed to get one because he was too busy, would approach Mrs. Roosevelt and then turn up as a dinner guest guest at the White House.

Roosevelt was amused by his wife's crafty ways, and he took them in good humor. For her part, she tried to be a good hostess and continued to travel around the country—and world—on behalf of her husband. Her gallivanting around produced many jokes about her. She was liable to turn up anywhere—in a West Virginia coal mine, a hillbilly cabin in Kentucky, and in an urban slum in a big city. Once, Texas Congressman Maury Maverick asked her to visit a prison in Baltimore that was experimenting with a program in which prisoners produced war goods. Mrs. Roosevelt accepted the invitation and the next day got up early and headed for Maryland. A little later President Roosevelt got up and found his wife gone. "Where's Mrs. Roosevelt?" he asked her secretary. "She's in prison," said the Secretary. "Well, I'm not surprised," laughed Roosevelt, "but, why?"

After Mrs. Roosevelt, things were never the same for the presidents' wives. Bess Truman, it is true, tried to return to the old ways and keep out of the public eye as much as she could. But even she felt obliged to accompany her husband on campaign trips in 1948 when he ran for president. His chances of beating Thomas Dewey, the Republican candidate, did not seem good, and his wife and daughter accompanied him on a barnstorming train trip across the country. On the trip Truman made five major speeches in the big cities, but also arranged for his train to stop at little towns en route, where he came out on the rear platform of the train to speak for a few minutes, blasting Wall Street and the right-wingers. When he finished with big ovations, he lifted his hand and cried, "How'd you like to meet the boss?" and brought Mrs. Truman out on the platform. The crowds cheered, and then he cried, "How'd you like to meet the boss's boss?" and brought Margaret out. Neither his wife nor daughter enjoyed the routine very much, but the crowds gathered on the tracks loved it, and no doubt it contributed to the surprise victory in November.

Truman's cross-country campaign set a precedent. In 1952, when Dwight D. Eisenhower was running for president against the Democratic candidate Adlai Stevenson, he scheduled a trip by train across the continent, stopping at both major cities and little towns the way Truman had done. Like Truman, Eisenhower spoke a few minutes to the crowds gathered around the tracks and then exclaimed, "How'd you like to meet Mamie?" Then, as the crowd cheered, Eisenhower's wife, bangs and all, came out with a friendly smile to greet the people. Mamie thoroughly enjoyed the act, but if she and Ike had had a little quarrel beforehand, he would say, "How would you like to meet Mrs. Eisenhower?"

Mamie Eisenhower's successor, Jackie Kennedy, took the traditional view of women's role in society when she married John F. Kennedy in 1953, a few months after he became a US senator. Though her interests lay in the arts, not in history and politics, she tried hard to be a good political wife. "The more I hear Jack talk about such intricate and vast problems," she said, "the more I feel like a complete moron." Kennedy was aware of her lack of interest in the political world. "Jackie is superb in her personal life," he once remarked. "But do you think she'll ever amount to anything in her political life?"

In 1960, however, when Kennedy announced his candidacy for the Democratic nomination for president, she offered to help in the campaign. Kennedy was dubious; he thought she was too aristocratic for the average voter. He said she had "too much status" and "not enough quo." The American people, he told her, just aren't ready for someone like you. "Guess we'll just have to run you through subliminally, in one of those quick flash TV spots so no one will notice." She was reduced to tears. But she was determined to become a good campaign wife, and she was soon surprising her husband by the way she took to campaigning. Her first public appearances by his side in 1960 were enormously successful. People loved to see her in public. It got so that sometimes Kennedy told friends, "As usual, Jackie's drawing more people than we are."

Jackie not only appeared by her husband's side on campaign trips; she even made a few speeches for him on her own. And when he won the 1960 election over Richard Nixon and she entred the White House, she turned out to be a major asset to him, particularly when they travelled abroad. She became a popular White House hostess; she also became a fashion leader, and the so-called "Jackie look" became popular for a time. On Inauguration Day, January 21, 1961, she wore a pillbox hat that had been especially designed for her. It was very windy that day, so when she stepped out of the presidential limousine, she put her hand up to the pillbox to keep it from flying away. But she put a slight dent in the hat, and the dent appeared in pictures for the newspapers. Soon after, American women started putting dents in their pillboxes, and designers even started producing them that way.

Mrs. Kennedy developed a special project soon after she entered the White House. She found the White House dingy and uninteresting and decided to have it renovated and furnished along historical lines. Once the White House was renovated the way she had arranged, she appeared on a television program making a tour of the place and pointing out its new design. As well as in the United States, Mrs. Kennedy attracted people abroad, particularly in France, where she impressed General DeGaulle by her skill in speaking French.

After Mrs. Kennedy, the trend among presidential wives was toward more activism. Like Jackie, Lady Bird Johnson had a special project—the beautification of the highways—and before long Congress passed a beautification law that was called the "Lady Bird Law." And so it went: Pat Nixon took up "volunteerism" as her project, Betty Ford concentrated on women's rights, and Rosalynn Carter emphasized mental health care as well as women's rights. Nancy Reagan decided not to bother with a special project when her husband became president in 1981, but the pressure to do something became so strong that she finally picked the crusade against drugs ("Just say no") as her speciality. And so it went: Barbara Bush's major interest was literacy, Hillary Clinton was interested in health reform and children's education, Laura Bush sponsored literary evenings in the White House, and Michelle Obama formed an organization to fight obesity by seeing to it that children ate healthier food.

No doubt Thomas Jefferson and the Founding Fathers (and their wives) would have been shocked by the idea of a president's wife bouncing out of the president's house whenever she wanted to take a trip, here and abroad. But today, the American public, men and women, are intensely curious about the woman who moves into the White House with her husband. They expect her to give interviews, make speeches, and take part in her husband's campaigns. They also want her to choose some special activity to spend time on, as well as to help, but not dominate, her husband in his work. One can't help wondering what would happen if a woman became president one day. Would her husband have a special project? And would he be called the "First Laddie"?

CHAPTER 24

The American Presidents and Shakespeare

On April 23, 1932, Shakespeare-lovers from around the country flocked up to Washington, DC, to attend the dedication of the handsome new Folger Shakespeare Library, with President Herbert Hoover and the First Lady Lou Henry Hoover sitting on a platform watching the ceremony. The main speaker was John Quincy Adams Jr., a descendant of Presidents John and John Quincy Adams who taught English literature at Cornell University and adored William Shakespeare. Professor Adams announced that with the new Folger Library, the capital city now had three great memorials that "stand out, in size, dignity and beauty, conspicuous above the rest: the memorials to Washington, Lincoln, and Shakespeare." He went on to point out that for the American people, the "great English dramatist" had become, through the years, "the supreme thinker, artist, poet. Not Homer, not Dante, not Goethe, not Chaucer, not Spencer, not even Milton, but Shakespeare was made the chief object of their study and veneration."

Professor Adams knew his history. Beginning in the late eighteenth century, when England's Shakespeare performers began coming to the United States to make the rounds, citizens of the new republic gradually became ardent fans of the great playwright, and some Americans came close to making him an honorary citizen. In the nineteenth century they quoted him in letters, read his plays aloud, and turned out in large numbers, even in the newly settled West, whenever presentations of his plays were available. Many a household owned just two books: the Bible and Shakespeare. Some Americans, still fiercely anti-British after the American Revolution and War of 1812, thought that the way Americans spoke English was closer to Shakespeare's language than the way the snobbish British spoke. The American people, according to the Shakespeare scholar Lawrence Levine, "were able to fit Shakespeare into their culture so easily because he seemed to fit it—because so many of his values and tastes were, or at least appeared to be, close to their own."

Some of America's presidents were enchanted by Shakespeare, too. George Washington had a collection of the Great Bard's plays in his library at Mount Vernon, and he attended at least two of the plays when he was in New York and Philadelphia. His successors varied widely in their interest. Some—James Madison, James Monroe, Andrew Jackson, Ulysses S. Grant, Warren G. Harding—seem to have had little or no interest in Shakespeare. Others—Rutherford B. Hays, Woodrow Wilson, John F. Kennedy— read and studied him in school and college, and as adults attended his plays from time to time without becoming passionate devotees. James A. Garfield took Shakespeare more seriously. He called him "the great William" and took his children to see the plays after reading Charles and Mary Lamb's *Tales from Shakespeare* to them. Bill Clinton liked to quote a passage from *Macbeth* that he memorized as a boy because as an adult the words were "still full of power for me." And George W. Bush, it was reported, "did three Shakespeares" one summer when he was president.

Theodore Roosevelt was a singularity. He began his career by dismissing Shakespeare's plays as crude and vulgar, and then, in 1909, when he was on a safari in Africa after leaving the White House, he began dipping into a Shakespeare collection he took along with him and, almost to his own surprise, was soon swept into the Shakespeare orbit. "You will be both amused to hear at last, when at fifty years old, I have come into my inheritance in Shakespeare," he wrote Henry Cabot Lodge and his wife. "I have never before really cared for more than one or two of his plays; but for some inexplicable reason the sealed book was suddenly opened to me on this trip. I still balk at three or four of Shakespeare's plays; but most of them I have read or am reading over and over again."

Four Presidents—John Adams, Thomas Jefferson, John Quincy Adams, and Abraham Lincoln—may be called Shakespeare-lovers. Unlike Theodore Roosevelt, they were drawn to his plays when they were young and remained ensorcelled the rest of their lives. They read and reread Shakespeare with mounting appreciation and went out of their way to attend productions of his plays time and again. More than that, they looked to him not only for good stories, fascinating characters, and a wonderful literary style, but also for insights into social behavior, political institutions, varied customs, and the meaning of life itself. John Adams called Shakespeare "the great master of nature" and the "great teacher of morality and politics," pronouncing him "that great

Master of every Affection of the Heart and every Sentiment of the Mind as well as of all the Powers of Expression." In one of Adams's writings, he quoted at length passages from one of Shakespeare's plays that he found less striking than usual, but, he explained, "The style in those quotations from Shakspeare [*sic*] has little of that fluency, and less of that purity which sometimes appears in his writings, but the sense is as immortal as human nature." For John Adams, Shakespeare was almost never lacking in substance and style.

John Adams's search for wisdom in the Great Bard began early. "Let me search for the Clue, which Led great Shakespeare into the Labyrinth of mental nature!" he wrote in his diary during December 1758. "Let me examine how men think. Shakespeare had never seen in real Life Persons under the Influence of all those Scenes of Pleasure and distress, which he has described in his Works, but he imagined how a Person of such a Character would behave in such Circumstances, by analogy from the Behaviour of others that were most like that Character in nearly similar Circumstances, which he had seen."

Shakespeare helped Adams out on one occasion when he was an undergraduate at Harvard. Somewhat shy as a student, he was surprised and pleased to be invited to join the Harvard Discussion Club when he was a junior and instructed, as a kind of initiation, to read Oedipus's speech from Alexander Pope's translation of *Thebais* (the Thebes) to the club members. Young Adams practiced furiously, pacing the floor as he declaimed the speech over and over again, but when the time came for him to perform before fifty or so students and some faculty members in the college library, he was so nervous that he mangled the words and bungled the gestures, to the great amusement of the audience When he reached the end of Oedipus's speech, he raised his hand high, then lowered it slowly, and pointed it at the students. "Don't shoot, Adams!" yelled one of his classmates. "For God's sake, spare a mother's son!" At that, the students exploded into wild laughter, and Adams rushed frantically out of the room. Afterward, he found the teasing he received extremely humiliating, and he vowed never to be caught in such a trap again.

Several months later young Adams had another chance. This time he did the choosing: a passage from Shakespeare's *Coriolanus* that contained the force, strength, and defiance he thought he needed to get even with his tormentors. He was more sure of himself as he began reading Coriolanus's speech, but when there were some titters in the audience, he lost his temper, slammed the book down, walked to the front, threw back his chest, and began reciting the speech ferociously to his classmates:

Look, sir, my wounds!
I got them in my country's service, when,
Some certain of your brethren roar'd and ran
From the noise of our own drums.

He increased his intensity:

You common cry of curs! whose breath I hate
As reed o' the rotten fens . . .
For you, the city, thus I turn my back:
There is a world elsewhere.

At that point Adams stood staring sternly at his audience for a moment,
and then walked to his seat. To his astonishment, the students began
clapping, pounding their shoes, and tossing compliments at the day's
orator. "Adams!" they cried, "You'll make the best orator of us all."
Remarked one student at the end of this meeting: "Coriolanus angry is
surely better than Oedipus scared."

In his college years Adams mastered the ancient classics and the
best writers of his day, and he came to love John Milton's poetry. For
understanding human nature, however, he put Shakespeare first. Adams
was forever referring to Shakespeare or quoting lines and passages from
the plays in his diary, letters, and chats with friends. In his journal he
once observed that a fellow who got drunk at a party he attended had
"railed and foamed" in "as wild mad a manner as King Lear." In a
letter he mentioned a woman friend who reminded him of Shakespeare's
"Patience on a monument, / Smiling at grief." There was a scene in
Henry VIII that he liked and thought it "may be very properly recommended to modern Monarks, Queens, and Favourites." When a question came up at a town meeting, he remarked that it was raised for the
first time "since Wm. The Conquerer, nay, since the Days of King Lear."
Of a woman he knew whose husband abused her, he declared, "Bela
really acts the Part of the Tamer of the Shrew in Shakespeare." One of
Adams's favorite quotations was: "If I would but go to hell for an eternal moment or so, I could be knighted." Another favorite was:

Take but degree away, untune that string
And hark, what discord follows! Each thing meets
In mere oppugnancy . . .
Then everything includes itself in power,
Power into will, will into appetite,
And appetite an universal wolf.

Each of these quotations, he was convinced, contained a deep understanding of social and ethical matters.

In a series of articles Adams wrote for the *Gazette of the United States* in 1790 and 1791, later published as *Discourses on Davila* (1805), he used a translation of the Italian historian Enrico Caterino Davila's history of the French civil wars in the sixteenth century, published in 1650, as a springboard for setting forth some of his own views on social and political institutions. To emphasize his ideas, he quoted seventy lines from *Troilus and Cressida*, in which Ulysses talks about the importance of "degree," or status, in human societies. In rejecting equality, Adams also stressed the need for a strong executive to avoid the anarchy he thought unbridled democracy was likely to produce. Adams's views upset his friend Thomas Jefferson and his republican followers; they thought he was leaning dangerously toward monarchism. He was not, of course, but he did think that his—and Shakespeare's— view of human behavior was more realistic than that of the Jeffersonian Republicans.

Adams and Jefferson drifted apart for a time after *Davila* and especially after Jefferson's triumph over Adams in the presidential election of 1800. But they had once been close friends, and they had long agreed on their respect and admiration for Shakespeare (and, years later, they famously renewed their friendship). In April 1786, before *Davila*, when the two men were in London, they had gone on a sightseeing trip to Shakespeare's Stratford-upon-Avon. Adams was deeply moved by the visit and wrote in detail about it afterward. "Stratford upon Avon is interesting as it is the scene of the Birth, Death and Sepulcher of Shakspeare [*sic*]," he began. Then came disappointment! "Three Doors from the Inn, is the House where he was born, as small and mean, as you can conceive. They shew Us an old Wooden Chair in the Chimney Corner where He sat. We cut off a Chip according to the Custom. A Mulberry Tree that he planted has been cutt down, and is carefully preserved for Sale. The house where he died has been taken down and the Spot is now only Yard or Garden." Adam's disgust mounted. "The curse upon him who should remove his Bones, which is written on his Grave Stone, alludes to a Pile of some Thousands of human Bones, which lie exposed in that Church." It got worse. "There is nothing preserved of this great Genius which is worth knowing—nothing which might inform Us what Education, what Company, what Accident turned his Mind to Letters and the Drama. His name is not even on his Grave Stone. An ill sculptured Head is sett up by his Wife, by the Side of his Grave in the Church. But painting and Sculpture would be thrown away upon his Fame. His wit, and Fancy, his Taste and Judgment, His Knowledge of Nature, of Life and Character, are immortal." Adams was thoroughly upset, even angered, by the tawdry tribute the British paid to the writer he admired so much.

Jefferson surely shared Adams's disgust. Still, the entry he made in his record of the sightseeing trip was about the fees he paid: "for seeing house where Shakespeare was born, 1 shilling; seeing his tomb, 1 shilling; entertainment, 4 shillings, 2 pence; servants, 2 shilling." Yet he owned more copies of Shakespeare's plays than Adams did, as well as four different commentaries on the plays, and he also sought to acquire pictures and busts of his hero. In Shakespeare, Jefferson insisted, there are "new sublimities which we had not tasted before." Years later, when he was president, he told John Bernard, the famous British actor, that Shakespeare, as well as Alexander Pope, "gave him the perfection of imagination and judgment, both displaying more knowledge of the human heart—the true province of poetry—than he could find elsewhere."

Like Adams, Jefferson came to Shakespeare early. As a boy, he delved into the plays in his father's library, and as a college student he headed for the playhouse in Williamsburg to see Shakespeare's plays and plays by others as often as he could. In 1760, when he was fifteen, he began writing his literary commonplace book, filling it with quotations from Shakespeare and other favorites. An early entry, from *Julius Caesar*, seemed to display a bit of rebellion against his mother's rule after his father's death: "Do not presume too much upon my love; / I may do that I shall be sorry for."

A gifted violinist, Jefferson also copied a passage from Shakespeare about music into his commonplace book:

The man who has not Music in Soul
Or is not touch'd with Concord of sweet Sounds,
Is fit for Treasons, Strategems and Spoils,
The Motions of his Mind are dull as Night,
And his Affections dark as Erebus:
Let no such Man be trusted.

Jefferson also liked political passages from plays such as *Henry IV*, *Coriolanus*, and *Troilus and Cressida*, and the comments on cowardice from *Julius Caesar*: "Cowards die many times before their deaths; / The valiant never taste of death but once."

After Jefferson became a lawyer, he could not resist mentioning Shakespeare in his legal writing. In a case involving the gradual transformation of seven units of land into nearly seventeen, he enjoyed himself by comparing it to Falstaff's mischievous exchange with Prince Hal in *Henry IV, Part 1*, during which the two rogues whom he proudly boasted he had bested became four, then seven, and then eleven.

Jefferson once said he could not live without books, and Shakespeare's plays were certainly among the indispensables. The reading schedule he once recommended was heavy: "From twelve to one read politics. . . . In the afternoon read history. . . . From dark to bedtime: belles lettres, criticism, rhetoric, oratory. . . . Read the best of the poems. . . . But among these Shakespeare must be singled out by one who wishes to learn the full powers of the English language." For Jefferson, reading Shakespeare not only helped form one's "style and taste"; it also produced insights into the English language itself.

Language fascinated Jefferson; he was something of a linguist. In his essay "Thoughts on English Prosody," he quoted at length from Shakespeare to show where he put the accent on words when giving a speech. But he was even more interested in the sources of the English language. He thought that if people knew something about the development of the language, they would appreciate Shakespeare's genius all the more. "We shall then read Shakespeare," he wrote, "with a superior degree of intelligence and delight, heightened by the new and delicate shades of meaning developed to us by a knowledge of the original sense of the same words." It was Jefferson's belief that research into the various country dialects spoken in England would reveal the development of the English language in all its richness. "When these local vocabularies are published and digested into one single one, it is probable we shall find that there is not a word in Shakespeare which is not now in use in some of the counties of England, from which we may obtain its true sense."

Like Adams, however, Jefferson was more struck by the moral truths he found in Shakespeare's plays than by their linguistic skill. These plays, he was convinced, like all the great works of fiction, help "fix us in the principles and practices of virtue" and in "an abhorrence" of vice. "I appeal to every reader of feeling and sentiment whether the fictitious murther of Duncan by Macbeth does not excite in him as great a horror of villainy, as the real one of Henry IV [of France] by Ravaillac as related by Davila." In the same way, "a lively and lasting sense of filial duty is more effectually impressed on the mind of a son or daughter by reading *King Lear*, than by all the dry volumes of ethics and divinity that ever were written."

John Adams shared Jefferson's view that reading Shakespeare sharpened one's moral sense. So did his son, John Quincy Adams, who met and admired Jefferson when he was in London as a youngster and was already deep into Shakespeare's plays at the time. When he was only ten, the younger Adams had already discovered the Shakespeare collections in his mother's bedroom closet and devoured *Much Ado about Nothing, The Tempest, As You Like It, The Merry Wives of Windsor,* and *King Lear*. "The humors of Falstaff scarcely affected me at all," he recalled, "but the incantations of Prospero, the loves of Ferdinand and Miranda, the more than ethereal brightness of Ariel, and the worse than beastly grossness of Caliban, made for me a world of revels, and lapped me in Elysium." Adams soon came to appreciate Shakespeare's clowns, too, and his youthful attraction to Shakespeare developed into deep appreciation as an adult. "My admiration for Shakespeare as a profound delineator of human nature and a sublime poet," he once wrote, "is but little short of idolatry."

As an undergraduate at Harvard, John Quincy Adams joined an informal club of about ten students who met every Saturday night to drink wine, exchange witticisms, and toss nicknames at each other, many of them coming from Shakespeare. Since he planned to become a lawyer, he decided, as his father had done, to get some practice in public speaking, since he really was not very good at it. As a junior, he got to recite Shakespeare's famous "All the world's a stage" passage one night before all the students in the college chapel. When he described the learned justice in the play "with fair round belly," everyone laughed because he was a bit plump himself. By the time he graduated John Quincy Adams had written and delivered seventeen orations, before various student organizations, that the students apparently liked. One of them dealt with *Othello*, his first venture into a Shakespeare critique.

When John Quincy Adams decided to talk about *Othello*, he must have known that his mother, Abigail Adams, disliked the play. Mrs. Adams was as warm an admirer of Shakespeare as her husband and son were, but when she saw the great English actress Sarah Siddons play Desdemona in a production of *Othello* in London in 1786, she had mixed feelings. As Desdemona, she found Siddons "as interesting beyond any actress I have ever seen," but to see her in the arms of *Othello*, a black man, came as a shock. *Othello*, played by John Kemble, in blackface, "was represented blacker than any African," she wrote afterward, and whether it was from "the prejudices of education" or from a "natural antipathy" to blacks, "my whole soul shuddered whenever I saw the sooty heretic Moor touch the fair Desdemona." *Othello* was "manly, generous, noble" in character, she admitted, but his color put her off. Her husband, who saw the play with her, was impressed by her "horror and disgust" every time the "sooty" actor touched Desdemona, even though she knew they were acting in a play. Mrs. Adams deeply regretted her feelings; she reminded herself that there was "something estimable" in every human being. The "liberal mind," she reminded herself, "regards not what nation or climate it springs up in, not what *color* or *complexion* the man is."

Years later, when Mrs. Adams's son gave his speech about *Othello* at a meeting of one of the student organizations at Harvard, he pointed out that the play was regarded as "the most perfect of all, that we owe to the immortal Shakespeare," and that "if we attended merely to the conduct of it, we may readily confess that few dramatic performances are better." Still, he went on to announce grimly that "the very foundation upon which the whole fabric is erected" was "injudicious, disgusting, and contrary to all probability." Like his mother, he simply could not believe that "a young woman so virtuous and Chaste as Desdemona" would, in Shakespeare's words, "Run from her gaurdage to the sooty bosom" of a Negro. John Quincy Adams praised the parts of the play he liked, but he seemed to think that the play's human improbabilities destroyed the pleasure one usually derived from Shakespeare's plays.

John Quincy Adams felt so strongly about *Othello*'s shortcomings that years later he published an article in the *New England Magazine* (1835) in which he expanded on his dislike for the play. Who can sympathize with Desdemona, the daughter of a Venetian nobleman, he wanted to know, who "falls in love and makes a runaway match with a blackamoor for no better reason than that he has told her a braggart story of his hair-breadth escapes in war. For this, she not only violates her duties to her father, her family, her sex, and her country, but she makes the first advance. . . . The blood must circulate briskly in the veins of a young woman, so fascinated, and so coming to the tale of a rude, unbleached African soldier."

For John Quincy Adams, the "great moral lesson" of *Othello* was that "black and white blood cannot be intermingled in marriage without a gross outrage upon the laws of Nature." On the stage, he wrote, Desdemona's "fondling" with Othello "is disgusting." The way she behaves is so repelling, he concluded, "that when Othello smothers her in bed, the terror and the pity subside immediately into the sentiment that she has her deserts." A few years later, when the British actress Fanny Kemble met Adams on her first trip to Boston, she recalled that he began "talking to me about Desdemona" and "assured me, with a most serious expression of sincere disgust, that he considered all her misfortunes as a very just judgment upon her for having married a 'nigger.'" Kemble was deeply offended by Adams's language. She told a friend that if some anti-abolitionist Americans produced the play, they might well change Iago's first soliloquy, "I hate the Moor!" to "I hate the nigger!"

John Quincy Adams contributed significantly to the antislavery cause in America when he served in Congress after leaving the White House, and, in 1841, he won freedom for slave mutineers aboard the Spanish ship *Amistad* in a case he argued before the US Supreme Court. Still, he remained proud of his piece on *Othello*. When the actor, James H. Hackett, with whom he exchanged letters about *Hamlet*, wrote to say he had heard about Adams's article on *Othello* and wanted to know whether he could procure it, John Quincy Adams happily decided that this "extension of my fame is more tickling to my vanity than it was to be elected President of the United States."

Othello was not the only the play that Adams disliked. He also had little liking for *King Lear*. The "old king," he complained, was "nothing less than a dotard." The "dotage of an absolute monarch may be a suitable subject of tragedy," he conceded, "and Shakespeare made a deep tragedy of it. But, as exhibited on the stage, it is turned into a comedy." He also complained that producers of *Romeo and Juliet* got into the habit of raising Juliet's age, fourteen in the play, to nineteen on the stage, thus spoiling Shakespeare's portrayal of an innocent young girl, accompanied by a nurse, by turning her into a mature young woman who knew her way around. For the rest, though, Adams's love for Shakespeare was mainly unrestrained. Like his father and Jefferson, he was forever quoting him in his diaries, letters, articles, and books, including the earnest *Lectures on Rhetoric and Oratory* (1810).

John Quincy Adams liked the way Coriolanus called Valeria the "moon of Rome," for he thought it conveyed the idea of "extraordinary chastity." He thought the advice given in *The Taming of the Shrew* was excellent: "Talk logic with acquaintance that you have / And practice rhetoric in your common talk." He adored these lines in *Titus Andronicus*: "She is a woman, therefore may be woo'd; / She is a woman, therefore may be won." There were other passages in Shakespeare Adams cited time and again, insisting that no repetition could make these lines "uninteresting." He regarded the passage in *Measure for Measure* commencing "Ay, but to die, and go we know not where" as one of the most thoughtful accounts ever written on how people feel at the end of their lives. As for his chance of becoming president in 1824, he followed what he called "The Macbeth policy": "If chance will have me king, why chance may crown me, / Without my stir."

Hamlet seems to have been Adams's favorite play. He thought it represented "the heart and soul of man in all their perfection and all their frailty." He quoted from it, commented on passages in it, and even published an article, "The Character of Hamlet," explaining his liking for the play in some detail. For Adams, the play focused on the clash between Hamlet's mind and heart, and revealed "every part of the character and conduct" of the young prince. Hamlet "reflects upon life, upon death, upon the nature of man, upon the physical composition of the universe," Adams noted; "he indulges in minute criticism upon the performance of the players; he comments upon a satire in Juvenal; he quibbles with a quibbling grave digger; he commemorates the convivial attractions of an old jovial table companion . . . and philosophized upon the dust of imperial Caesar, metamorphized into the bung of a beer barrel." Adams himself thought that the man's passions and appetites placed him "on a level with herds of the forests," but that "by our reason we participate of the divine nature itself." He adored *Hamlet*'s soliloquy with Guildenstern commencing, "What a piece of work is man!" In short, for John Quincy Adams, *Hamlet* was "the Master Piece of the drama—the Master Piece of Shakespeare—I had almost said the Master Piece of the human mind."

If John Quincy Adams's favorite play was *Hamlet*, Abraham Lincoln's was *Macbeth*, though he liked *Hamlet* and *Othello*, too. The reasons for his choices were the same as those of Adams: the stunning insights into the way people feel, think, and behave. Of all the plays Lincoln read, he turned most often to *Macbeth*; he cherished it.

Unlike the other White House Shakespeareans, Lincoln had a meager education; he spent a few months in a "blab" school, where the pupils recited their lessons aloud. But from almost the beginning, he took to books the way the Adamses and Jefferson did, and as a young man he seemed to be reading all the time, when standing, sitting, and even when walking. He devoured the selections from Shakespeare included in William Scott's *Lessons in Elocution* (1825) and committed them to memory. And in New Salem, Illinois, he befriended Jack Kelso, a friendly fellow "with the soul of a poet," who took him farther down the road to Shakespeare-land. Kelso loved Shakespeare and fishing "above all else," it was said, and Lincoln loved Shakespeare, "but not fishing." Still, the two sat for hours on the bank of the Sangamon River, fishing, quoting Shakespeare, and arguing about the plays.

Later on, when Lincoln was a clerk in a general store in New Salem, he sneaked in some Shakespeare when he was not waiting on customers. And when he became a lawyer and rode the circuit, he usually carried a much-used copy of *Macbeth* with him. He even mentioned Shakespeare in some of his court cases. Defending some minors who had signed a contract they could not pay for, he "slowly got up" in the courtroom, and "in his strange, half-erect attitude and clear, quiet accent began: 'Gentlemen of the Jury, are you willing to allow these boys to begin life with this shame and disgrace attached to their character? The best judge of human character that ever wrote has left these immortal words for all of us to ponder.'" Then he quoted:

> Good name in man, or woman, dear my lord,
> Is the immediate jewel of their souls.
> Who steals my purse steals trash; 'Tis something, nothing;
> 'Twas mine, 'tis his, and has been slaves for thousands;
> But he that filches from me my good name
> Robs me of that which not enriches him,
> And makes me poor indeed.

Lincoln's first speech in Congress in December 1847 contained Shakespeare, too. He was responding to President James K. Polk's call for a declaration of war. Lincoln spoke for the antiwar congressmen who were convinced that Polk provoked the war himself by sending troops into land belonging to Mexico. In his speech in the House of Representatives, the young congressman from Illinois demanded to know exactly where the "spot" was where Polk said American blood was shed. He posed eight questions about the "spot," and his queries came to be known as the "Spot Resolutions." Lincoln was of course thinking of *Macbeth* when he emphasized the word "spot." In the play, the guilt-ridden Lady *Macbeth* rubs her hands to remove the red traces of her crime and cries out: "Out, damned spot! out, I say! . . . What, will these hands ne'er be clean?"

When Lincoln became president in March 1861, he now had access, for the first time, to theaters in Washington that presented the plays he had come to admire so much, with distinguished performers, British and American, playing the parts he knew so well. If he liked the performance of an actor, he usually invited him to visit the presidential box for a chat and later entertained some actors in the White House. During his presidency he attended more than a hundred plays in Washington, many of them Shakespeare's, sometimes with his wife Mary and son Tad and sometimes with his secretaries. The plays—comedies, histories, tragedies—gave him peace and respite from the stresses and strains of the Civil War presidency. Once, one of his assistants saw him in a Washington theater entranced by the gifted James H. Hackett's performance as Falstaff in *Henry IV*, and he could not help thinking: "He has forgotten the war. He has forgotten Congress. He is out of politics. He is living in Prince Hal's time." Lincoln came to believe that Shakespeare's comedies were best seen on the stage, while reading the tragedies was perhaps even more important than seeing them staged.

Lincoln loved reading Shakespeare to his friends and associates. His secretary John Hay recalled the time the president took him to the Soldiers' Home and "read Shakespeare to me, the end of *Henry VI* and the beginning of *Richard III*, until my heavy eyelids caught his considerate notice and he sent me to bed." During his private entertainments at the White House, Lincoln liked to sit by the fire and read Shakespeare aloud for the guests. Once, at Fort Monroe, he began reading *King John* to one of the officers there, and when he reached the passage where Constance bewails the loss of her child, "his voice trembled," according to the officer, and "he was deeply moved." Putting the book down, he asked the officer, "Did you ever dream of a lost friend and feel that you were having a sweet communion with that friend, and yet a consciousness that it was not a reality?" "Yes," replied the officer. "I think almost anyone may have had such an experience." "So do I," said Lincoln thoughtfully. "I dream of my dead boy, Willie, again and again." He bowed his head and wept.

One of Lincoln's favorite plays was *Othello*. He was eager to see it performed in Washington, and when he did get to see it, one of his secretaries, who was with him, was struck by "the keen interest with which he followed the development of Iago's subtle treachery. One would have thought that such a character would have had few points of attraction for a man to whose nature all its peculiar traits were so utterly foreign. Perhaps he was fascinated by the very contrast." Lincoln insisted on talking to the Iago performer between acts, with "a very near approach to excitement."

Lincoln had none of the revulsion that John Quincy Adams had for the character of Othello. Later on, when newly formed black regiments distinguished themselves in the siege of Petersburg, Virginia, in 1864, the president was enormously pleased. He recalled a story some of his friends in Chicago told him about the reaction of their black servant to a presentation of the play, "with the distinguished actor, Edwin Forrest playing Othello. Asked afterward what he thought of the play, the servant said thoughtfully: 'Well, layin' aside all sectional prejudices and any partiality I may have for the race, derned ef I don't think the nigger held his own with any on 'em.'" Lincoln though the black soldiers had bravely "held their own" on the battlefield.

Lincoln made friends with several Shakespearean actors—Edwin Booth (Hamlet), Edwin Forrest (Lear), John McCullough (Edgar)—but the one he got to know best was James H. Hackett. He liked Hackett's portrayal of Falstaff so much that he let the actor know of his admiration. Extremely pleased by the recognition, Hackett sent the president an autographed copy of the book he had written about Shakespeare, with a note of appreciation. When Lincoln wrote back, to thank him, he made some comments of his own on some of Shakespeare's plays. "For one of my age I have seen very little of the Drama," he told Hackett:

> The first presentation of Falstaff I ever saw was yours, here
> last winter or spring. Perhaps the best compliment I can pay,
> is, to say, as truly as I can, I am very anxious to see it again.
> Some of Shakespeare's Plays, I have never read, whilst others
> I have gone over perhaps as frequently as any unprofessional
> reader. Among the latter are Lear, Richard Third, Henry
> Eighth, Hamlet, and especially Macbeth. I think none equals
> Macbeth. It is wonderful. Unlike you gentlemen of the pro-
> fession, I think the soliloquy in Hamlet commencing "O, my
> offense is rank," surpassed that commencing "To be; or not
> to be." But pardon this small attempt at criticism. I should
> like to hear you pronounce the opening speech of Richard
> the Third.

Delighted by Lincoln's praise, Hackett had the letter printed as a broad-side entitled "A Letter from President Lincoln" to be circulated in

Washington. But the newspapers got wind of it and began making snide remarks about Lincoln's comments on some of Shakespeare's plays. The *New York Herald* was particularly nasty. The editor dismissed the letter as an "awkward speech" written in "decidedly self taught grammar" by a man who was one of a "crowd of arrogant pretenders to taste," and then added sarcastically:

> [The president] has displayed a variety of attainment, a depth of knowledge, a fund of anecdotes, a power of analysis and correct judgement that stamp him as the most remarkable man of the age. It remained for him to be a dramatic critic of the first order and the profound commentator on Shakespeare. The Falstaff of our age has been honored with an autograph letter from the American autocrat just as Shakespeare was honored with an amicable letter from King James the First and which we are told that most learned prince and great patron of learning was pleased with his own hands to write.

Greatly embarrassed by the assaults on Lincoln, Hackett wrote the president to apologize, and in his return the president refrained from chiding the actor for publicizing his letter. "Give yourself no uneasiness on the subject," he wrote. "I certainly did not expect to see my note in print; yet, I have not been much shocked by the comments on it. They are a fair specimen of what has occurred to me through life. I have endured a great deal of ridicule, without much malice; and have received a great deal of kindness, not quite free from ridicule. I am used to it." For Lincoln, the pleasure of seeing Hackett play Falstaff far outweighed the pain of abuse from the press.

But Lincoln was not silenced by the sneers. His love of Shakespeare was so deep that he could not help expressing his opinions about the plays he knew to the actors he chatted with in the theater and sometimes invited to the White House for talks. Not only did he let them know that he preferred a later soliloquy in *Hamlet* to the famous "To be, or not to be" passage; he also criticized players who he thought misinterpreted lines in the plays or omitted lines he considered essential to the mood of the scene. The fact is that Shakespeare had become such an inextricable part of Lincoln that it is hard to imagine him without the great English writer.

Sometimes Lincoln had fun with Shakespeare. Since he regarded himself as ugly, he once singled out a passage in *King Richard the Third* that he thought fit himself perfectly. At the outset of the play, he noted, Richard complains bitterly about his homeliness:

Cheated of feature by dissembling nature,
Deform'd, unfinish'd, sent before my time,
Into this breathing world, scarce half made up,
And that so lamely and unfashionable
That dogs bark at me as I halt by them.

But more often Lincoln took Shakespeare seriously. He regarded himself as a fatalist—it softened the sadness of things for him—and he turned to Shakespeare to explain his way of thinking. "What is to be will be," he told a congressman one day, "or rather I have found all my life as Hamlet says: 'There is a divinity that shapes our ends, Rough-hew them how we will.'"

In March 1864, when the painter Francis B. Carpenter met with Lincoln to do a large painting of the president reading the Emancipation Proclamation to members of his cabinet, he was struck by the president's immersion in Shakespeare during the days he spent with him. "It matters not to me whether Shakespeare be well or ill acted," he quoted Lincoln as telling him, "with him the thought suffices." Later Lincoln mentioned his favorite soliloquy in *Hamlet*—that of King Claudius about murdering his brother—and then, throwing himself into the spirit of the scene, he "repeated this entire passage from memory, with a feeling and appreciation unsurpassed by anything I witnessed on the stage." When Lincoln finished, he turned to the opening of *King Richard the Third*, where Richard appears on the stage and commences, "Now is the winter of our discontent." Most actors playing the part, he told Carpenter, begin with "a flourish" and proceed in "sophomore style." They get it wrong, he insisted, for Richard appears just after the crowning of Edward, and he is "burning with repressed hate and jealousy." To prove his point, Lincoln took over the role himself, repeated Richard's soliloquy from memory, and rendered it "with a degree of force and power that made it seem like a new creation to me," Carpenter remembered. The painter simply could not help putting down his palette and brushes when Lincoln finished, applauding him heartily, and telling him that he "was not sure that he had made a mistake in the choice of a profession," to Lincoln's great amusement.

But Carpenter saw Lincoln's melancholy side, too. "In repose," he wrote, "it was the saddest face I ever knew. There were days when I could scarcely look into it without crying. The first week of the battle of the Wilderness he scarcely slept at all." Carpenter knew also that Shakespeare's comedies always raised Lincoln's spirits. "The spirit which held the woe of Lear and the tragedy of Hamlet would have broken, had it not also had the humor of The Merry Wives of Windsor and the merriment of a Midsummer Night's Dream."

Yet even Shakespeare's comedies could not help during the bloody battle of the Wilderness. One day, John W. Forney, a Philadelphia journalist, overheard Lincoln cry out: "My God! My God!" when he learned that twenty thousand men had been killed and wounded during the fighting. "I cannot bear it! I cannot bear it!" Later that week, Forney found him "ghastly pale, dark wings under his caverned eyes, hair brushed back from his temples," hunched in a chair reading his favorite tragedy. "Let me read you this from *Macbeth*," Lincoln exclaimed when he saw Forney. "I cannot read it like Forrest, but it comes to me tonight like a consolation," and he quietly read the passage:

> Tomorrow, and tomorrow, and tomorrow,
> Creeps in this petty pace from day to day,
> To the last syllable of recorded time;
> And all our yesterdays have lighted fools
> The way to dusty death. Out, out, brief candle!
> Life's but a walking shadow; a poor player
> That struts and frets his hour upon the stage,
> And then is heard no more. It is a tale
> Told by an idiot, full of sound and fury
> Signifying nothing.

Shakespeare was with Lincoln to the end. On Sunday, April 9, 1865, with the war over, he was returning to Washington on the *River Queen* from City Point, Virginia, where he had visited the front, and he talked Shakespeare to his companions, read aloud to them, and recited his favorite passages from memory. He spent most of his time on *Macbeth*. "The lines after the murder of Duncan," recalled the Marquis de Chambrun, a foreign visitor, "when the new king falls a prey to moral torment, were dramatically dwelt on. Now and then he paused to expatiate on how exact a picture Shakespeare here gives of a murderer's mind when, dark deed achieved, its perpetrator already envies his victim's calm sleep." Lincoln's companions were struck by the slow, quiet way he read the lines:

> Duncan is in his grave;
> After life's fitful fever, he sleeps well,
> Treason has done his worst; nor steel, nor poison,
> Malice domestic, foreign levy, nothing
> Can touch him farther.

When Lincoln finished, he paused for a moment, and then read the lines slowly over again. "I then wondered," reflected one of his friends, "whether he felt a presentiment of his approaching fate."

White House History: The Presidents and the Theatre, January 2012.

CHAPTER 25

The Inauguration of
Barack Obama

My book, *Presidential Inaugurations*, published in 2001, covered all the inaugural ceremonies from George Washington to George W. Bush, and in a chapter entitled "2001—Into the Twenty-First Century" called attention to Bush's clumsy dancing at the inaugural balls held in his honor. "I confess I'm not the world's greatest dancer," admitted President Bush, "but you're going to have to suffer through it."

Barack Obama was Bush's successor in the White House. Since he was a better dancer than Bush, it seemed only fair to add a chapter on his swearing-in as president in 2009. It was, in fact, a remarkable inauguration: the first black citizen to become America's chief executive.

★ ★ ★

On January 20, 2009, Barack Hussein Obama took his oath as forty-fourth President of the United States, and, with a black father from Kenya and a white mother from Kansas, he became the first African-American citizen to become the nation's Chief Executive.

Obama's inauguration was a major event in American history. A few years earlier, the idea that a black man could become America's president seemed unthinkable to most people. But Obama's credentials were impeccable: He was intelligent, well-educated, articulate, and socially concerned, and, as a Democratic senator from Illinois, he had learned something about politics in Washington. Black leaders like Jesse Jackson, who had tried for the presidency himself years before, were overjoyed at Obama's victory in his race against Republican Senator

John McCain of Arizona during the presidential campaign of 2008. But so were thousands of Americans, black and white. It was "a landmark in American history," exclaimed journalist Nicholas Lemann. "Obama is a star." To *Time* magazine's Joe Klein, the "sheer fun of the inauguration, the world-record number of interracial hugs and kisses, augurs a new heterodox cultural energy." Even right-winger Jonah Goldberg admitted that he was "proud of and excited by the fact that we have inaugurated the first black president of the United States." He called it, "a wonderful—and wonderfully American—story."

The times, though, were inauspicious. By the time Obama became President, the United States had fallen into the worst economic downturn since the Great Depression of the 1930s, and in the Middle East the nation was embroiled in two wars, in Iraq and Afghanistan, which seemed unending. But Obama was hopeful and determined, and, when running for President, he took an optimistic view of what he could do, with the help of the American people, to improve his country's well-being. "Today," he declared in his inaugural address, "I say to you that the challenges we face are real, they are serious, and they are many. They will not be met easily or in a short span of time. But know this, America: they will be met."

Obama helped shape the festivities surrounding his inauguration, and many of the inaugural activities before and after he took his oath bore the stamp of his personality. A great admirer of Abraham Lincoln, he decided to make a slow-moving, whistle-stop train trip to Washington, the way Lincoln did for his inauguration in 1861, but starting in Philadelphia, not Springfield, Illinois, where Lincoln began his journey. "While our problems may be new," he told the crowd assembled in Philadelphia on Saturday, January 17, "what is required to overcome them is not. What is required is the same perseverance and idealism that our founders displayed. What is required is a new declaration of independence, not just in our nation, but in our own lives—from ideology and small thinking, prejudice and bigotry"—an appeal (as Lincoln put it) "to our better angels." When he finished, the train sounded its whistle, started moving, and the conductor yelled, "Welcome aboard the inaugural train!"

The first stop for the inaugural train was Wilmington, Delaware, where Vice President-elect Joseph R. Biden and his family joined the Obamas, and the next was Baltimore, where Obama made another speech. "We recognize that such enormous challenges will not be solved quickly," he reminded the people gathered in the downtown square. "There will be false starts and setbacks, frustrations and disappointments. I will make some mistakes, and we will be called to show patience even as we act with fierce urgency." As the train continued its journey to Washington, the tracks were lined with people, bundled in winter jackets, waving frantically, and then bursting into loud cheers whenever the train stopped and Obama and Biden stepped out to greet them personally. Arriving at Union Station in Washington after a seven-hour trip that usually took only two hours, Obama, his wife, and their two little girls, Malia and Sasha, were escorted to Blair House, where they stayed until inauguration day. Before reaching Washington, the presidential party celebrated the forty-eighth birthday of Obama's wife Michelle on the train.

Obama made the rounds of Washington in the days before his inauguration on January 20. He visited wounded soldiers in the Walter Reed Army Medical Center and then joined teenagers building a house at a Youthwork Center, explaining that it was good for him to work there, "because I'm moving into a new house, and I may have to do a few touch-ups here and there." He also attended a dinner honoring Arizona Senator John McCain, whom he had defeated in the 2008 campaign, and called him an "American hero," adding: "We might not always agree on everything in the months to come. We will have our share of arguments and debates. John is not known to bite his tongue, and if I'm screwing up, he's going to let me know." The following day he devoted to honoring Martin Luther King Jr. (whose ninetieth birthday was coming up), calling on Americans everywhere to observe a day of service to others. The response was tremendous. Thousands of people around the country made care packages for the soldiers serving overseas, opened soup kitchens for the homeless, worked on affordable housing for the poor, and cleaned up neglected parks, neighborhoods, and waterways. Obama visited some of the projects himself, and he took in a "Day of Service" at the Calvin Coolidge High School in the Northwest. Obama "doesn't envision this call to service as a one-day event," noted the *Washington Post*. "He is intent on creating a culture of service."

The most spectacular pre-inaugural gathering took place on the Mall in front of the Lincoln Memorial, where an enthusiastic crowd of four hundred thousand people, extending all the way to the Washington Monument, gathered for a two-hour salute to "the man who will be America's first black president and to the nation that elected Barack Obama to the White House despite centuries of racial divisiveness." Bruce Springsteen "strummed a guitar," reported the *Washington Post*, "and led a chorus through a rendition of 'The Rising.'" John Mellencamp and Mary J. Blige "also warmed up their vocal chords." Actress-singer Queen Latifah paid tribute to the great singer Marian Anderson, who, denied an appearance at Washington's Constitutional Hall in 1939 because of her race, performed beautifully for an "adoring crowd" at the Lincoln Memorial soon after. "This afternoon," Queen Latifah explained, "we are celebrating not just the inauguration of a new President, but the ongoing journey of the American people." Hollywood actors—Tom Hanks and Denzel Washington—also appeared on the stage. "We are in this together," Washington told the audience, adding "This is why the ceremony name was three simple words: We are One."

The Lincoln Memorial crowd not only greeted the singers and speakers warmly; people also cheered lustily whenever the Jumbotrons, stationed at various places on the Mall, flashed a huge shot of the president-elect for them to see. And when Obama himself finally appeared on the stage, they went wild with joy and excitement. "Hello, America," Obama hailed them. "I want to thank all the speakers and performers for reminding us, through song and through words, just what it is that we love about America." Glancing at the marble statue of Lincoln, he called attention to the Civil War President, "who in so many ways made this day possible," and was still "watching over the union he saved." Obama had great hopes for the future, he told the audience, because "Americans of every race and religion and station came here because you believe in what this country can be and because you want to help us get there." He recognized "the uncertainty about the future—about whether this generation of Americans will be able to pass on what's best about this country to our children and their children. I won't pretend that meeting any one of these challenges will be easy." But "despite all of this—despite the enormity of the task that lies ahead—I will stand here today as hopeful as ever that the United States of America will endure—that it will prevail—that the dream of our founders will live on in our time."

Inauguration Day was clear and cold. But people from all over the country gathered in Washington—almost two million—to see Obama sworn in as President. His supporters spread out for miles on the National Mall, and Joe Klein thought it "may have been the happiest crowd ever to grace the nation's capital." Washington's subways were so jam-packed that the stationmaster shouted, "Don't panic!" and then began a rhythmic chanting, "O-bam-a! O-ba-ma!" and the crowd picked it up and continued the chant as the trains moved on. "The mass of humanity sparkled with thousands of camera flashes," observed reporters, "shimmered with waving flags, and echoed with a chant of 'O-bah-mah!'" All day long Obama's name seemed like magic to the people celebrating his inauguration.

In one long line outside the Mall, some teenagers started singing, "We're off to see Obama—the wonderful president of ours!" The people nearby joined in the fun. There were a few protesters on the Mall, to be sure, but far more vendors, selling chocolate bars and Obama incense. "However people voted, whatever their background," observed David Axelrod, one of Obama's advisers, "I think there is a pervasive sense of pride among Americans about another barrier broken. It's an affirmation that we live our ideals." In Harlem, Katrina Foye, a black city worker watching the inauguration on television, had tears in her eyes when Obama came to take his oath. "This is the moment black people have been waiting for," she sighed, "from a time when we thought none of us could ever be president. It's liberating. It's not just for black people. The country can be itself."

Obama rose early on inauguration day and went through his morning workout in his family's temporary quarters in Blair House, and then attended services in St. John's Church, across from the White House. After that, the appropriate inaugural procedures took over, built up through the years since Washington's simple inauguration in 1789. Back from church, the Obamas headed for the White House, where the outgoing President, George W. Bush, and his wife Laura, welcomed them to the Blue Room for coffee. Vice President-elect Joseph Biden and his wife were there, too, as were the outgoing Vice President Dick Cheney and his wife Lynn. Around 10:45 a.m., after some small talk, the Bushes and Obamas left the White House for the ceremony at the Capitol. A few days before the inauguration, *New York Times* columnist Thomas Friedman had suggested that Obama emphasize energy-saving at his inauguration by "getting rid of the black stretch limos and double-plated armored Chevy Tahoes inching down Pennsylvania Avenue, and use no vehicles that get less than 30 miles a gallon." Obama certainly favored the conservation of energy, but, for security reasons, he rode in the usual carefully guarded presidential limousine on his trip to the Capitol.

Once the Obamas were on the inaugural platform facing west, Rick Warren, a conservative Evangelical minister from southern California, gave the invocation. "We know today," he declared, "that Dr. King and a great crowd of witnesses are shouting in heaven!" He ended his prayer by invoking the name of Jesus four times: in Hebrew (Yeshua), Arabic (Issa), Spanish (Jesús), and English (Jesus). It was clear, noted one reporter, that "he was not about to compromise his evangelical Christian tradition to please the religiously diverse audience who might hope to hear a more inclusive prayer at a presidential inauguration." But Obama made up for it in his speech. "We know that our patchwork heritage is a strength, not a weakness," he told his audience. "We are a nation of Christians and Muslims, Jews and Hindus, and nonbelievers." He was the first President to mention secularists in his address.

Poetry and music preceded the installation of Obama in office. Elizabeth Alexander recited a poem, "Praise Song for the Day," which she had written for the occasion, and Aretha Franklin, the "Queen of Soul," sang "My Country 'Tis of Thee." Wearing an "outsized, glamorized, church-lady hat," Franklin sang, it was said, "with the flamboyance of a gospel hymn." There was quieter music, too, on the program. A quartet made up of Yo Yo Ma (cello), Itzhak Perlman (violin), Anthony McGill (clarinet), and Gabriela Montero (piano) performed a composition entitled "Air and Simple Gifts," composed by John Williams for the ceremony. Because the sharp cold and wind that day might have wreaked havoc on some of the instruments, the members of the quartet made a recording of the music two days before, and now ran it off and accompanied it in perfect synchronization as they played. "Famous (Frigid) Fingers Played Live," reported the *New York Times*, "But the Sound Recorded." It "would have been a disaster if we had done it any other way," explained Pearlman afterward. "This occasion's got to be perfect. You can't have any slip-ups." There was in fact nothing unusual about the recording. "Truly, weather made it just impossible" to do without it, said a member of the Joint Committee on Inaugural Ceremonies. "No one's trying to fool anybody. Inaugural musical performances are routinely recorded ahead of time for just such an eventuality." No one, of course, wanted "a wacky intonation minutes before the President's swearing-in."

Unfortunately, the swearing-in didn't go as smoothly as the quartet's music. After US Supreme Court Justice John Paul Stevens swore Joseph Biden in as vice president, Chief Justice John Roberts stepped forward to administer the presidential oath to Obama. His wife, Michelle, held the Bible for him that Lincoln had used for his first inauguration in 1861. Both Roberts and Obama were graduates of Harvard Law School, but that didn't prevent them from having "a hard time," noted the *New York Times*, "getting through the constitutional oath of office." There was a false start by Obama, who began responding before Roberts had completed the first phrase in the oath, and he ended saying the first two words, "I, Barack," twice. Then Roberts recited the first few words of the oath incorrectly. Instead of saying, "That I will faithfully execute the office of the president of the United States," he said, "That I will faithfully execute the office of the president to the United States faithfully." Obama was a little bewildered by the error, and paused uncertainly after saying "that I will execute." Roberts then tried again, but although he put the word *faithfully* back into its proper place, he left out the word *execute* this time. Obama then repeated Roberts's error of putting the word *faithfully* at the end, instead of where it belonged. From then on, though, the two men handled the rest of the thirty-five-word oath competently.

At the luncheon in Congress following the inauguration, the Chief Justice told the President the mistake was his fault, and even though the bungled oath-taking was fully acceptable, they agreed to have another try at it. The following afternoon, the two met in the White House Map Room, with some reporters present, for a second try. "Are you ready to take the oath?" Robert asked formally. "Yes, I am," responded Obama. "And we're going to do it very slowly." And so they did. Obama didn't have a Bible handy this time, but he insisted that the oath was binding anyway. After the ceremony, he told reporters with a smile that he and the Chief Justice had decided to do the ceremony over "because it was so much fun."

Obama's inaugural address, following the original oath, went off splendidly. He had worked hard on it and took seriously the advice of his gifted speechwriters. The "main task of an inauguration speech," he told an interviewer some weeks before, "is to try to capture as best I can the moment we are in," and then "project confidence that if we take the right measures . . . we can once again be that country, that beacon for the world." In preparing for his speech he looked over some of the best inaugural speeches of the past: Lincoln's second inaugural was so superb, he thought, that he felt "intimidated" by it; JFK's speech in 1961 he found "extraordinary." But Theodore Sorensen, the writer who had helped Kennedy with his speech, expected much from Obama. He called him "the most eloquent presidential candidate since JFK" and said he hoped to hear Obama deliver "the most eloquent speech since JFK's forty-eight years ago." He was not alone in his expectations. *New York Times* columnist Gail Collins put it simply: "Barack Obama is a celebrated speaker, and our hopes are unusually high."

For most people Obama lived up to his reputation as a fine speaker on inauguration day. He began his speech by praising George W. Bush "for his service to our nation as well as the generosity and cooperation he has shown throughout this transition." But almost at once he mentioned the crisis at home and abroad he had inherited from the Bush administration. "Our nation is at war, against a far-reaching network of violence and hatred. Our economy is badly weakened, a consequence of greed and irresponsibility on the part of some, but also our collective failure to make hard choices and prepare the nation for a new age." He also spoke of other problems facing the nation: health care, the shortage of good schools, and waste of energy. And, he added, there was "a nagging fear that America's decline is inevitable." Still, he insisted, "we gather because we have chosen hope over fear, unity of purpose over conflict and discord." It was now our task, he said, to live up to the "God-given promise that we are all equal, all are free and all deserve a chance to pursue their full measure of happiness."

From generalities Obama proceeded to specifics. "The state of the economy calls for action, bold and swift," he declared, "and we will act, not only to create new jobs but to lay a new foundation for growth. We will build the roads and bridges, the electric grids and digital lines that feed our commerce and bind us together. We will restore science to its rightful place, and wield technology's wonders to raise health care's quality and lower its cost. We will harness the sun and the winds and the soil to fuel our cars and run our factories. And we will transform our schools and colleges and universities to meet the demands of a new age. All this we can do. And all this we will do."

What about the dangers of big government (except when at war) that his predecessors in the White House, beginning with Ronald Reagan, had warned against? Obama swept aside the warnings against government and declared that the "question we ask today is not whether our government is too big or too small, but whether it works—whether it helps families find jobs at a decent wage, care they can afford, a retirement that is dignified. Where the answer is yes, we intend to move forward. Where the answer is no, the programs will end." But what about the "free market," which, unregulated, was supposed by many Americans to produce a prosperous economy? Obama conceded that the power of the market "to generate wealth and expand freedom is unmatched," but he also pointed out that the present crisis "has reminded us that without a watchful eye, the market can spin out of control—and that a nation cannot prosper when it favors only the prosperous." The implication of course was that the market needed some kinds of restraints to keep it from getting out of hand.

When Obama came to discuss foreign policy, he placed great emphasis on the long-held responsibility of the United States since World War II to spread its views of freedom and justice around the world. "America," he said, "is a friend of each nation and every man, woman, and child who seeks a future of peace and dignity, and . . . she was ready to lead once more." At the same time, prudence, humility, and restraint were to accompany America's leadership abroad. "We will begin to responsibly leave Iraq to its people," he promised, "and forge a hard-earned peace in Afghanistan." We will also "work tirelessly to lessen the nuclear threat, and roll back the specter of a warming planet." As for the Muslim world, "we seek a new way forward based on mutual interest and mutual respect." We will, he told the Muslims, "extend a hand if you are willing to unclench your fist."

Obama concluded his address by reminding Americans of the ideals motivating the men and women who founded this country:

> This is the meaning of our liberty and our creed, why men and women and children of every race and every faith can join in celebration across this magnificent Mall, and why a man whose father less than sixty years ago might not have been served at a local restaurant can now stand before you to make a most sacred oath. . . . With hope and virtue, let us brave once more the icy currents, and endure the storms that may come. Let it be said by our children's children that when we were tested we refused to let this journey end, that we did not turn back nor did we falter; and with eyes fixed on the horizon and God's grace upon us, we carried forth that great gift of freedom and delivered it safely to future generations.

Obama's speech was warmly received. *Time* magazine's Joe Klein called it "resolute, suffused with sobriety; reflecting a tough-minded realism at home and abroad," and he also liked the "simplicity of the words" and "lack of pomp and bombast." Columnist Rosa Brooks was struck by the fact that Obama "referred only elliptically to his status as our first black president. He didn't talk about black people or white people. He did something simpler. He talked about 'us.' This is what gave Obama's speech its power. His generous vision of an America that includes all of us, belongs to all of us, shapes and is shaped by all of us." In a lengthy editorial summing up Obama's major points in his address, the *New York Times* concluded that most of his speech "filled us with hope that with Mr. Obama's help, this battered nation will be able to draw together and man itself." For *Newsday*'s Tom Brune, Obama "delivered a confident, almost sober speech, rooted in history and aimed at the future, with the primary themes of responsibility and change."

There were criticisms too. Republicans resented the implied disapproval of the Bush administration's policies in much of what he said in his address. And some liberals, like Princeton economist Paul Krugman, were disappointed by what they regarded as his "conventionality." Krugman wondered whether "the platitudes in his inaugural address" were a sign that "he'll wait for the conventional wisdom to catch up with events. If so, his administration will find itself dangerously behind the curve." *Washington Post* columnist Jim Hoagland singled out Obama's phrase about extending a hand to an unclenched fist as "the dominant foreign-policy metaphor of the new administration," but warned that it made the United States "vulnerable" too. And William Safire, Richard Nixon's speechwriter years before, said he thought the unclenched fist phrase was "quotable if it is original, but I think I've seen it before." He then revealed that in 1989, George H. W. Bush, George W.'s father, had declared: "This is the age of the offered hand. To the world, too, we offer new engagement and a renewed vow: we will stay strong to protect the peace. The offered hand is a reluctant fist; but once made, strong, it can be used with great effect." Safire seemed amused that Obama shared some of the older Bush's ideas.

Two other passages in Obama's speech attracted special interest. One was the "warmly familiar metaphor" that Obama made use of in calling for action: "Starting today, we must pick ourselves up, dust ourselves off, and begin again the work of remaking America." It turned out that two of the lines came from a song entitled "Pick Yourself Up," with lyrics by Dorothy Field and music by Jerome Kern, appearing in a movie called Swing Time (1936), starring Fred Astaire and Ginger Rogers, with the following lines used several times:

"I pick myself up,
Dust myself off,
Start all over again."

The second passage attracting attention was the quotation from George Washington toward the end of the address. Instead of using the first President's emphasis in his first inaugural on the "sacred fire of liberty" and the "experiment" in republican self-government, Obama utilized Washington's far less known words to the soldiers at Valley Forge in 1777: "Let it be told to the future world . . . that in the depths of winter, when nothing but hope and virtue could . . . survive, that the city and the country, alarmed at one common danger, came forth to meet [it]."
Praise for Obama outweighed criticism. Michael Kinsley, a no-nonsense public intellectual, called Obama "one of the greatest public speakers now practicing that art." And in the *London Times*, conservative columnist Andrew Sullivan observed that instead of seeing the world in "black and white terms," Obama "sees it as a series of interconnected conflicts that can be managed by pragmatic solutions, combined with a little rhetorical fairy dust and willingness to offer respect where Bush provided merely contempt." In Cairo, Egypt, and in Lebanon there was some approval for Obama's outreach to the Muslim world, and even Cuba's aging and ailing Fidel Castro conceded that the new president seemed "honest." In Japan some youngsters liked Obama's grit (mojo?) so much that they turned his last name into a Japanese verb, *obamo*, meaning determined to get things done no matter what the odds were.

After Obama's address, Joseph E. Lowrey, a seventy-six-year-old black minister from the deep south who had been active in the civil rights movement, gave the benediction, praying for "that day when black will not be asked to get in back, when brown can stick around, when yellow will be mellow . . . when the red man can get ahead, and when the white will embrace what is right." With the inaugural ceremony over, the Obamas joined members of Congress for lunch in the Capitol's Statuary Hall, where Massachusetts friend Senator Edward M. ("Ted") Kennedy joined the lawmakers honoring the new president. But Kennedy was being treated for brain cancer at the time, and after exchanging jokes with his colleagues for a few minutes, he suddenly went into a seizure and had to be rushed to the hospital. Obama hurried to Kennedy's side as he was being wheeled out, and left the room with him. When he returned, he sighed, "This is a joyous time, but it's also a sobering time." Kennedy, he said, had been a "warrior for justice" during his forty-six years in the Senate: not only did he help pass Lyndon Johnson's landmark civil rights legislation; he also helped make Obama's ascent to the presidency possible. After leaving the luncheon, Obama and his wife boarded the armored presidential limousine to drive down Pennsylvania Avenue to the White House. The Obamas waved at the crowd along the way, and twice they left the limousine to walk part of the way, as some of their predecessors had done.

After freshening up a bit in his new home, Obama went out to the White House reviewing stand to watch the lengthy afternoon parade in his honor. It contained thirteen thousand individuals, representing more than ninety organizations, 217 horses, eleven Native American tribes, ten college bands, and three ten-foot papier-mâché dragons imported from China. There were six military divisions in the inaugural parade, each led by a military band. Since the president is the civilian commander-in-chief of the armed forces, Obama followed the precedent that Ronald Reagan had initiated in 1981, returning salutes from professional military officials with civilian salutes of his own. (Most presidents before Reagan had avoided military etiquette because they were not in uniform and represented the principle, dear to the Founding Fathers, of civil supremacy over the military.) Like Reagan, Obama gave snappy salutes. Pentagon officers were delighted by his becoming one of them, so to speak. "Anyone in the military," commented one reporter, "could tell that Mr. Obama took the time to practice the first, crisp salute that he executed on January 20." It was almost as if he had risen from the ranks to become the Constitution's commander in chief.

If Obama was good at saluting, he was also a skilled dancer, and he and his wife attended all ten of the inaugural balls that evening, dancing at times to the song, "At Last," a hit for Glenn Miller in 1941, to the delight of the guests. "While it was a gospel and soul inauguration," remarked *New York Times* writer Jon Pareles the next day, "it was also a hip-hop inauguration. Rappers who are charismatic, articulate, self-made successes, may well see Mr. Obama as one of their own; he also gives them someone to boast about besides himself." At one ball, though, Obama accidentally stepped on his wife's hem, "revealing," teased one writer, "that the new president might be better on the basketball court than on the dance floor."

Obama spent seven hours swinging and swaying at the different dancing parties, including the Youth, Neighborhood Google/You Two, and Hip-Hop Balls, but his entreaty before leaving them was always the same: "We are going to need you, not just today, not just tomorrow, but this year, for the next four years, and who knows after that, because together, we are going to change America."

CHAPTER 26

They Really Said It: Quotes from the Presidents and Their Wives

Quotations have long fascinated me, some for their beauty, others for their insights, and still others for their humor. In 1967, a book of mine on the various uses of quotations—*Quotemanship: The Use and Abuse of Quotations for Polemical and Other Purposes*—was published and attracted a lot of attention. Years later, my friend John George, a specialist in political science, and I came up with a book about quotations that we called *They Never Said It* (1989), in which, as the book covers explained, we "examine hundreds of misquotations, incorrect attributions, and blatant fabrications, outlining the origins of the quotes and revealing why they should be consigned to the historical trashcan."

Abraham Lincoln never said, "You cannot fool all the people all the time," and Thomas Jefferson never said, "That government is best which governs least." Nor did Mark Twain say this about one of the attractive showgirls of his day: "I would rather go to bed with Lillian Russell stark naked than with Ulysses S. Grant in full military regalia." Our book dealt with more than Americans. We even showed that Marie Antoinette never said of the starving peasants, "Let them eat cake," and that Charles Darwin never dreamed of saying, "How I wish I had not expressed my theory of evolution, as I have done."

I am presenting the presidents and their wives here chronologically, and I'm including the years that they spent in the White House. I'm also giving each quotation I cite a brief title summing up the gist of the quote. Needless to say, some of the quotations are among my favorites.

★ ★ ★

George Washington (1789–97)

Foreign Policy—"Why forego the advantages of so peculiar a situation? Why quit our own to sit upon foreign ground . . . ? It is our true policy to steer clear of permanent alliances with any position or portion of the foreign world."

Declaring War—"The Constitution vests the power of declaring war with Congress, therefore no offensive expedition of importance can be undertaken until after they shall have deliberated on the subject, and authorized such a measure."

Love—"Love is a mighty pretty thing," but it "is too dainty a food to live on *alone*, and ought not to be considered further than as a necessary ingredient for that matrimonial happiness which results from a combination of causes; none of which are of greater importance than that the partner should have good sense, a good disposition, a good reputation, and financial means."

Friendship—"It is easy to make acquaintances, but very difficult to shake them off, however irksome and unprofitable they are found to be after we have once committed ourselves to them." The solution to the problem is to "be courteous to all, but intimate with few, and let those few be well tried before you give them your confidence; true friendship is a plant of slow growth."

Hiring Workers—When Washington was seeking a carpenter and a bricklayer for his Mount Vernon estate, he remarked: "If they are good workmen, they may be of Asia, Africa, or Europe. They may be Mohametans, Jews or Christians of any Sect, or they may be atheists."

Political Parties—Hs warned Americans to "moderate the fury of party spirit, to warn against the mischiefs of foreign intrigue, to guard against the impostures of pretended patriotism."

Martha Washington

Filthy Democrat—When Mrs. Washington found a dirty mark on the wall of the living-room after entertaining some Congressmen, she exclaimed: "Ah, that was no Federalist. None but a filthy democrat would mark a place his good-for-nothing head in that manner."

President's House—"I live a very dull life here, and know nothing that passes in town."

John Adams (1797–1801)

On Alexander Hamilton—"the bastard brat of a Scots' peddler . . ."

On Tom Paine—"a mongrel between pig and puppy, begotten by a wild boar on a bitch wolf . . ."

On Paine's Common Sense—"a poor, ignorant, malicious, short-sighted, crapulous mass . . ."

Reducing Eternal Principles—"What can be more mad than to represent the eternal, almighty, omnipresent Cause and Principle of the universe by statues, pictures, coins, and medals?"

Forming the United States—"It will never be pretended that any persons employed [in creating America's government] had interviews with the gods, or were in any degree under the inspiration of Heavan, more than those at work upon ships or houses, or laboring in merchandise or agriculture; it will forever be acknowledged that these governments were contrived merely by the use of reason and the senses."

Choosing to Laugh—"I cannot contemplate human affairs, without laughing or crying. I choose to laugh."

Presidential Elections—"I look at the presidential election as I do at the squabbles of little girls about their dolls and at the more serious wrangles of little boys, which sometimes come to blows, about their rattles and whistles. It will be a mighty bustle about a mighty bauble."

Congress—"Oh! the wisdom, the foresight and the hindsight and the rightside and the leftside, the northsight and the southside, and the eastsight and the westsight that appeared in that august assembly."

Congress in Session—"In Congress, Nibbling and quibbling—as usual. There is no greater Mortification than to sit with half a dozen Witts, deliberating upon a Petition, Address or Memorial. These great Witts, these subtle Cricks, these refined Geniuses, these learned lawyers, these wise Statesmen, are so fond of showing their Parts and Powers, as to make their Consultations very tedious."

Denounces the Eighteenth Century—"The Age of Folly, Vice, Frenzy, Brutality, Daemons, Buonaparte, Tom Paine, or the Age of the Burning Brand from the Bottomless Pit, or anything but the Age of Reason."

Adams's Sarcasm—"The history of our Revolution will be one continued Lye from one end to the other. The essence of the whole will be that *Dr. Franklin's electoral rod, smote the earth and out sprung General Washington. That Franklin electrified him with his rod—and thence forward these two conducted all the Policy, Negotiations, Legislatures, and War.*"

To Abigail—"Oh, that I had a bosom to lean my head upon! But how dare you hint or lisp a word about 'sixty years of age.' If I were near I would soon convince you that I am not above forty."

Abigail Adams
Remember the Ladies—From a letter sent to her husband when he was in Philadelphia discussing independence in the Continental Congress: "I long to hear that you have declared an independency. And, by the way, in the code of laws which I suppose it will be necessary for you to make, I desire you would remember the ladies and be more generous and favorable to them than your ancestors. Do not put unlimited power into the hands of the husbands. Remember, all men would be tyrants if they could. If particular care and attention is not paid to the ladies, we

are determined to foment a rebellion, and will not hold ourselves bound by any laws in which we have no voice or representation. That your sex are naturally tyrannical is a truth so thoroughly established as to admit of no dispute." Calling her "saucy," Adams wrote back: "Depend on it, we know better than to repeal our masculine systems. Although they are in full force, you know they are little more than theory. We dare not exert our power in its full latitude." But his wife refused to accept his teasing and she shot back: "I cannot say that I think you are very generous to the ladies, for, whilst you are proclaiming peace and good-will to men, emancipating all nations, you insist upon retaining an absolute power over wives." Actually, Adams treated Abigail more or less as an equal when it came to serious matters.

Woman as Lordess—"I will never consent to have our Sex considered in an inferiour point of light. Let each planet shine in their own orbit. God and nature designed it so. If man is Lord, woman is Lordess—that is what I contend for, and if woman does not hold the Reins of Government, I see no reason for her not judging how they are conducted."

Life in Motion—"I begin to think that a calm is not desirable in any situation in life. Every object is beautiful in motion; a ship under sail; trees gently agitated with the wind, and a fine woman dancing, are three instances in point. Man was made for action and for bustle too. I believe I am quite out of conceit with calms."

Iniquitous Slavery—"I wish most sincerely there was not a slave in the province. It allways appeared a most iniquitous scheme to me—fight ourselves for what we are daily robbing and plundering from those who have as good a right to freedom as we have."

Black Othello—She "lost much of the play," she confessed, "from the sooty appearance of the Moor. Perhaps it may be early prejudice; but could not separate the African color from the man, nor prevent that disgust and horror which filled my mind every time I saw him touch the gentle Desdemona; nor did I wonder that Brabantio thought some love potion or some witchcraft had been practised to make his daughter fall in love with what she scarcely dared to look upon."

A Freeman in Black—"The Boy is a Freeman as much as any of the Young Men, and merely because his Face is Black, is he to be denied instruction, how is he to be qualified to procure a livelihood? Is this the Christian principle of doing to others as we would have others to do us? . . . I have not thought it any disgrace to my self to take him into my parlour and teach him both to read and write. . . . I hope we shall all go to Heaven together."

Thomas Jefferson (1801–09)

Women and Politics—"The tender breasts of the ladies were not formed for political convulsions."

The Rights of Conscience—"Our rulers can have authority over such natural rights only as we have submitted to them. The rights of conscience we never submitted, we could not submit. We are answerable for them to our God. But, it does me no injury for my neighbor to say there are twenty gods, or no god. It neither picks my pocket nor breaks my leg."

Monied Corporations—"I hope we shall crush in its birth the aristocracy of our monied corporations which dare already to challenge our government to a trial of strength and bid defiance to the laws of our country."

Justice in America—"I tremble for my country when I reflect that God is just."

Healthy Body—"Exercise and recreation are as necessary as reading; I will say rather more necessary, because health is worth more than learning. A strong body makes the mind strong."

James Madison (1809–17)

Father of the Constitution—"You give me credit to which I have no claim, in calling me 'the writer of the Constitution of the U.S.' This was not, like the fabled Goddess of Wisdom, the offspring of a single brain. It ought to be regarded as the work of many heads & many hands."

Civil Rights—"The civil rights of none shall be abridged on account of religious belief or worship, nor shall any national religion be established, nor shall the full and equal rights of conscience be in any manner, or any pretense, infringed."

Congressional Chaplains—"The establishment of the chaplainship to Congress is a palpable violation of equal rights, as well as of Constitutional privilege." Madison thought that if Congressmen wanted chaplains, they should pay for them themselves: "How small a contribution from each member of Congress would suffice for the purpose! How just it would be in its principle! How noble in the exemplary sacrifice to the genius of the Constitution and the divine right of conscience." He felt the same about chaplains in the armed forces.

Congress and War—"In no part of the Constitution is more wisdom to be found than in the clause which confines the question of war or peace to the legislature, and not to the executive department. . . . War is in fact the true nurse of executive aggrandizement. In war, a physical force is to be created; and it is the executive will which is to direct it. In war, the public treasures are to be unlocked; and it is the executive hand which is to dispense them. . . . It is in war, finally, that laurels are to be gathered, and it is the executive brow they are to encircle. The strongest passions and most dangerous weaknesses of the human breast; ambition, avarice, vanity, the honorable or venial love of fame, are all in conspiracy against the desire of duty of peace."

Protection of All Religions—The law was "meant to comprehend, with the mantel of its protection, the Jew and the Gentile, the Christian and the mahometan, the Hindoo and infidel of every denomination."

Dolley Madison

Politics—"Politics is the business of men. I don't care what offices they may hold, or who supports them. I care only about people."

Lack of Political Talents—In a letter to her husband, Dolley referred to "her want of talents" when it came to politics, and to her "diffidence in expressing those opinons always imperfectly understood by her sex."

James Monroe (1817–25)

Political Parties—"Surely our government may go on and prosper without the existence of parties. I have always considered their existence as the curse of the country."

John Quincy Adams (1825–29)

American Foreign Policy—"Wherever the standard of freedom and independence has been or shall be unfurled, there, will be America's heart, her benedictions and her prayers. But she goes not abroad in search of monsters to destroy. She is the well-wisher to the freedom and independence of all. She is the champion and vindicator only of her own."

Dislike of Andrew Jackson—"I would not be present to see my darling Harvard disgrace herself by conferring a Doctor's degree upon a barbarian who could scarcely spell his own name."

Criticism of Shakespeare's Othello—"Who can sympathise with the love of Desdemona?—the daughter of a Venetian nobleman [who] falls in love and makes a runaway match with a blackamoor [Othello]. . . . The great moral lesson of the tragedy of 'Othello' is, that black and white blood cannot be intermingled in marriage without a gross outrage upon the law of nature. . . . Upon the stage, her fondling with Othello is disgusting." JQA angered British actress Fanny Kemble by saying that Desdemona should have died for marrying "a nigger."

JQA and Louisa—There were "frailties of temper in both of us; both being quick and irascible, and mine being sometimes harsh."

Louisa Adams

Unsocial House—"There is something in the great unsocial house which depresses my spirit beyond expression and makes it impossible for me to feel at home or to fancy that I have a home any where."

Hanging and Marriage—"Hanging and marriage are strongly assimilated."

Andrew Jackson (1829–37)

Harvard Degree—"I shall have to speak in English," he told the students, "not being able to return your compliment in what appears to be the language of Harvard. All the Latin I know is E Pluribus Union."

South Carolina Nullification—When South Carolina threatened to nullify a tariff bill Jackson had signed, he threatened to enforce the law by leading troops to battle. "Suppress the rebellion, sir," he cried; "root out the treason, sir; with ruthless hand! Assemble a force sufficient to crush any uprising at any point; assume as constitutional commander-in-chief, the immediate command and take the field in person, sir! Hang every leader and every false counsellor of that infatuated people, sir, by martial law, irrespective of his name, or political or social position—*the higher, the worse!* . . . For my part, I declare that I will enforce the laws of the United States if I should have to depopulate the State of traitors and repeople it with a better and wiser race!"

Rights of the Weak—"I . . . believe . . . that just laws can make no distinction of privilege between the rich and poor, and that when men of high standing attempt to trample upon the rights of the weak, they are the fittest object for example and punishment. In general, the great can protect themselves, but the poor and humble, require the arm and shield of the law."

James K. Polk (1845–49)

No Leisure—"No president who performs his duties faithfully and conscientiously can have any leisure."

Zachary Taylor (1849–50)

War—"My life has been devoted to armies; yet I look upon war at all times, and under all circumstances, as a national calamity, to be avoided if compatible with national honor."

Millard Fillmore (1850–53)

Casting Presidents Adrift—"It is a national disgrace that our presidents . . . should be cast adrift, and perhaps be compelled to keep a corner grocery for subsistence. . . . We elect a man to the presidency, expect him to be honest, to give up a lucrative profession, perhaps, and after we have done with him we let him go into seclusion and perhaps poverty."

An Honorary Degree in Latin—Fillmore refused an honorary degree in Latin from Oxford University in England because he couldn't read Latin: "I have not the advantage of a classical education and no man should, in my judgment, accept a degree he cannot read."

Franklin Pierce (1853–57)

In Retirement—What should a president do after leaving office: "There's nothing left . . . but to get drunk."

James Buchanan (1857–61)

Champagne in Small Bottles—"Pints are very inconvenient in this house, as the article is not used in such small quantities."

Abraham Lincoln (1861–65)

Cruel Opponents—"It is a little singular that I, who am not a vindictive man, should have always been before the people for election in canvasses marked for their bitterness."

Laughter—"I laugh because I must not cry; that is all—that is all."

Labor—"Labor is prior to, and independent of, capital. Capital is only the fruit of labor, and could never have existed if labor had not first existed. Labor is the superior of capital, and deserved much higher consideration."

God's Purpose—"The will of God prevails. In great contests each party claims to act in accordance with the will of God. Both may and one must be wrong. God cannot be *for* and *against*, the same thing at the same time. In the present civil war, it is quite possible that God's purpose is something different from the purpose of either party."

Enemies—"Am I not destroying my enemies when I make friends of them?"

Governing others—"No man is good enough to govern another man without that other's consent."

Democracy—"As I would not be a slave, so I would not be a master. This expresses my idea of democracy."

Know-Nothings—"I am not a Know-Nothing. That is certain. How could I be? How can anyone who abhors the oppression of Negroes, be in favor of degrading classes of white people? Our progress in degeneracy appears to be pretty rapid. As a nation, we began by declaring that '*all men are created equal*.' We now practically read it 'all men are created equal, except negroes.' When the know-nothings get control, it will read, 'all men are created equal, except negroes, *and foreigners and Catholics*.' When it comes to this, I shall prefer emigrating to some country where they make no pretense of loving liberty—to Russia, for instance, where despotism can be taken pure, without the base alloy of hypocrisy."

How It Feels to Be a President—"You have heard about the man tarred and feathered and ridden out of town on a rail? A man in the crowd asked how he liked it, and his reply was that if it wasn't for the honor of the thing, he would much rather walk."

Mary Todd Lincoln

Looks Like a President—"Yes, he is a great favorite everywhere. He is to be president of the United States some day; if I had not thought so I never would have married him, for you can see he is not pretty. But look at him! Doesn't he look as if he would make a magnificent president?"

Andrew Johnson (1865–69)

Lowly Status—"I am a mechanic, and when a blow is struck, on that class, I will resent it. I know we have an illegitimate, swaggering, bastard, scrub aristocracy which assumes to know a great deal, but which, when the flowing veil of pretension is torn off, is seen to possess neither talents nor information on which one can rear a useful superstructure."

Ulysses S. Grant (1869–77)

The Mexican War—The Mexican War was "one of the most unjust wars ever waged by a stronger against a weaker nation. It was an instance of a republic following the bad example of European monarchies in not considering justice in their desire to acquire additional territory."

Music—"I know only two tunes; one is 'Yankee Doodle' and the other isn't."

Regrets—"Twice in my life I killed wild animals, and I have regretted both acts ever since."

Soldier-Farmer—"The truth is I am more of a farmer than a soldier . . . . I never went into the army without regret and never retired without pleasure."

Julia Grant

Leaving the White House—"Oh, Ulys, I feel like a waif, like a waif on the world's wide common."

Rutherford B. Hayes (1877–81)

Importance of Public Schools—"The want of public schools in any quarter of the Union is an injury to the whole Union, as the success of republican institutions rests upon the intelligence & capacity for self government of the whole people & of all the states."

Lucy Webb Hayes

A Woman's Mind—"It is acknowledged by more persons" that a woman's mind "is as strong as a man's. . . . Instead of being considered the slave of man, she is considered his equal in all things, and his superior in some."

Benjamin Harrison (1889–93)

Policing the World—The United States has "no commission from God to police the world."

Grover Cleveland (1885–89, 1893–97)

Business and Fishing—"There can be no doubt that the promise of industrial peace, of contented labor and of healthful moderation in the pursuit of wealth . . . would be infinitely improved if a large share of the time which has been devoted to the concoction of trust and business combinations had been spent in fishing."

Ex-Presidents—"And still the question, 'What shall be done with our ex-presidents?' is not laid to rest; and I sometimes think Watterson's solution of it, 'Take them out and shoot them' is worthy of attention."

William B. McKinley (1897–1901)

Anti-Imperialism—"We want no wars of conquest; we must avoid the temptation of territorial aggression. Wars should never be entered upon until every agency of peace has failed . . . peace is preferable to war in almost every contingency."

Imperialism—McKinley defended taking over the Philippines from Spain after the Spanish-American War in 1898 because the Filipinos were "unfit for self government" and it was America's duty "to take them and to educate the Filipinos, and uplift and Christianize them, and by God's grace do the very best we could by them."

Ida Saxton McKinley

Her Beloved Husband—To a friend she exclaimed, "Do you mean to say that you would prefer England to a country ruled over by my husband????"

Theodore Roosevelt (1901–9)

Armchair and Parlor Jingoes—"One of the commonest taunts directed at men like myself is that we are armchair and parlor jingoes who wish to see others do what we only advocate doing. . . . I cannot afford to disregard the fact that my power for good, whatever it may be, would be gone if I didn't try to live up to the doctrines I have tried to preach. Moreoever, it seems to me that it would be a good deal more important from the standpoint of the nation as a whole that men like myself should go to war than that we should stay comfortably in offices at home and let others carry on the war we have urged."

Books a Statesman Should Read—poetry and novels as well as books on history, government, science, and philosophy. The important thing was to "know human nature, to know the needs of the human soul; and they will find this nature and these needs set forth as nowhere else by the great imaginative writers, whether of prose or poetry."

The Malefactors of Great Wealth—"It may well be that the determination of the government (in which, gentlemen, it will not waver) to punish certain malefactors of great wealth, has been responsible for some of the trouble (on the stock market). . . . I regard this contest as one to determine who shall rule this free country—the people through their government agents, or a few ruthless and domineering men whose wealth makes them pecuiliarly formidable because they hide behind the breastworks of corporate organization."

Soft Living—"The things that will destroy America are prosperity at any price, peace at any price, safety first instead of duty first, the love of soft living and the get-rich-quick theory of life."

A Short Speech—During the campaign of 1912, TR was shot just before giving a speech, and he told the audience: "I am going to ask you to be very quiet and excuse me from making a long speech. I'll do the best I can, but there is a bullet in my body."

On Woodrow Wilson—a "damned Presbyterian hypocrite" and a "Byzantine logothete . . ."

Action—"Get action; do things; be sane; don't fritter away your time; create, act, take a place wherever you are and be somebody; get action."

War—"No triumph of peace is quite so great as the supreme triumphs of war."

Obligation of the Rich—A "man of great wealth owes a particular obligation to the state because he derives special advantage from the mere existence of government."

The Joy of Life—"I rarely took exercise merely as exercise. Primarily

I took it because I liked it. Play should never be allowed to interfere with work; and a life devoted merely to play is, of all forms of existence, the most dismal. But the joy of life is a good thing, and while work is the essential in it, play also has its place."

The President on the Battlefield—Soon after TR became president, a worried citizen begged him not to let his fighting spirit plunge the United States into war. "What!" cried TR, "a war, and I cooped up here in the White House. Never!" He made it clear he would be at the front if war broke out while he was president. Wasn't he civilian commander-in-chief?

The White House—"I had a corking time in the White House."

Edith Roosevelt

Taming TR—"Theodore, I do wish you'd do your bleeding in the bathroom. You're spoiling every rug in the house."

William Howard Taft (1909–13)

Losing His Try for Reelection—"No one candidate was ever elected ex-president by such a large majority."

Leaving the White House—"I'm glad to be going—This is the lonesomest place in the world."

Woodrow Wilson (1913–21)

Conservatism—"A conservative is someone who makes no changes and consults his grandmother when in doubt."

Disagreement—"I am sorry for those who disagree with me. Because I know they are wrong."

Preparing Speeches—"If I am to speak ten minutes, I need a week for preparation; if fifteen minutes, three days; if half an hour, two days; if an hour, I am ready now."

God's President—"God ordained that I should be the next president of the United States. Neither you nor any other mortal could have prevented that!"

Woodrow and Ellen Wilson Read Proof—"The soup comma my dear comma is delicious semi colon Maggie is an excellent cook period No wonder exclamation You taught her period Thank you comma Woodrow period"

Submitting the Versailles Treaty to the Senate—"The stage is set, the destiny disclosed. It has come about by no plan of our conceiving, but by the hand of God which led us into this war."

Warren G. Harding (1921–23)

Modesty—"I am a man of limited talents from a small town."

Making a Speech—"Well, I never saw this before. I didn't write this speech and don't believe what I just read."

Corruption in his Administration—"I have no trouble with my enemies. I can take care of my enemies in a fight. But my friends, my goddamned friends, they're the ones who keep me walking the floor at nights!"

Chatterbox—"I like to go out into the country and bloviate."

The Helpful Government—"I would like the government to do all it can to mitigate."

Avoiding Chaos—"Speaking our sympathies, uttering the conscience of all the people, mindful of our right to dwell amid the good fortunes of rational, conscience-impelled advancement, we hold the majesty of righteous government with liberty under the law to be our avoidance of chaos and we call upon every citizen in the Republic to hold fast to that which made us what we are, and we will have orderly government safeguard the onward march to all we ought to be."

Wisdom—"Despite all the deprecation I cannot bring myself to accept the notion that the inter-relation among our men and women has departed."

Mind Your P's—"Progression is not proclamation nor palaver. It is not pretense nor play on prejudice. It is not of personal pronouns, nor perennial pronouncement. It is not the perturbation of a people passionately wrought nor a promise proposed."

Florence Harding

The People's House—When people started peeking into the White House windows after Harding's inauguration in 1921, Mrs. Harding cried: "Let em look if they want to! It's their White House!"

Calvin Coolidge (1923–29)

The Commonplace—"When my countrymen turn their attention again to the commonplace, I shall know that American institutions are secure."

Unemployment—"The final solution for unemployment is work."

Taciturnity—"If you don't say anything, you won't be called upon to repeat it."

Keep Still—"Four-fifths of all our troubles in this life would disappear if we would only sit down and keep still."

Grace Coolidge

Quiet Partner—"If I had manifested any particular interest in a political matter, I feel sure I should have been properly put in my place."

Herbert Hoover (1929–33)

Unemployment—"When a great many people are unable to find work, unemployment results."

Fishing—Fishing is "the chance to wash one's soul with pure air, with the blue water. It brings meekness and inspiration from the decency of nature, charity toward tackle-makers, patience toward fish, a mockery of profits and egos, a quieting of hate, a rejoicing that you do not have to decide a darned thing until next week. And it is discipline in the equality of men—for all men are equal before fish."

War—"Older men declare war. But it is youth who must fight and die."

Capitalists—"The only trouble with capitalism is capitalists.

They're too damned greedy."

More on War—"War is a losing business, a financial loss, a loss of life and an economic degeneration. . . . It has but few compensations and of them we must make the most. Its greatest compensation lies in the possibility that we may instill into our people unselfishness."

Lou Hoover

Women in Politics—"Women should get into politics. They should take a more active part in civic affairs, give up some of their time devoted to pleasure for their duty as citizens. Whether we are wanted in politics or not, we are here to stay and the only force that can put us out is that which gave us the vote. The vote itself is not a perfect utility. It is perfected the way it is used."

Franklin D. Roosevelt (1933–1945)

Government's Inherent Duty—"While it isn't written in the Constitution, nevertheless it is the inherent duty of the Federal Government to keep its citizens from starvation."

Freedom and Security—"We have come to a clear realization of the fact that true individual freedom cannot exist without economic security and independence. Necessitous men are not free men. People who are hungry and out of a job are the stuff of which dictatorships are made. In our day those economic truths have become accepted as self-evident. We have accepted, so to speak, a second Bill of Rights under which a new basis of security and prosperity can be established for all—regardless of station, race or creed."

Four Political Outlooks—"A radical is a man with both feet firmly planted—in the air. A conservative is a man with two perfectly good legs who, however, has never learned to walk forward. A reactionary is a somnambulist walking backward. A liberal is a man who uses his legs and his hands at the behest of his head."

FDR and Eleanor—"Never get into an argument with the Missus, you can't win. You think you have her pinned down here . . . but she bobs up right away over there somewhere! No use—you can't win!"

The American System—"Why do we have to be 'socialist' or 'capitalist'? The United States is a big enough country to have several systems going at once. It has brains and tolerance enough to accomodate them. We don't have to force everything into some doctrinaire model."

Disliked Economic Abstractions: "People aren't cattle, you know!"

Atom Bombs?—There "will be no invasion of Japan. We will have something that will end our war with Japan before any invasion takes place."

Eleanor Roosevelt

Chatting at Meals—"You don't just sit there and look at each other!"

Arguing with Franklin—"Without giving me a glance or the satisfaction of batting an eyelash, he calmly stated as his own the policies and beliefs he had argued against the night before! To this day I have no idea whether he had simply used me as a sounding board, as he so often did, with the idea of getting the reaction of the person on the outside, or whether my arguments had been needed to fortify his decision and to clarify his own mind."

Serving Franklin's Purposes—"When I went to Washington I felt sure that I would be able to use opportunities which came to me to help Franklin gain the objectives he cared about—but the work would be his work and the pattern his pattern. He might have been happier with a wife who was completely uncritical. That I was never able to be, and he had to find it in other people. Nevertheless, I think I sometimes acted as a spur, even though the spurring was not always wanted or welcome. I was one of those who served his purposes."

Harry Truman (1945–53)

Worship of Money—"One of the difficulties, as I see it, is that we worship money instead of honor. A billionaire in our estimation is much greater in the eyes of the people than the public servant who works for the public interest. It makes no difference if the billionaire rode to wealth on the sweat of little children and the blood of underpaid labor."

His Unfavorite Songs—"'The Missouri Waltz' is a ragtime song and if you let me say what I think, I don't give a damn about it, but I can't say it out loud because it's the song of Missouri. It's as bad as 'The Star-Spangled Banner' as far as music is concerned."

Choice in Life—"My choice early in life was either to be a piano player in a whorehouse or a politician." Then he added, "To tell the truth, there's hardly a difference."

Trouble in the World—"We should realize that much of the trouble in the world today is the result of false ideas of racial supremacy."

Economist—"Get me a one-handed economist! All my economists say, 'on the one hand . . . , but on the other.'"

Hell—"Give 'em hell, and if they don't take it, give 'em more hell."

Sympathy with the Little Fellow—"My own sympathy has always been with the little fellow, the man without advantages, with no pull at the seat of the mighty."

The Interests of the People—"Is the government of the United States going to run in the interests of the people as a whole, or in the interest of a small group of privileged big businessmen?"

Treatment of the Indians—"The treatment of the Indians by the white settlers at both South America and North America was a disgrace and always will be. . . . The list of mistreatment and treachery toward the Indians is almost endless. Practically every great chief ended up murdered or a prisoner."

On General Douglas MacArthur—"I fired him because he wouldn't respect the authority of the president. I didn't fire him because he was a dumb son-of-a-bitch, although he was, but that's not against the law in general. If it was, half to three-quarters of them would be in jail."

On Richard Nixon—"Nixon is a shifty-eyed, goddam liar, and people know it."

Riding a Tiger—"Within the first few months, I discovered that being a president is like riding a tiger. A man has to keep riding or be swallowed."

Bess Truman

Presidential Wife—"A woman's place in public is to sit beside her husband, be silent, and be sure her hat is on straight."

Policy with Reporters—"Just keep on smiling and tell 'them' nothing."

Nothing for the Public—"I am not the one who is elected. I have nothing to say to the public."

Dwight D. Eisenhower (1953–61)

Military-Industrial Complex—"We must guard against the acquisition of unwarranted influence, whether sought or unsought, by the military-industrial complex."

Knowing War—"The people who know war, those who have experienced it . . . I believe are the most earnest advocates of peace in the world."

Hatred of War—"I hate war, as only a soldier who has lived it can, as one who has seen its brutality, its futility, its stupidity."

Military Thefts—"Every gun that is made, every warship launched, every rocket fired signifies, in the final sense, a theft from those who hunger and are not fed, those who are cold and are not clothed."

On Joe McCarthy—"I will not get in the gutter with that guy!"

Keeping the Peace—"The United States never lost a soldier or a foot of ground in my administration. We kept the peace. People ask how it happened—by God, it didn't just happen, I'll tell you that."

The Last of the Long-Winded Speakers—"I am the punctuation—the period," he said, and sat down. Afterward, he said it was one of his most popular addresses.

John F. Kennedy (1961–63)

Not Interested in Vice-Presidential Nomination—"Let's not talk so much about vice. I'm against vice in any form."

US Limitations—"We must face the fact that the United States is neither omnipotent or omniscient—that we are only 6 percent of the world's population; that we cannot impose our will upon the other 94 percent of the world's population; that we cannot right every wrong or reverse each adversary; and therefore there cannot be an American solution to every world problem."

The City of Washington—"Washington is a city of Southern efficiency and Southern charm."

Ending War—"Mankind must put an end to war, or war will put an end to mankind."

Helping the Poor—"If a free society cannot help the many who are poor, it cannot save the few who are rich."

How to Handle Enemies—"Forgive your enemies, but never forget their names."

The Real Things in Life—"There are three things which are real: God, Human Folly, and Laughter. The first two are beyond our comprehension, so we must do what we can with the third."

Catholic Democrat—"I am not the Catholic candidate for president. I am the Democratic Party's candidate for president who happens also to be a Catholic. I do not speak for my church on public matters, and the church does not speak for me."

Practice What It Preaches—"It should be clear that a nation can be no stronger than she is at home. Only an America which practices what it preaches about equal rights and social justice will be respected by those whose choice affects our future."

The Presidency—"The American presidency is a formidable, exposed, and somewhat mysterious institution."

People Not Ready for Jackie—"The American people just aren't ready for someone like you. I guess we'll just have to run you through subliminally in one of those quick flash TV spots so no one will notice."

Jackie Kennedy

Not a First Lady—"The one thing I do not want to be called is First Lady. It sounds like a saddle horse."

Hairdo and the Presidency—"All the talk over what I wear and how I fix my hair has me amused, but it also puzzles me. What does my hairdo have to do with my husband's ability to be president?"

Told What to Do—"People have told me ninety-nine things that I had to do as First Lady, and I haven't done one of them."

Men and Their Wives—"I don't think there are any men who are faithful to their wives. Men are such a combination of good and evil."

Raising Children—"If you bungle raising your children, I don't think whatever else you do well matters very much."

Losing Anonymity—"It's frightening to lose your anonymity."

Old-Fashioned—"I'm an old-fashioned wife, and I'll do anything my husband asks me to do."

Taking Good Care of JFK—"My life revolves around my husband. His life is my life. It is up to me to make his home a haven, a refuge, to arrange it so that he can see as much of me and his children as much as possible—but never let the arrangements ruffle him, never let him see that it is work. . . . I want to take such good care of my husband that, whatever he is doing, he can do better because he has me. . . . His work is so important. And so exciting."

Introducing a White House Secretary—"And this is a young lady who is supposed to be sleeping with my husband!"

Lyndon B. Johnson (1963–69)

Ulcers—"I don't have ulcers. I give 'em."

The Vice Presidency—"The vice-presidency is filled with trips around the world, chauffeurs, men saluting, people clapping, chairmanship of councils, but in the end it is nothing. I detested every minute of it."

Politics—"I seldom think of politics more than eighteen hours a day."

Why He Kept FBI Director J. Edgar Hoover On Longer—"Well, it's probably better to have him inside the tent pissing out, than outside pissing in."

Talking—"I'd rather talk to you than hear the voice of Jesus."

Being President—"Being president is like being a jackass in a hailstorm. There's nothing to do but stand there and take it."

The Kind of President He Wants to Be—"I do not want to be the president who built empires, or sought grandeur, or extended dominion. I want to be the president who educated young children to the wonders of their world . . . who helped to feed the hungry and to prepare them to be taxpayers instead of tax-eaters . . . who helped the poor to find their own way and who protected the right of every citizen to vote in every election . . . who helped to end hatred among his fellow men and who promoted love among the people of all races and all regions and all parties . . . who helped to end war among the brothers of this earth."

Can't Swim—"If one morning I walked on top of the water across the Potomac River, the headline that afternoon would read, 'President Can't Swim.'"

Not Ivy-Leaguer—"I don't believe I'll ever get credit for anything I do in foreign affairs, no matter how successful it is, because I didn't go to Harvard."

No Favorites—"There are no favorites in my office. I treat them all with the same general inconsideration."

Where He Was Born—A German official told Johnson, "I understand you were born in a log cabin, Mr. President." "No, Mr. Chancellor, I was born in a manger."

Criticism—Of a Kennedy aide he once said, "He doesn't have sense enough to pour piss out of a boot with the instructions written on the heel."

On Nixon's Speeches—"Boys, I may not know much, but I know the difference between chicken shit and chicken salad."

Vietnam vs. Great Society—"The kids were right. I blew it. I knew from the start that if I left the woman I really loved—the Great Society—in order to fight that bitch of a war . . . then I would lose everything at home. All my hopes . . . my dreams."

Lady Bird Johnson

On LBJ—"Lyndon stretches you. He always expects more of you than you're really mentally or physically capable of putting out. Somehow that makes you try a little bit harder, and makes you produce a little more. It is a very good fertilizer for growth; it's all very tiring."

Instructions to Chief Usher—"Anything that's done here, or needs to be done, remember this: my husband comes first, the girls second, and I will be satisfied with what's left."

LBJ Loved People—"You have to understand, my husband loved people. All people. And half the people in the world were women. You don't think I could have kept my husband away from half the people. He loved me. I know he only loved me."

The Women Plodders—"Through the centuries, women have been the plodders. Good works go forward in proportion to the number of vital and creative and determined women supporting them. When women get behind a project, things happen."

Boasting—"Call it corny, if you will, but I want to boast about America."

Richard M. Nixon (1969–74)

Presidential Recreation—"Recreation is a means to an end, not the end in itself. You don't want to be president so that you can have fun. You want to have fun so that you can be a better president."

All-Powerful President—"When the president does it, that means it is not illegal."

Losing an Election—"The voters have spoken—the bastards."

Shaking Hands—"Sometimes at the end of the day, when I'm smiling and shaking hands, I want to kick them."

Standing Pat—"America can't stand pat. We can't stand pat for the reason that we're in a race, as I have indicated. We can't stand pat because it is essential with the conflict we have around the world, that we not just hold our own."

The Moon and Peace—"Any culture which can put a man on the moon is capable of gathering all the nations of the earth in peace, justice, and concord."

Gerald Ford (1974–77)

The Status of Things—"Things are more like they are now than they have ever been."

Lincoln—"If Lincoln were alive today, he'd roll over in his grave."

As Golfer—"I know I am getting better at golf because I am hitting fewer spectators."

Betty Ford

A Housewife's Work—"Being a good housewife seems to me a much tougher job than going to the office and getting paid for it. What man could afford to pay for all the things a wife does, when she's a cook, a mistress, a chauffeur, a nurse, a baby-sitter? But because of this, I feel women ought to have equal rights, equal social security, equal opportunities for education, an equal chance to establish credit."

Sleeping with the President—"Something else no one seems to expect is for a First Lady to sleep with the president. This," she told a guest, "is our bedroom, and that is our bed. We are the first president and First Lady to share a bedroom in an awfully long time. To my great surprise, though, people have written me objecting to the idea of a president of the United States sleeping with his wife."

Jimmy Carter (1977–81)

Meeting Film Stars—"It is a real thrill to meet the famous people here tonight. I hope I don't get to know too much about you!"

Civil Rights—"The passage of the civil rights acts during the 1960s was the greatest things to happen to the South in my lifetime. It lifted a burden from the whites as well as the blacks."

Outsider—"I have been accused of being an outsider," said Carter when running for president in 1976. "I plead guilty. Unfortunately, the vast majority of Americans . . . are also outsiders."

Lust in His Heart—"I've looked on a lot of women with lust. I've committed adultery in my heart many times. This is something that God recognizes I will do—and I have done it—and God forgives me for it. But that doesn't mean that I condemn someone who not only looks on a woman with lust, but who leaves his wife and shacks up with somebody out of wedlock. Christ says, don't consider yourself better than someone else because one guy screws a whole bunch of women while the other guy is loyal to his wife. The guy who's loyal to his wife ought not to be condescending or proud because of the relative degree of sinfulness."

Ronald Reagan (1981–1989)

No American Government—"I used to fantasize what it would be like if everyone in government would quietly slip away and close the doors and disappear. See how long it would take the people of this country to miss them. I think that life would go on, and people would keep right on doing the things they are doing, and we would get along a lot better than we think."

Politics—"Politics is not a bad profession. If you succeed there are many rewards. If you disgrace yourself, you can always write a book."

Presidential Performer—"I've sometimes wondered how you could be president and not be an actor."

Leaving the White House—"As soon as I get home to California, I plan to lean back, kick up my feet and take a long nap. . . . Ah, come to think of it, things won't be all that different after all!"

Hard Work—"It's true that hard work never killed anybody, but I figure, why take the chance?"

Nancy Reagan

Advice to Presidents' Wives—"First, be yourself, and do what you're interested in. Next, don't be afraid to look after your husband and speak out, when necessary, to either him or his staff." Above all, be realistic about what lies ahead: "Once you're in the White House, don't think it's going to be a glamorous, fairy-tale life. It's very hard work with high highs and low lows. Since you're under a microscope, everything is magnified, so just keep your perspective and your patience."

George H. W. Bush (1989–93)

After the Inauguration—"I'll play a good deal of tennis, a good deal of horseshoes, a good deal of fishing, a good deal of running . . . and some reading. I have to throw that in for the intellectuals out there."

Good Question—"It's a very good question, very direct, and I'm not going to answer it."

Broccoli—"I do not like broccoli. And I haven't liked it since I was a little kid and my mother made me eat it. And I'm president of the United States and I'm not going to eat any more broccoli."

Opinions—"I have opinions of my own—strong opinions—but I don't always agree with them."

Drugs—"I'm going to be coming out here with my own drug problem."

Country-Western Music—"The guy over there at Pease—a woman, actually—she said something about a country-western song, you know, about the train, a light at the end of the tunnel. I only hope it's not a train coming the other way. Well, I said to her, 'Well, I'm a country-music fan. I love it. always have. Doesn't fit the mold of some of the columnists, I might add, but nevertheless—of what they think I ought to fit in, but I love it. . . . But nevertheless, I said to them you know there's another one the Ditty Nitty Gritty Great Bird [Nitty Gritty Dirt Band]—that they did. And it says if you want to see a rainbow you've got to stand a little rain. We've had little rain. New Hampshire has had too much rain. A lot of families are hurting."

Barbara Bush

Did Bush have an affair?—"How can George Bush have an affair? He can't stay up past ten o'clock!"

Answering Reporters' Questions about Abortion—"Now, listen, you can try this every way you know—I'm not going to discuss that. But that really—first of all, I don't think it's very presidential. I don't think it's—it's—it's not—I don't think it's—I'm not going to talk about it. I'm—because, see, if I start talking about one issue, then I have to move into another and another and another."

Bill Clinton (1993–2001)

Character—"Character is a journey, not a destination."

Oval Office—When one of Clinton's friends was overwhelmed by the sight of the president's office, Clinton exclaimed: "Don't let it get you. This is the crown jewel of the Federal penal system."

Hillary Rodham Clinton

Her Love for Bill: "I'm not sitting here like some little woman standing by her man like Tammy Wynette. I'm sitting here because I love and respect him."

A President's Wife—"What I hope is that each woman . . . will be free to be who they are. If that means being a full-time career person not involved in the issues of the day but very much wrapped up in . . . her own career that should be a choice that we respect. If it's a more traditional role in which the primary focus is in supporting the family that is there and the person who holds the office, that is the position we should respect. If it is a more active public role, then I think we ought to be very happy about that."

George W. Bush (2001–2009)

God's Choice—"I believe that God wants me to be president."

Limits of French Langugage—"The problem with the French is that they don't have a word for 'entrepreneur.'"

War-Peace—"I just want you to know that when we talk about war, we're really talking about peace."

Trustworthiness—"Well, I think if you say you're going to do something and don't do it, that's trustworthiness."

America's Role in the World—"I just don't think it's the role of the United States to walk into a country and say, 'We do it this way, so should you.' . . . I think one way for us to end up being viewed as 'the ugly American,' is for us to go around the world saying, 'We do it this way, so should you.'"

Bush's Dad—When asked whether he consulted his father for guidance, he replied, "You know, he is the wrong father to appeal to in terms of strength. There is a higher father that I appeal to."

Barack Obama (2009–?)

The Kind of Government He Prefers: "The question we ask today is not whether our government is too big or small, but whether it works—whether it helps families find jobs at a decent wage, care they can afford, a retirement that is dignified. Where the answer is yes, we intend to move forward. Where the answer is no, programs will end."

Michelle Obama

Military Families—"It hurts. These are people who are willing to send their loved ones off to perhaps give their lives, the ultimate sacrifice. Yet they're living back at home on food stamps. It's not right, and it's not where we should be as a nation."

INDEX

Adams, Abigail, 186, 222–23
Adams, John: and Adams, Abigail,
  186; campaign of 1800, 89–90;
  comments on philosophers,
  125–28; love of Shakespeare,
  194–97; quotations by, 221–22
Adams, John Quincy, 200–3, 225
Adams, Louisa, 225
asylum, 42–43

bigotry, religious: Hoover's
  opposition to, 93; Newport
  statement, 58–59; Washington's
  opposition to, 41–45, 55–60.
  See also Jews, American;
  religious freedom
Bill of Rights, 132, 133
Blaine, James G., 27–28
Bryan, William Jennings: and
  anti-imperialism, 33; free silver
  issue, 31–32, 33; ovations
  and gifts, 30; presidential
  campaigns, 29–37; on trusts,
  33, 35
Buchanan, James, 226
Bush, Barbara, 239
Bush, George H. W., 89, 176–82, 239
Bush, George W., 240
Bush-Speak, 176–82

campaigns, presidential: 1852
  contest, 61–73; campaign of
  1800, 89–91; candidates' importance in, 38; civilian versus general, 61–73; electioneering,
  18–19, 26–27, 37; front-porch,
  26–30; military men, dangers of,
  65–66; and money, 4; and
  political parties, 19–20; and
  religion, 89–94; stump speak-

ing, 18, 20, 27–32, 31, 34, 35;
  and Washington, George, 18–19
candidates, presidential: Blaine,
  James G., 27–28; Bryan, William
  Jennings, 29–37; Douglas,
  Stephen A., 22–23; Garfield,
  James A., 26–27; Grant, Ulysses
  S., 24–25, 79–83; Greeley,
  Horace, 24–26; Harrison,
  William Henry, 20, 28–29;
  McKinley, William, 30, 33, 34;
  Parker, Alton B., 34; Pierce,
  Franklin, 61, 63, 64–65, 68–69;
  Roosevelt, Theodore, 33–37;
  Scott, General Winfield, 20–22,
  61, 65–67, 69–71; Taft,
  William Howard, 34–37;
  Washington, George, 18–19.
  See also campaigns, presiden-
  tial; citizen soldiers; electioneer-
  ing; religion; soldiers, profes-
  sional; stump speaking; wives,
  presidents'
Carter, Jimmy, 238
Catholics, 49–51, 94. *See also* church
  and state, separation of;
  Kennedy, John F.; Washington,
  George
church and state, separation of,
  46–49, 93–94. *See also*
  Constitution
citizen soldiers, 62–64, 70–73.
  See also Pierce, Franklin
civil supremacy: and Eisenhower,
  Dwight, 74, 77, 83–84, 88;
  Newburgh crisis, 104–10; and
  presidential salutes, 39–40;
  and Taylor and Grant, 80; and
  Washington, George, 72, 95–
  112. *See also* citizen soldiers;

241